Erotic Triangles

CHICAGO STUDIES IN ETHNOMUSICOLOGY

A series edited by Philip V. Bohlman, Bruno Nettl, and Ronald Radano

EDITORIAL BOARD

Margaret J. Kartomi

Anthony Seeger

Kay Kaufman Shelemay

Martin H. Stokes

Bonnie C. Wade

Erotic Triangles

Sundanese Dance and Masculinity in West Java

HENRY SPILLER

The University of Chicago Press   Chicago and London

HENRY SPILLER is associate professor in the Department of Music at the University of California, Davis.

The University of Chicago Press, Chicago 60637
The University of Chicago Press, Ltd., London
© 2010 by The University of Chicago
All rights reserved. Published 2010.
Printed in the United States of America
19 18 17 16 15 14 13 12 11 10   1 2 3 4 5

ISBN-13: 978-0-226-76958-5 (cloth)
ISBN-13: 978-0-226-76959-2 (paper)
ISBN-10: 0-226-76958-5 (cloth)
ISBN-10: 0-226-76959-3 (paper)

Library of Congress Cataloging-in-Publication Data
Spiller, Henry.
        Sundanese dance and masculinity in West Java / Henry Spiller.
            p. cm. — (Chicago studies in ethnomusicology)
        ISBN-13: 978-0-226-76958-5 (cloth : alk. paper)
        ISBN-10: 0-226-76958-5 (cloth : alk. paper)
        ISBN-13: 978-0-226-76959-2 (pbk. : alk. paper)
        ISBN-10: 0-226-76959-3 (pbk.)
        1. Dance—Indonesia—Jawa Barat. 2. Sundanese (Indonesian
        people)—Music. 3. Masculinity in music. I. Title. II. Series:
        Chicago studies in ethnomusicology.
    GV1703.I532J389559 2010
    792.809'92232—dc22

                                        2009053688

♾ The paper used in this publication meets the minimum requirements of the American National Standard for Information Sciences— Permanence of Paper for Printed Library Materials, ANSI Z39.48–1992.

Contents

List of Figures and Tables vii
Preface ix
Acknowledgments xv

1 Discourses of Sundanese Dance 1

2 Drumming and Power 43

3 *Ronggeng* and Desire 76

4 Dance Events and Freedom 104

5 The Erotic Triangle of Sundanese Dance 143

6 Triangulating Sundanese Dance 181

Notes 211
References 223
Index 239

Figures and Tables

FIGURE P.1. Aep Diana plays *kendang* xiii

FIGURE P.2. Key for *kendang* notation xiii

FIGURE 1.1. *Ketuk tilu* in Paneungteung 3

FIGURE 1.2. *Bajidoran* performance at Cikaum 5

FIGURE 1.3. A man dances at a wedding 6

FIGURE 1.4. Pusbitari brochure 16

FIGURE 1.5. Triangle model for wedding dance event 42

FIGURE 2.1. *Tepak kocak* 47

FIGURE 2.2. *Dogdog* 49

FIGURE 2.3. *Terbang/rebana* 50

FIGURE 2.4. Aep Diana's notation for standard *jaipongan* pattern 51

FIGURE 2.5. "Trundling" *kendang* motive 53

FIGURE 2.6. Variation of *kendang* motive that leads to a *goong* stroke 54

FIGURE 2.7. *Kendang* motive that leads to a *goong* stroke 54

FIGURE 2.8. Syncopated pattern leading to *goong* pattern 55

FIGURE 2.9. One of Tosin Mochtar's *tepak melem* cadential patterns 56

LIST OF FIGURES AND TABLES

FIGURE 2.10. *Keupat kendor* 60

FIGURE 2.11. Dance accompaniment scheme from 1893 65

FIGURE 2.12. Standard phrase (*pola ibing*) for *jaipongan* 70

FIGURE 2.13A. Choreographic scheme for "Banda Urang" 72

FIGURE 2.13B. Choreographic scheme for "Daun Pulus/Keser Bojong" 72

FIGURE 2.13C. Choreographic scheme for "Adumanis" 72

FIGURE 4.1. *Goong* and three *ketuk* from a *ketuk tilu* ensemble 113

FIGURE 4.2. Basic *kendang* phrase for *dangdut* 135

FIGURE 5.1A. Part of a *tari kursus* choreography 154

FIGURE 5.1B. Part of a *tari kursus* choreography 154

FIGURE 5.1C. Part of a *tari kursus* choreography 154

FIGURE 5.2. Schematic representation of Sundanese dance events 167

FIGURE 5.3. Seeger's model of tactile, audio, and visual communication 169

FIGURE 5.4. Tactile, audio, and visual elements in the dance-event triangle 170

FIGURE 5.5. Dance-event triangle's aesthetic teams 172

FIGURE 6.1. Dance-event triangle geometry 183

FIGURE 6.2. *Ketuk tilu* in Paneungteung 186

FIGURE 6.3. *Bajidor* in Subang 188

FIGURE 6.4A. *Jaipongan* 191

FIGURE 6.4B. A man dances at a wedding 192

FIGURE 6.5. Puppet ogres dance *jaipongan* 195

FIGURE 6.6. *Tari baksa* 202

TABLE 4.1. Effort-shape adjectives 129

TABLE 5.1. Summary of *tari kursus* core movements 152

TABLE 5.2. Comparison of three "Lenyepan" choreographies 155

Preface

Erotic Triangles is the culmination of a research quest that had its beginnings during my undergraduate student years at the University of California, Santa Cruz (UCSC), in the mid-1970s, when I first became captivated by Sundanese dance and music. UCSC is fortunate to have an accomplished Sundanese dance drummer, Undang Sumarna, on its faculty. What immediately intrigued me was the way Pa Undang's drumming seemed to bring to life the dancing it accompanied. Over the years, my engagement with Sundanese performing arts deepened, and I began to develop a glimmer of an understanding of how this close correlation between gesture and sound was achieved.

Most of the dances we performed at UCSC were presentational dances, designed for the stage and meant to be watched, and the students who studied and performed dance at UCSC were mostly women. I learned, however, that these dances, as well as the way the drumming accompanied them, developed in the context of improvised social dancing by men. I found both novel and fascinating the notion that men dancing with other men could be an arch-masculine activity, and I tried to find out as much as I could about what I imagined to be the purest forms of Sundanese men's dancing—*ketuk tilu* and *tayuban*. My first extended trip to West Java in the early 1980s coincided with the explosion of popularity of *jaipongan*, a very modern kind of dancing that exhibited many of the qualities in which I was interested, but ketuk tilu and tayuban were virtually nonexistent. During subsequent trips to Indonesia, however, I came to understand that despite the dearth of traditional

PREFACE

ketuk tilu and tayuban, Sundanese men's dancing was alive and well in myriad forms, if one knew what to look for. Simply put, this book forms my ideas about exactly what to look for into an erotic triangle that represents the essence of Sundanese men's dancing.

The Sundanese

Sundanese culture remains virtually unknown to the West. Approximately thirty million people speak the Sundanese language and identify themselves as Sundanese—considerably more than better-known Indonesian groups such as the Balinese. Yet all too often American journalists (and their automated spell-checkers) render the name as "Sudanese"— and even provide the laughably inaccurate "clarification" that it refers to a place in Africa. Perhaps the fact that there is no place called Sunda is a contributing factor to this obscurity. The Sundanese homeland is the highland areas of western Java. Java is among the largest islands in modern Indonesia, and certainly the most densely populated. Parahyangan ("land of the gods") is an old Sundanese name for the area; the Dutch colonists who controlled the area for several centuries rendered the name Preanger, and today it is still called Priangan. In Indonesian languages, the word *Sunda* typically is used not as a noun, but as an adjective, as in *basa Sunda* (Sundanese language) and *tanah Sunda* (Sundanese homeland). The modern Indonesian province of Jawa Barat (West Java) is roughly coterminous with the Sundanese homeland.

Languages

Most Sundanese people speak at least two languages: Sundanese (*basa Sunda*, the regional language, rich with local associations) and Indonesian (*bahasa Indonesia*, the national language of Indonesia). Although I have studied Sundanese, I have never become conversant in it, and most of my interactions with people during my trips to West Java were conducted in Indonesian. My Sundanese interlocutors used both Indonesian and Sundanese technical terms when discussing music and dance, and I have attempted to provide English translations or equivalents for these terms following their first introduction.

The rich landscape of Sundanese arts has not received much attention in European-language scholarship, despite the minor "world beat" popularity of some Sundanese recordings released in the West (such as the Dian recording *Sangkala*, released in the United States as Icon

x

Records 5501). It is beyond the scope of this book to provide even cursory discussions of all the genres and forms of Sundanese music and dance mentioned in it. Instead, I refer the reader to several readily available sources that provide up-to-date and accurate overviews. My own *Focus: Gamelan Music of Indonesia* (Routledge, 2008) includes background information about gamelan music in Indonesia and detailed introductions to Sundanese *gamelan salendro, gamelan degung*, and dance. Relevant articles in *Southeast Asia*, volume 4 of the *Garland Encyclopedia of World Music*, include Sean Williams's "Java: Sunda" (1998b); Endo Suanda's "Java: Cirebon" (1998); and René Lysloff and Deborah Wong's "Popular Music and Cultural Politics" (1998). The second edition of *The New Grove Dictionary of Music and Musicians* contains an excellent overview, written by Simon Cook, of Sundanese music (2001), in addition to the many auxiliary articles it cross-references. The *New Grove* is also available online.

Names

Citing Sundanese names (and Indonesian names in general) presents a problem for scholarly writing. Although some Indonesians go by only one name, most Sundanese use at least two names, but these do not necessarily represent the exact equivalents of American given names and surnames. Sundanese parents typically give their children a formal name (or several) at birth, but these are rarely used. Instead, individuals are commonly addressed throughout their lives by nicknames, which may or may not be derived from their formal names. People rarely call others by name without using some sort of title or honorific; which title to use depends on the status of both interlocutors as well on as the relationship between them. In some cases, an individual's formal name may change, but her or his nickname typically remains constant (even if the honorifics used to address that person do not). For example, one of my teachers in Bandung gives his full name as Otong Rasta. Rasta was his father's name, and Otong cites it to establish himself as an heir to his father's store of knowledge and skill. Given our teacher-student relationship, I cannot imagine calling him anything but Pa Otong ("Pa" is an honorific reserved for men, generally those older than the addresser). Because he is a musician, however, he is more commonly referred to as Mang Otong ("Mang" is a familiar address for an uncle, but frequently is applied to musicians or artisans of some standing). Another distinguished musician with whom I studied went by the name Entis Sutisna; Sutisna was his formal name, but his nickname was Entis (derived from Sutisna). Again, I addressed him as Pa Entis, but many others called him Mang Entis.

PREFACE

Under these circumstances, to cite these men as Rasta and Sutisna seems ludicrous. On the other hand, it is difficult to decide which title to use—Pa or Mang. My imperfect solution is to use a complete name when introducing informants for the first time in each chapter, and to subsequently refer to them using the names by which they are best known, without any titles. I have taken a slightly different tack when citing published works by Indonesian authors, however; these names I have treated as any American bibliographer would—as if the final name in an author's moniker were his or her surname. It should also be noted at this juncture that some Sundanese authors have published under various names and alternate spellings. Thus, Irawati Durban, Irawati Durban Arjo, and Irawati Durban Ardjo are three name variations for the same person. Atik Soepandi also published under the name Atik Supandi, and so on.

Drumming Transcriptions

Sundanese dance drumming has an important role in this book, so a number of transcriptions of drum parts are included. I employ a system for transcribing drumming that I have devised and refined beginning with my first encounters with Sundanese drumming. It is accessible to readers familiar with Western staff notation and has appeared in print several times (cf. Spiller 1993, 1996, 1999, 2001). Sundanese drummers typically use a set of barrel-shaped drums called *kendang*, which includes one large drum (*kendang indung*), both heads of which the drummer plays, as well as one or more small drums (*kulanter*), only one head of which is used. Figure P.1 shows Aep Diana, drummer of the Rawit Group, playing a set of kendang. In the photograph, Aep's hands are hitting both heads of the kendang indung. A couple of kulanter, one on its side, one on its end, are visible in the foreground. Another kulanter is out of sight, accessible to Aep's right hand. Aep's set is supplemented by another kendang indung sitting on one of its heads, as well as a cymbal on a stand. The drummer can vary the timbre of the strokes by using different hand techniques, by hitting different parts of the drum head, and, in the case of the larger, lower-pitched head of the kendang indung, by changing the head tension with the heel of his foot. Two Sundanese musicologists, Atik Soepandi and Maman Suaman, have developed a standardized set of drum syllables to represent kendang strokes, and it is on their system that my staff-based notation is based (Soepandi and Suaman 1980).

My notation system uses a standard five-line staff. A drum stroke's relative pitch is indicated by which line or space the notehead occupies.

xii

PREFACE

P.1 Aep Diana plays *kendang* (photo: Henry Spiller, 1999).

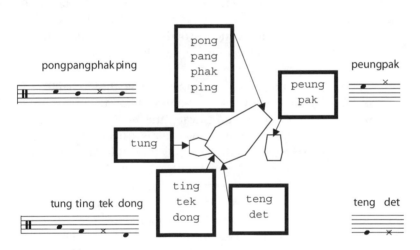

P.2 Key for *kendang* notation.

A stroke's decay is indicated by the notehead's shape; an x-shaped notehead indicates a stopped, rapid decay, while a regular notehead indicates a ringing decay. Rhythm is indicated with standard Western note values, except that dotted bar lines mark off the four-beat units from which typical drum patterns (and gamelan pieces) are constructed. The dotted bar

PREFACE

lines intersect the accented beats of the unit, making temporarily moot the controversial issue of whether accents are heard at the units' beginnings (as most Western-trained ears hear them) or ends (where a gamelan musician's rhythmic sensibility would place them). This system quickly communicates a drum part's rhythm and overall pitch contour to readers who are familiar with Western notation. The schematic drawing of a set of kendang (from the drummer's vantage) in figure P.2 maps the standardized mnemonic syllables (see Soepandi and Suaman 1980) to the drums on which they are produced and the symbols with which they are represented in my notation system.

Organization

The first chapter introduces some of the key concepts involved in my analysis: the panorama of Sundanese dance and some of the discourses around it, Sundanese ideas of masculinity and sexuality and how *malu* (shame) helps to regulate these ideas, and how masculinity, malu, and freedom govern Sundanese dance events. Chapter 1 also introduces how Sundanese dance might be conceived as an erotic triangle; each of the next three chapters introduces one side of that triangle, along with theoretical foundations for considering the sides in the context of the triangle. By providing a detailed investigation of attitudes toward drums, drum sounds, drumming techniques in Sundanese music, chapter 2 focuses on how Sundanese drumming operates and on the way in which it represents power. Chapter 3 investigates the female singer-dancers—*ronggeng*—who are emblems of the dance events. Chapter 4 explores the landscape of Sundanese men's dance events up to the early twenty-first century and investigates changes and continuities in event protocols.

Chapter 5 opens with an exploration of *tari kursus*—a presentational dance genre with roots in participatory men's dancing—and explains how viewing it as an erotic triangle helps to make sense of the discourse that surrounds it. The chapter culminates in a synthesis of all the ethnographic data and theoretical musings from the preceding chapters to create a wide-ranging "trigonometry" of Sundanese dance events. Finally, chapter 6 applies this trigonometry to a selection of recent Sundanese performances to explore the relationship of participatory men's dance traditions to the presentational genres that reference them and explore why some of these new genres seem to be more successful at transforming Sundanese dance—and Sundanese values—than others.

Acknowledgments

I include information gathered during several trips to West Java: the first for four months in 1981; short trips in 1988, 1996, 2001, and 2008; and ten months of research funded by the Fulbright Program in 1998–99. My research trips to Indonesia, as well as archival research trips to the Netherlands, have been supported by the University of California, Berkeley, Center for Southeast Asia Studies; the UC Berkeley Graduate Division; the American Association for Netherlandic Studies (AANS); California Polytechnic State University; Kenyon College; a Whiting Foundation summer research grant; and the University of California, Davis. I am grateful to all of them. Funding for this project's central research trip in 1998–99 was provided by an Institute of International Education (IIE) Fulbright fellowship. I would like to thank the Indonesian Institute of Science (Lembaga Ilmu Pengetahuan Indonesia—LIPI) for facilitating my research, and Iyus Rusliana, former director of the Indonesian Academy of the Arts (Sekolah Tinggi Seni Indonesia—STSI) in Bandung, for sponsoring my stay in Indonesia. The faculty and staff of STSI assisted me in countless other ways as well. The American-Indonesian Exchange Foundation (AMINEF), under the direction of John B. Situmeang, administered the Fulbright grant and facilitated my research in Indonesia. I would like to express special thanks to Nelly Paliama of AMINEF for her tireless support and good humor before, during, and after my stay in Indonesia.

I have been extremely fortunate in this quest to have received wisdom and encouragement from a host of indi-

ACKNOWLEDGMENTS

viduals and organizations. I thank first of all my teachers in West Java, who have generously shared with me their knowledge and feelings about Sundanese music and dance. Ade Komaran, Tosin Mochtar, Otong Rasta, Abay Subardja, Entis Sutisna, and Yus Yusdianawijaya each spent hours teaching, playing, and discussing music and dance with me. Other individuals who took time to discuss their art with me include Irawati Durban Ardjo; Sujana Arja; Enoch Atmadibrata; Idjah Hadidjah; Euis Komariah; Ana Mulyana; Wahyu Roche; Ismet Ruchimat and his wife, Ati; Nano S.; Tati Saleh; Nugraha Sudiredja; and Tjetjep Supriadi; I am grateful for their time and insights. I spent a lot of time in Bandung tagging along with two *lingkung seni* (literally, arts circles), and the members of these groups always made me feel welcome and went out of their way to support my research. I thank everybody associated with the Bandung Zoo's lingkung seni, especially Hasibun Arief, Edi Kusnadi, Salam Mulyadi, Abdul Rozak, Asep Suparma, and Dohot Tarmana. The Rawit Group generously tolerated my tagging along to their gigs and did all they could to make my trips with them enjoyable. I thank all the members, including Ace, Adang, Ade, Iin Angraeni, Caca, Cece, Dedi, Lia Mustika Dewi, Endang, Aep Diana, Asep Dodi, Honi, Iman, Jajang, Ade Komaran, Ana Mulyana, Nana, Nia, Oman, Nining Setianingsih, and Yani for their good humor and hospitality.

My research has been immeasurably enriched by friends in Bandung who have provided companionship, advice, and local know-how, including Ben Arcangel; Matt Ashworth and his wife, Hendrawati; Andrew Bouchard; Simon and Oom Cook; Endo and Marjie Suanda and their children, Ata and Umay; and Benjamin Zimmer. In Indonesia, Budi Affandie and Tati Haryanti provided excellent transcriptions of Sundanese-language song texts and recordings of performances.

I have also received considerable intellectual and moral assistance from family, friends, and colleagues. I would like to especially thank Mary Anne Barnheiser, Katherine Bergeron, Kathy Foley, Mary Ann Smart, R. Anderson Sutton, and Andrew Weintraub for reading and commenting upon significant portions of this manuscript as it developed. Much of the present work found its first expression in my 2001 dissertation, which I wrote at UC Berkeley. I thank the members of my dissertation committee—Benjamin Brinner, Lawrence Cohen, and Bonnie Wade— for their thoughtful readings and excellent suggestions. I am grateful to Michael Ewing, Laura McColm, Rae Ann Stahl, Sean Williams, and Benjamin Zimmer for sharing their knowledge of things Sundanese. My partner, Michael Seth Orland, has supported this work in many different ways—by discussing ideas with me, providing close and critical readings of the manuscript at many stages, and providing unending physical and emotional support.

The editorial and production staff of the University of Chicago Press deserves my sincere gratitude. The series editor, Philip V. Bohlman, provided support and encouragement from the moment the project came to his attention. The deep engagement with ethnomusicology and the keen literary sense of the editor, Elizabeth Branch Dyson, refined the final form of the book. Her assistant, Anne Goldberg, and the production editor, Carol Saller, simplified the complexities of the publishing process. And the copy editor, Barbara Norton, polished my prose with great skill, attention to detail, and sensitivity.

I would like to thank two remarkable Sundanese musicians and friends living in the United States who have contributed immeasurably to my love and understanding of Sundanese music. My first gamelan teacher, Undang Sumarna, is an inexhaustible source of inspiration and always reminds me not to take myself too seriously. Burhan Sukarma's brilliant musicianship never fails to amaze me. His humble deference to "tradition" somehow never conflicts with his penchant for incorporating new materials and unorthodox ideas into his work.

Although this scholarly inquiry, like scholarship of all sorts, strives to proffer universal wisdom based on impartial inquiry and analysis, in the final analysis, this is a very personal book. In retrospect, I believe that this Sundanese approach to music, dance, and manliness appealed to me precisely because it represented a different approach to masculinity, an alternative to those typically available to American men. I believe that I have always been something of a "wannabe" dancer, uncomfortable with the idea of moving my body at all—uncomfortable even drawing attention to the fact that I inhabited one. Sundanese music, drumming, and dance have provided me an outlet for exploring my own masculine identity and for legitimating to me the idea that there are many ways to articulate a coherent identity. In any case, Sundanese music and dance have proved to be among the most important matters in my life, and I cherish this opportunity to share them with others.

In closing, I would like to dedicate this book to my mother, Marion Hahn Spiller (1916–2004). Her unflappable confidence in me and my various exploits—many of which would have made other mothers despair—never failed to strengthen my own resolve. Given my own complex sense of malu, I probably would have feigned embarrassment when she proudly shared this book with her wide and diverse group of friends.

ONE

Discourses of Sundanese Dance

It is an everyday occurrence in the Sundanese areas of West Java, Indonesia: men get up and dance. Businessmen, pedicab drivers, civil servants, and students alike find the combination of animating rhythms played on drums and the beguiling voice of a female entertainer to be irresistible, so they cast aside their everyday modest demeanors and make spectacles of themselves by gyrating their hips and waving their arms in time with the drums. Some get so carried away that they sidle up to the singer—even touch her. The musical styles to which they dance are quite varied, ranging from staid folkloric ketuk tilu ensembles, through modern gamelan music, to the global pop sounds of contemporary *dangdut*. Equally varied are the occasions at which such activities take place—village ceremonies, weddings, political rallies, and nightclubs, among others. What remains constant is the men's enthusiastic willingness, given the right conditions, to breach ordinary standards of comportment in order to dance.

This book develops the argument that men's dancing persists in myriad forms in West Java because it satisfies a crucial need: through dancing, participants explore and enact the contradictions inherent in Sundanese gender identities. The combination of drumming and a female voice in effect grant men permission to "perform"—literally, onstage—the behaviors that constitute their own masculine identities that they unconsciously enact all the time. The conventional protocols of Sundanese improvised dance,

CHAPTER ONE

such as ambiguity about whether dancers "lead" or "follow" the drumming, and the subtle ways in which men's perceived freedom to move in whatever ways they like is constrained by musical structures, provide aesthetic metaphors for important contradictions of masculinity. Because virtually every Sundanese man, woman, and child understands the conventions that surround men's dancing, any dance event provides a potent forum for both reinforcing and contesting the conventional gender values that such events model. Furthermore, the powerful meanings conveyed by participatory dance inhere as well in modern presentational, staged dance performances that reference the conventions of participatory genres without inviting any actual participation.

How to analyze such a vast and complex array of cultural practices? A structuralist approach that identifies common patterns underlying all of the practices runs the risk of ignoring the roles of individuals in the process and excising Sundanese dance from its historical context. By the same token, interpretive approaches are in danger of understating the strength of the persistent underlying value systems that drive people's beliefs and behaviors. In this book, I selectively combine divergent theoretical approaches to build multiple perspectives on the detailed ethnographic data upon which it is based. This interdisciplinary approach reconciles structuralist ideas with poststructuralist approaches to enable an eclectic, heterodox, yet compelling reading of Sundanese cultural practices.

Opening Scenarios

To begin, I introduce a few real-life scenarios that illustrate some of the contexts in which amateur men's dancing is likely to occur.

Scenario 1: Ketuk tilu in Lembang

The setting: The small rural community of Paneungteung, near Lembang (nestled in the mountains north of Bandung), in August 1999. Salam Mulyadi, a noted exponent of the genre of Sundanese men's social dancing known as ketuk tilu, has invited me to join him as he performs at an annual ritual, sponsored by Paneungteung and the surrounding communities, to ensure that enough water is available for the upcoming growing season. Although ketuk tilu is the quintessential Sundanese amateur men's dance, it is rarely encountered in modern West Java. Salam explains to me that this is one of the very few remaining occasions in

1.1　*Ketuk tilu* in Paneungteung (photo: Henry Spiller, 1999).

and around Bandung at which one could encounter ketuk tilu in a non-folkloric context.

The scene: A temporary raised stage (with a roof but no walls; see fig. 1.1) has been built in the front yard of the village head's house. The large banner that flaps in the wind at the rear of the stage identifies the musical group that is to perform as Lingkung Seni Manggu Sari.[1] The rear of the stage is occupied by some musical instruments: a *goong* (a large hanging bossed gong), three *ketuk* (small bossed gongs laid horizontally), a kendang (a set of double-headed barrel drums), and a *rebab* (a two-stringed spike fiddle). Most of the instruments are miked, and there are several more microphones set up for singers and an emcee.

We head first for the house's interior. I am invited into a small room off the main living area, in which a variety of *sesajen* (offerings) are set up, over which the couple who own the house and are sponsoring the ceremony pray and light incense. At about 9:25 A.M., the program onstage begins.

The action: After the elderly hostess, who is known in the community for her spiritual power, has finished singing the sacred invocatory song "Kidung" to the accompaniment of three musicians who play the instruments (a single musician handles the goong and the three ketuk) and others have given a few obligatory speeches, the dancing begins. Several female performers dressed in brightly colored formal outfits sit on a

CHAPTER ONE

bench at stage right, ready to dance with male spectators. For each ketuk tilu dance number, one, two, or three men mount the stage and dance, each with his own partner selected from among the female performers, to the accompaniment of the instrumentalists and a couple of seated singers. At times, some of the female dancers also take turns singing. Each man dances with his own idiosyncratic style, and some are clearly more skilled at dancing than others, but everybody's movements are coordinated closely with the various rhythmic patterns that the drummer plays. In the middle of each number, the tempo quickens, the dancers *nyembah* (make a gesture of respect) to one another, and the female performers return to their bench while the men, at times joined by other men, follow a leader in a serpentine dance around the stage (cf. Herdiani 1996; Sumiati 1996b).

As the morning brightens into afternoon, people passing by on the road across the irrigation canal occasionally stop to watch the goings-on. The biggest crowds gather when the action onstage is something other than ketuk tilu, such as *penca silat* (Sundanese martial arts) or jaipongan (a modern style of dancing based loosely on ketuk tilu). All in all, however, the event is sparsely attended.

Scenario 2: Bajidor in Subang

The setting: Cikaum (near the town of Purwadadi) in northern Subang, in June 1999, about 10 P.M. The choreographer and dance scholar Mas Nanu Muda and his brother, Nana, have brought me to a performance of *bajidoran* (a kind of dance event that centers around male dance fanatics known as *bajidor*) featuring the Leunyay Group and sponsored by the village as part of their annual *bersih desa* ("cleaning the village") festival. The village is quite remote, but the performance has attracted an enormous crowd. The road is choked with people going to and fro and just hanging around, and portable food carts are set up everywhere. Nana points out to me that the people gathered in a large cluster under a long, narrow canopy on the outskirts of the performance area were gambling.

The scene: The stage is very high—five feet off the ground. The front of the stage is covered with a banner printed with the group's name and contact information. The whole stage is very, very brightly lit, and colored lights flash above the stage. Speaker towers worthy of a Grateful Dead concert, about ten feet high, flank the stage and blast earsplittingly amplified music. On either side of the stage, facing center stage, are kendang players, and between these drummers is a line of ten or so seated female performers who wear matching tight pink outfits, enormous wigs,

1.2 *Bajidoran* performance at Cikaum (photo: Henry Spiller, 1999).

and thick, pale makeup. In the center sits Yayah Leunyay, the group's star performer. Gamelan instruments are set up behind the women and the drummers (see fig. 1.2).

The action: The floor below the stage is crowded with men dancing—alone, in couples, in small groups. At times the emcee's amplified voice cuts through the din of the gamelan, calling out the name of a dancer. The man whose name has been called approaches the stage and selects his favorite female performer, who comes to the edge of the stage. Once there, he gives her money in exchange for the opportunity to *egot*—hold hands and sway together. The men's movements are loosely coordinated; they move as a unit, dancing to flurries of drumming, pausing when the drumming pauses. But each man's particular movement style is unique: some are funny, some are debonair; some are aggressive and locomotive, some are understated and stationary. While they are not dancing, the men sit close to the stage sipping Guinness stout mixed with Red Bull energy drinks. From the sidelines, other men, women, and children passively observe the activities.

Scenario 3: A Man Dances at a Wedding

The setting: Wisma Cahaya Garuda, a large hall in a newer section of western Bandung that can be rented for private functions, in 1996. My drum

CHAPTER ONE

1.3   A man dances at a wedding (photo: Henry Spiller, 1996).

teacher, Tosin Mochtar, has invited me to observe him and his lingkung seni perform for a Sundanese wedding.

The scene: The bride and groom, dressed in elaborate formal outfits, sit regally on a couch on the stage, surrounded by the rest of the wedding party. First, the lingkung seni presents an *upacara adat* ("traditional ceremony")—a pageant that draws upon traditional characters and symbols to cast the newlywed couple as aristocrats for a day and welcome them (and their guests) to the reception (cf. Swindells 2004). Following the upacara adat, the performers present a selection of choreographed dances, some *degung kawih* (solo songs accompanied by a small, distinctly Sundanese type of gamelan called *gamelan degung*), and karaoke singing accompanied by a solo keyboard.

The action: While three female dancers in matching costumes perform their carefully rehearsed jaipongan dance to an accompaniment featuring gamelan and a female singer, one of the guests—a middle-aged man dressed in fastidiously pressed slacks and a silky batik shirt—enters the performance area and begins to dance along (see fig. 1.3). I was surprised that nobody pulled him aside discreetly to suggest he stay out of the dancers' way. The dancers themselves did not acknowledge the interloper, but neither did they seem particularly irked by him. Sometimes he danced facing the women, approaching them, while at other times he faced away from them. I asked Tosin who he was and why he got up and danced. Tosin shrugged and said he was a guest, and that he felt like dancing.

Overview of Sundanese Dances

All three of these scenarios took place within the context of some sort of ritual. In post-independence West Java, there are nonritual contexts for dancing as well—recitals by faculty and students at the government-sponsored college-level arts institute (Sekolah Tinggi Seni Indonesia [STSI]),[2] television entertainment, benefit concerts for various charitable causes, cultural shows at hotels and restaurants, nightclubs—but many performances are presented within the framework of some sort of ceremony. Despite this shared ritual context, the three scenarios represent (in very broad strokes) an overview of modern Sundanese dances. The first is a self-consciously traditional ritual performance. Its location is determined through ritual conventions—in this case, the location of the irrigation system—and the various actions each participant takes are imbued with symbolic intention and meaning. The second is a vibrant, contemporary social dance scene. Although the participants understand the event's ritual significance, their main motivation for dancing is to entertain themselves. The third is a staged presentational dance, with trained, costumed dancers. Again, despite the ceremonial setting, the performance is apprehended as entertainment and spectacle by the audience.

These three contexts fit rather closely with a common framework for describing contemporary Sundanese dance, such as that presented by Iwan Natapradja in his article "Sundanese Dances" (1975). Natapradja describes four categories: (1) ritual and ceremonial dances, (2) self-defense dance, (3) social dances, and (4) performing dances (1975:103–5). These serve as an outline for my overview of contemporary Sundanese dance.

Ritual and Ceremonial Dances

Premodern Sundanese life centered around agricultural pursuits—the cycle of planting and harvesting rice. Throughout West Java, farming communities pay homage to the rice goddess, Nyi Pohaci, also known as Dewi Sri. A few communities still perform music and dance featuring *angklung* (shaken bamboo rattles) and *dogdog* (conical drums) to accompany the carrying of the newly harvested rice from the fields to the storehouses. Although each region has its own version of angklung ensembles—the

CHAPTER ONE

Sundanese culture journal *Kawit* once reported twenty-one distinct varieties (Masunah, Milyartini, Yukara, Karwati, and Hermawan 2003:4)—all the ensembles embody the spirit of cooperation that is important to agricultural success. Each musician plays a single angklung, which provides only a single pitch. Melodies and ostinatos emerge only when the entire group performs intricately coordinated interlocking parts. Angklung ensembles are quite mobile, and the musicians may also be considered dancers.

For a possible glimpse into the Sundanese past, urban and rural Sundanese alike look to small, self-isolated communities of Baduy—a small group that speaks a dialect of the Sundanese language and fiercely adheres to an old-fashioned, technologically limited agricultural lifestyle and an animistic belief system (Wessing 1977). Sometimes the Baduy are dubbed the "Amish of Indonesia" because of their iconoclastic cultural practices. According to one legend, they are descendants of the rulers of the Pajajaran kingdom (1333–1579 CE)—the last independent Sundanese political entity—who fled to the hinterlands when driven from their court by invaders from the central Javanese Mataram kingdom (Ekadjati 1995:60–61). Although the legend is almost certainly not based in fact, it does reflect the fact that it is to the Baduy that modern Sundanese attribute authenticity. The performance of music and dance in Baduy communities is regulated by the annual one-crop dry rice agricultural cycle. The angklung are played only during the three-month planting season and are "put to sleep" for the rest of the year (Zanten 1995:527). Angklung performance is associated with the planting of rice: the sound of the angklung awakes the rice goddess (Ekadjati 1995:100–101; Zanten 1995:532).

Such ritual performances are full of symbolic significance, much of which is eloquently explicated by the practitioners. They characterize the bamboo from which the angklung are made as part of Dewi Sri herself (according to legend, when the goddess was interred in the earth, all sorts of useful plants, including several varieties of bamboo, sprung up from different parts of her body). The sleeping goddess is awakened by the music and dancing to ensure her cooperation in growing a bountiful crop, and the cooperative music making models the cooperative enterprise of dry rice farming (Masunah, Milyartini, Yukara, Karwati, and Hermawan 2003:10).

Some ceremonial music traditions persist even after their original ritual functions have disappeared. Wet rice farming allows for multiple crops each year, making an annual ritual obsolete. In some communities, angklung traditions simply died out; in other locales, they were re-

DISCOURSES OF SUNDANESE DANCE

fashioned to be suitable for other kinds of celebrations—for example, life-cycle ceremonies such as weddings and circumcisions. In the several Sundanese localities where diehard musicians maintain traditional angklung ensembles, their mobility has made them an ideal component of Indonesian Independence Day (August 17) parades. As ceremonial performances are recontextualized, their symbolism becomes abstract and more difficult to explain.

Penca silat

Fighting arts are cultivated all over the Malay world, usually designated with the umbrella term *silat*. The Sundanese version of such self-defense practice is called penca silat. In addition to learning physical and mental discipline and secret techniques for besting an opponent, which some Sundanese characterize as the *buah* (fruit) of penca silat, students also study and perform dances based on the fighting movements they study. The dance aspect is considered to be the *kembang* (flower) of penca (Atmadibrata, Dunumiharja, and Sunarya 2006:22–23; Wilson 2002:75). Penca silat is a popular entertainment for a variety of occasions. In performance a musical ensemble, called *kendang penca* (two sets of kendang drums, a small gong, and a shawm called *tarompet*), accompanies the movements. Because it can be regarded as self-defense rather than dance, it is popular even among those Sundanese Muslims whose interpretation of the Qur'an prohibits participation in music and dance activities.

Penca silat has long been an object of Sundanese ethnic identification. According to Shoto Fukuoka, penca silat music was broadcast in the early days of the Bandung branch of the national radio station, Radio Republik Indonesia (RRI), on Sunday mornings, in alternation with gamelan degung music (2003:101). Schoolchildren study penca silat as a form of physical education, and there are quite a few penca silat organizations devoted to the study and proliferation of various styles of penca silat throughout West Java. Performances of penca silat—fighting demonstrations, dance performances, and displays of esoteric *elmu* (magical power)—have been and continue to be popular at weddings, circumcisions, and other celebrations.

Musical accompaniment for penca silat comprises five named rhythmic patterns, called *tepak*.[3] The slower tepak have two sections, which are alternated. In the first, the dancers perform combinations of fighting movements that increase in intensity as the gong stroke approaches but come to a dramatic stop just before the stroke. The second section, called *mincid*, involves warily walking around as if circling an opponent.

CHAPTER ONE

Social Dances

Dance events involving amateur male dancers who interact with professional female entertainers have been part of the landscape of Sundanese dance (as well as other Indonesian dance traditions) for centuries. The basic outline of these dance events once again relates to agricultural mythology. To explain the phenomenon of the Earth's latent fertility, Sundanese ancestors mapped it to a fertility system over which they had more direct control—human sexuality. The fundamental metaphor is that the earth, symbolized by the female rice goddess, is inseminated by masculine powers of heaven in the form of precipitation (Sumardjo 2005a). The ancestors enacted the process in dance events, in which female entertainers were personifications of the rice goddess, and the men in a community collectively represented the masculine power of the rain.

In current Sundanese discourse, dance events intended for common people accompanied by small ensembles of traditional musical instruments are generally lumped into a single category—ketuk tilu—although there are time- and place-specific names for particular versions as well. A nineteenth- and twentieth-century aristocratic equivalent, which featured the same female entertainers but were accompanied by a full gamelan ensembles, is generally called *tayub* or tayuban. An updated version of ketuk tilu, called *kliningan* or bajidoran, thrives in and around the minor Sundanese urban centers of Subang and Karawang (as described earlier in scenario 2). Bajidoran involves traditional gamelan instruments and female performers, but it also makes room for modern popular musical styles and new styles of dancing, such as *triping* ("tripping"), a choreographic interpretation of the euphoric state induced by the drug ecstasy.

Men are the main participants in social dances past and present; ordinary women rarely dance in public. Although women might enjoy watching the men in their lives perform, they leave the female dance roles to professional entertainers, who were generally thought to be of questionable moral character. Some aristocrats dutifully studied European ballroom dances as part of their effort to assimilate the niceties of upper-crust Dutch lifestyles (Sumarsam 1995:68, 78). In the 1950s there were efforts to popularize an Indonesian couple dance (i.e., a social dance to be danced by a man and a woman as a couple, in the manner of European couple dances). According to Enoch Atmadibrata, these attempts were not well received because people associated women who danced with prostitution, and so men did not want their wives and daughters to

DISCOURSES OF SUNDANESE DANCE

dance in public (personal communication, June 21, 1999; Atmadibrata 1998:4–5; Somantri 1953a).

At the beginning of the twenty-first century, the most popular social dancing (in West Java, as well as in other parts of Indonesia) is done to the accompaniment of *dangdut*, a versatile pan-Indonesian popular music genre characterized by its eponymous drum groove: "dang" is a typical onomatopoeic representation of a low-pitched drum sound, while "dut" represents a drum stroke with a rising pitch. Dangdut songs feature diatonic harmony, usually played on guitars and electronic keyboards, and lyrics that typically are in the national language—Indonesian—although some dangdut songs may be cast in local and regional languages such as Sundanese.

The stigma attached to women who dance in public has lessened, but not completely disappeared, since Indonesian independence. Indonesia participated in the worldwide popularity of disco in the last decades of the twentieth century, and young, urban, modern-thinking women are happy to dance with other women and even with men in nightclubs. This attitude has rubbed off onto more traditional performances as well, so that in the 1990s it was not impossible to see women taking part in social dances at weddings, usually in groups. However, such activities rarely went on without comments about the female dancers' bravery in the face of strong social taboos. The superstar singers who dominate the dangdut scene are sometimes male but more often female, and female superstars inherit the sullied reputation of their artistic ancestors. Inul Daratista, whose suggestive pelvic-thrusting dance style (called *ngebor*—"drilling") was deemed pornographic by some, for example, in 2003 found herself at the center of a national controversy about Indonesian morals (Weintraub 2008:368).

Presentational Dances

The current Sundanese presentational dance repertoire includes a host of choreographed dances; these are generally divided into the categories *wayang*, *topeng*, *kursus*, *kreasi baru*, and *rakyat*. In recent years, the first four categories (excluding rakyat dances) have often been grouped together under the umbrella term *tari klasik* (classical dance). Wayang dances depict characters from the Sundanese versions of the Indian epics *Ramayana* and *Mahabharata*, and sometimes from the indigenous Indonesian *Panji* and *Menak* stories. The most obvious context for such dances is *wayang wong* (wayang stories presented with multiple dancers, who may provide dialogue and song as well). Itinerant wayang wong troupes once

CHAPTER ONE

performed for both the upper and lower classes in West Java around the turn of the twentieth century (Rusliana 1989). In the early twentieth century, some Sundanese aristocrats entertained themselves by producing wayang productions that they themselves directed and danced; such productions were called *wayang priya* or *wayang priyayi* (Durban Ardjo 1998:51; Rusliana 1989:15).[4] These Sundanese creations were based on models from the court traditions of central Java and as well as village-style topeng (masked dance) from Cirebon. Nowadays, solo wayang dances and duets most often are performed as independent pieces, outside of the framework of a drama. Wayang dancers wear character-specific costumes and assume fictional personalities; they also conform to the physical build of the portrayed character and affect his or her mannerisms. Most wayang dances include movements that are unique to the character as well as movements common to other presentational genres.

In topeng dances, characters are portrayed with masks as well as movement. Topeng dances are associated with the northern coastal region of Cirebon, where some villages maintain vibrant traditions of topeng dancing. The village style involves a single dancer, called a *dalang topeng*, who portrays four or five masked characters in succession. Dalang typically came from a long line of topeng dancers who regard their lineage as an important component of their ability to dance effectively. Although the characters they portray have specific names (drawn from several Indonesian epic stories), the dances represent character types rather than specific characters. The characters are danced in sequence, and a full performance lasts eight hours (Rogers-Aguiniga 1986; Suanda 1981, 1983, 1985, 1988, 1996).

In the 1940s and 1950s several prominent Sundanese dancers, notably R. Nugraha Sudiredja and Ono Lesmana, learned topeng dances from peripatetic Cirebonese topeng dancers, who came periodically to Bandung, Sumedang, and other Sundanese cities to perform and teach (Suryabrata 1974:540). They drew upon these experiences to create uniquely Sundanese topeng dances by changing the costume, movements, and choreography to conform to their own aesthetic ideals. Nugraha's "Tiga Kedok" (Three Masks), "Kencana Wungu," and "Menak Jingga" (both named eponymously for characters from the Javanese *Damarwulan* epic story) dances are frequently taught and performed. Since the 1970s Sundanese dancers have attempted to learn original Cirebonese styles from topeng masters and to reproduce more faithfully the costumes and movement styles. Because each family of dalang topeng (and, indeed, each individual dalang) cultivates a unique style, this practice has resulted in a proliferation of topeng dances.

Tari kursus (called *ibing keurseus* in Sundanese) originated in the early twentieth century as a method for learning aristocratic social dancing. By the middle of the century, it had become a presentational dance genre in its own right, one that came to occupy a central position among Sundanese presentation dance genres. Natapradja characterizes kursus as "probably the principal and basic dance in Sunda today" (1975:105; see also Murgiyanto 1998:504; Soepandi and Atmadibrata 1976:85). Its basic movement vocabulary and formal structure provide a framework for other presentational dance choreographies (Atmadibrata 1977:9).

Kreasi baru (new creations) reflect a blending of old, traditional Sundanese elements with new concepts. Many also reflect some of the fundamental changes in Indonesian culture since the revolution and independence (1945–50), especially nationalism. Decades after his death in 1963, R. Tjetje Somantri remains West Java's most famous choreographer, and his dances are frequently performed; they are perhaps the best-known Sundanese dances within and outside of West Java.

Rakyat Dances

In the late 1970s a new presentational genre of dancing appeared on the scene: jaipongan. Although jaipongan incorporated elements of other presentational dances, as well as of penca silat, its most obvious source was bajidoran—a modern version of nonaristocratic social dance popular in the Subang region just north of Bandung. Within about ten years, however, jaipongan came to assume a hallowed place in the canon of Sundanese "traditional" dance. Its success and appeal inspired other choreographers to adapt other local dance traditions to the stage; these adaptations are generally called rakyat dances (the term "rakyat" suggests the common people and might be translated as "folk").

Jaipongan's lightning-quick transformation from innovation to tradition underscores the rapid changes that characterize Sundanese artistic practices over the past century as well as the Sundanese public's ability to assimilate into the canon of Sundanese tradition new forms that probe contemporary issues and values. The creation of a new category called tari klasik—which, in effect, fabricates a history for staged presentational dances—also demonstrates that designating something as "traditional" or "classical" in West Java does not necessarily mean that something is old, only that it somehow suits contemporary notions of traditional Sundaneseness. Although these different dance genres have different histories and precedents, the development of each over the course of the twentieth century is inextricably intertwined with that of all the others.

CHAPTER ONE

Most trained contemporary dancers have experience in all of them, and together they form a kind of canon of modern "traditional" Sundanese dance.

Discourses of Sundanese Dance

Sundanese dance in the modern era encompasses a wide variety of forms, genres, and contexts. Some overview descriptions of Sundanese dance begin with a division into two basic categories: *joged* and *ibing* (Atmadibrata 1980; Hood 1967:464); scholars who take this tack are probably following the model provided in an influential article by M. Soeriadiradja and I. Adiwidjaja.[5] In this formulation, joged refers to genres performed by the lower classes, while ibing refers to various genres first cultivated by upper-class Sundanese. A 1955 article about Sundanese dance in the *Star Weekly* makes the distinction more bluntly, stating that there are two levels of Sundanese dance: coarse (*kasar*) and refined (*halus*) (Seni Tari Sunda dalam Perajaan Pehtjun 1955).

It is not clear that historically any such clear distinction was ever drawn between aristocratic and common people's dancing. In West Java there were no regional centers of elite culture with the kind of wide influence wielded by the *kraton* (palaces) of central Java (Narawati 2003b:112; Natapradja 1975:103). The closest equivalents were the *kabupaten* (provincial government seats), which did not have the financial resources to develop, maintain, and preserve exclusive dance traditions such as those of central Java (Wright 1978:2.2). The Sundanese aristocrats indeed patronized music and dance, but they often relied on artists who also served the surrounding community. Music and dance traditions were thus centered in Sundanese artistic families rather than in the courts (Harrell 1980:211). In any case, since Indonesian independence the democratization and urbanization of West Java have blurred any distinctions there may once have been between ibing and joged (Atmadibrata 1980:211), and new genres have been created and popularized that fit conveniently into neither category.

In the twenty-first century, the label "traditional" is applied to a wide variety of Sundanese dance styles and genres, many with roots in various pre-twentieth-century dance forms. Staged dance performances often take the form of a sort of a revue in which a variety of contrasting dances are presented by professionally trained performers wearing elaborate, colorful costumes. The English-language brochure for Irawati Durban

Ardjo's dance company, Pusbitari (see fig. 1.4), gives a sense of the range of modern Sundanese presentational dance; it advertises staged adaptations of a local village ritual ("Gotong Singa," based on a traditional ceremony from the town of Subang), both lower-class ("Kembang Kalang") and upper-class ("Gawil") men's improvisational dances, and wayang ("Graeni"), topeng ("Klana"), and aristocratic female ("Badaya") dances. Pusbitari also includes emblematic dances from other Indonesian ethnic groups in its repertoire.

Many dancers establish their credentials by studying at STSI Bandung. Although dancers may specialize in one style of dancing or another, most urban dancers are capable of performing "traditional" dances drawn from a variety of repertoires; the STSI curriculum exposes its students to many different dance genres, all of which have been subjected to a certain amount of revision with regard to choreography and standardization by the time they are included in the official course of study.

Some Sundanese Dance Histories

Men's dancing that blurs the lines between performer and observer is a recurring theme in a variety of Sundanese dance genres. Most historians of Sundanese music and dance agree that there is little concrete information on which to base histories of Sundanese dance before the beginning of the twentieth century, but they do generally acknowledge that men of both the upper and the lower classes indulged in dance parties facilitated by professional female singer-dancers, with various sorts of musical accompaniment. It is clear that the entire corpus of presentational Sundanese dances, suitable for performing on stages, emerged only during the course of the twentieth century. Prior to the 1900s most Sundanese dance was participatory; presentational dances were limited to a few specialized contexts and venues. Sundanese dance historians generally maintain that the context and repertoire for presentational dances designed for stage performances developed out of agricultural, ceremonial, and recreational dances. Most of these narratives reveal, however, an unspoken prejudice that presentational dance is a culminating cultural achievement. They imply that there is little place in the modern world for amateur, improvised dancing, even though such dancing may have provided an important inspiration or influence in the development of a uniquely Sundanese style. For many historians, men's improvisational dance is little more than a missing link in the evolution of Sundanese presentational dance.

1.4 Pusbitari brochure (original brochure). Used with the permission of Irawati and Pusbitari Dance Company.

ENOCH ATMADIBRATA'S MODEL   The Sundanese dancer, choreographer, and scholar Enoch Atmadibrata has written many books and articles on Sundanese music and dance. In his earlier works he divides contemporary Sundanese dance into six categories: village ritual and ceremonial dances, *penca* (martial arts), social dances, *wirahma sari* dances (literally, "essence of rhythm," referring to a particular dance club), wayang (theater based on epic stories) dances, and topeng (masked) dances (Atmadibrata 1980:212–14; Soepandi and Atmadibrata 1976:70). Implicit in the ordering of his six categories is a progression from simple to complex, from functional to aesthetic, from participatory to presentational. He characterizes his first category as "the most ancient" and implicitly characterizes it by a certain archaic, primitive joy. The third category, "social dance," derives its refinement from the influence of wayang dance, a presumably more advanced category (Atmadibrata 1980:212).

Although he allows for cross-influences among dances, Enoch's model confers the highest aesthetic value on the presentational dances. The distinctions between the final three categories are not great compared to the qualities that distinguish the first three; they are all dances one might study at STSI Bandung and perform on a stage. Privileging them as separate categories is another strategy for stressing their evolutionary superiority.

In his later writings, however, Enoch groups the last three categories into a single category, *ibing pintonan* ("dances for watching"), that is, presentational dances (e.g., Atmadibrata 1997a:5), and he adds a category called *ibing silaturahmi* ("fellowship dances"), that is, participatory dances, restoring a bit of status to the notion of amateur dancing. These new categories reflect some rethinking on Enoch's part: in 1999 he was eager to revive the tradition of recreational dancing, not only to remind people of its social benefits, but also to promote its potential as a form of exercise.

Conspicuous by their absence in Enoch's model are dances that other critics call *kreasi baru* (new creations)—presentational, choreographed, staged dances—that have been composed and performed since Indonesian independence. Ironically, Enoch himself has made several notable contributions to modern Sundanese choreography, but in this particular analysis he did not incorporate them into his vision of traditional dance. I speculate that part of Enoch's project is to map out an "unchanging tradition" reminiscent of the "invented tradition" critiqued by Hobsbawm, who suggests that traditions are "invented" and that they represent "a set of practices . . . governed by overtly or tacitly accepted rules . . . which

CHAPTER ONE

seek to inculcate certain values and norms of behaviour by repetition, which automatically implies continuity with the past" (Hobsbawm 1983:1). Acknowledgment of modern pieces with known authors might undermine this goal.

SOEDARSONO'S MODEL Like Enoch Atmadibrata, the Indonesian dance scholar Soedarsono's project is to legitimize presentational dances as traditional dances with a long history. Unlike Enoch, however, Soedarsono is not Sundanese, and he seeks to situate Sundanese dance within the broader context of emerging Indonesian nationalist performing arts. Soedarsono pays very little attention in his 1974 *Dances in Indonesia* to the dance genres outlined by Enoch Atmadibrata. He dismisses dances from what he characterizes as the "Period of Primitive Society" literally with a single sentence: "Dances in West Java were still magical and sacred and in accordance with the primitive social structure of the time, they must have been very primitive too" (Soedarsono 1974:120).

In the "Period of Feudal Society" Soedarsono suggests that the Sundanese assimilated topeng dance from north Java as well as various central Javanese styles and thereby "developed a style of [their] own" (1974:123), although he is vague about details. Under the heading "People's Dances" Soedarsono briefly covers a few genres that Enoch might have placed in several different categories. Soedarsono notes that these dances were popular among common people "before independence" (1974:127), implying that they are no longer practiced and have no relevance in modern Indonesia.

In the bulk of Soedarsono's chapter on West Java, a section titled "Sundanese Dancing in Modern Society," he speaks of post-independence choreographers who cultivate and develop Sundanese dances, both those of the court and those of the common people. The dividing line between the two has been eliminated, and both have become Indonesian dances, Sunda style (Soedarsono 1974:129).

The resulting dances are in two categories: classical and modern. Classical dances employ themes deemed to be traditional, such as wayang stories, while modern dances depict nontraditional themes. Surprisingly absent from either category are the abstract *kursus* dances which many critics regard as a central genre in the Sundanese dance milieu (e.g., Murgiyanto 1998:504). Interestingly, Soedarsono mentions R. Tjetje Somantri as a notable choreographer of the modern dances, but does not mention that Tjetje also choreographed most of the dances he describes as classical as well, or that the supposedly classical dances he describes were choreographed during the same time period as the modern ones.

President Soeharto's New Order (Orde Baru) regime (1965–98) promoted the compilation of pan-Indonesian culture from the most attractive "peaks of culture" of the many ethnic groups and regions that comprise the modern Indonesian nation—an idea that dates from the foundation of the Indonesian nation, in 1945, in the Undang-undang Dasar (constitution) (Yampolsky 1995). According to John Pemberton, the New Order policies were designed to create an Indonesian "tradition" that encapsulated a "national treasury of inherited cultural wealth" consistent with the values of the national government (Pemberton 1994:11, 267). Pemberton attributes to New Order cultural policy a rather insidious project of amalgamating historically and politically grounded local customs into a monolithic tradition that was "free of political and historical implications, a culture dedicated to, as if by nature, its own celebration" (1994:15). Acts that once had a specific object in central Java, such as offerings or other devotions to local place spirits, are now made on behalf of "tradition" itself; tradition feeds upon itself in a closed, tightly spinning loop that leaves no room for deeper significance. Soedarsono's approach to rewriting Sundanese dance history (and, for that matter, the history of other Indonesian dance traditions) is consistent with these goals.

IRAWATI DURBAN ARDJO'S MODEL Irawati Durban Ardjo recounts the development of Sundanese presentational dance in her books *Perkembangan tari Sunda* (1998) and *Tari Sunda tahun 1880–1990* (2007). She concentrates on one organization, Badan Kesenian Indonesia (Indonesian Arts Group—BKI), and its two leading figures, R. Tjetje Somantri and Tubagas Oemay Martakusuma. The success of the dances that came out of this organization, she concludes, stems from their anticipation of the nascent Indonesian government's requirements for staged arts (Durban Ardjo 1998:2).

Irawati's dance history begins in earnest in 1880. She divides the hundred years between 1880 and 1980 into three periods. In the first period the raw materials of dance are already fully formed, namely tayub (dance for aristocratic dance events), wayang, topeng, kursus, penca, and dance from central Java. During this first period (1880–1942) Tjetje studied and mastered these various raw materials, and Oemay experimented with Sundanizing central Javanese dance. In the second period (1942–58) the two men pooled their knowledge and ideas to stage choreographed dances. Toward the end of this period their organization, BKI, achieved the height of its prestige. The third period, 1958–80, involves the spread and development of these BKI works throughout West Java (Durban

CHAPTER ONE

Ardjo 1998:xxxiii). In another publication Irawati suggests that subsequent developments and innovations in Sundanese stage dance involve a larger role for female dancers and choreographers, as well as research into "traditional forms" for inspirations for new choreography (Durban Arjo 1989:174). Irawati's presentation of this model as a flowchart (1998: xxxiii) suggests that she envisions Sundanese dance history as a progression from "raw materials" to modern, presentational dance.

PRIVILEGING PRESENTATIONAL DANCE   Other writers on Sundanese dance present variations of these approaches. Iwan Natapradja, for example, adopts Enoch Atmadibrata's model rather closely, although he follows Enoch's later practice of grouping the last three of the six categories together under the rubric "performing dances" (Natapradja 1975:103). Sal Murgiyanto, however, tends in his descriptions of Sundanese dance to include men's amateur improvisational dance forms that are left out by the other writers (Murgiyanto 1991, 1998).

In response to a "peaks of culture" cultural policy, Sundanese artists working in the Soeharto period indeed focused on finding or inventing Sundanese dance traditions that could represent Sundanese culture on national and international stages. West Javanese regional culture, with its emphasis on participatory dance and titillating female performers, apparently required "conservation, guidance, and development" (*pelestarian, pembinaan, pengembangan*) to be deemed suitable for national and international consumption, and provincial West Javanese government regulations outlined how to accomplish this (Jurriëns 2004:34–36). According to R. Anderson Sutton (writing on Sulawesi), the art forms that succeed in this milieu are those that are "attractive and sanitized," exhibit "readily observable physical skill," and leave a "strong visual impression" (Sutton 2002:189, 133).

Historians contributed to the fabrication of an appropriate Sundanese dance tradition—the kind of rewriting of dance history that Acciaioli calls a "cunning strategy" to relativize local traditions and make their value aesthetic rather than ritual (Acciaioli 1985:151–52). Despite an emphasis on participatory, improvisational dance in the past and the key role such dancing plays in Sundanese culture, these modern histories of Sundanese dance focus instead on documenting the relatively recent development of presentational dances. They present dance as a primarily visual experience for spectators and minimize the kinesthetic experiences of participants (including performers and engaged spectators). The progression of twentieth-century Sundanese dance presented in these histories valorizes attempts to professionalize dance, to solidify a boundary between performer and audience, and to disenfranchise the men in the audience who might be inspired to dance along, relegating them to the role of observers. Dance is envisioned as a visual symbol of Sundanese ethnic identity and West Javanese regional identity within larger Indonesian and international arenas, despite the persistent and long-standing practice in the Sundanese arts of active audience participation. In these narratives, men's improvisational dance is reduced to the role of the missing link between the unknown past and modern, presentational forms in the evolution of Sundanese dance. The implication is that there is no place in the modern world for amateur, improvised dancing, despite the significance of such dancing as source material for a Sundanese presentational dance style.

Dance in the Present: Exploring Gender Identities

Although modern Sundanese narratives of music and dance history acknowledge the existence of men's improvisational dance, they tend to downplay its significance by characterizing it as merely *hiburan* (entertainment). The only importance that such histories ascribe to amateur dancing is as an antecedent to more serious, developed forms of presentational dance. I assert, however, that there is still a social function in the practice of improvisational men's dance: to delineate and explore gender identities, in particular masculine identities.

As this chapter's three opening scenarios suggest, men's dancing in the present often takes place within the contexts of rituals of some sort. The brief overview of Sundanese dance that followed the scenarios identified agricultural rituals as a site for the development of men's dancing and suggested that the protocols of improvisational dance were rooted in fertility symbolism.

Only one of the scenarios—the irrigation-system ritual near Lembang—could be characterized as unequivocally agricultural in nature. The social values that grew out of an agricultural past, however (division of labor between men and women, ways of structuring families and kinship networks, and means of accruing social status), underlie modern, nonagricultural Sundanese culture. And so the ritual practices that affirmed these social values persist into modern rituals, such as weddings, and even into the sorts of ritual behavior that urbanites prefer to call "fun." The overt gender symbolism of agricultural rituals—the fertile feminine goddess, the masculine heavenly powers that inseminate her via the rain—continues to provide foundational metaphors for the Sundanese understanding of the cosmos and the world of human relations

CHAPTER ONE

by mapping the bounty of the natural world onto particular gender behaviors, roles, and identities. By gender identities, I mean the matrix of ideas, behaviors, and assumptions that result in the division of people into at least two distinct categories that we typically characterize as "sex" or "gender." Although "male" and "female" seem to be, on the surface, quintessentially natural categories, the notion that these categories are social constructs has been widely discussed in recent decades (cf. Butler 1990, 1993; Ortner and Whitehead 1981).

Gender identities and gendered behaviors lie at the heart of all Sundanese dance. In the discourse of wayang dances, for example, individual named characters are classified first into gender (male or female) and then into various subcategories, such as *satria lenyep* (most refined male), *satria lanyap* (refined male), *ponggawa* (warrior), and *raksasa* or *danawa* (coarse or monstrous male) (Arcangel 2006; Natapradja 1975:105–6; Soepandi and Atmadibrata 1976:89–90). Comparing these male categories with the two classifications for female wayang characters—*putri lenyep* (most refined female) and *putri lanyap* (refined female)—immediately suggests a fundamental difference between the range of socially acceptable masculine behaviors and socially acceptable feminine ones. Men may be coarse in public; women apparently may not. To dance these characters, performers draw upon a treasury of stereotyped gestures and movements as well as different kinds of costuming. In wayang performances, the dancer's own physical characteristics determine to a certain extent which characters he or she might portray; rarely is a tall, husky, or unattractive man well received in performing refined *satria* dances, while a slightly built, handsome man is fated to be typecast in such roles. In current practice, female dancers often perform refined male roles. It is extremely unusual and considered inappropriate, however, for a man to perform a female character in wayang dances (Arcangel 2006:65).

Cirebonese village-style topeng presents a much different approach to gender roles and identities. A single performer (the dalang topeng), wearing a single costume, presents a range of characters, each of which is distinguished by gesture, movement, and mask. Some of the characters portrayed are clearly masculine, while others tend toward the feminine. Topeng's gender symbolism extends beyond the sex of the characters— the white color of the mask for the most refined dance, "Panji," symbolizes semen, while the red color of the coarsest dance, "Rahwana" (or "Klana"), symbolizes menstrual blood. Although both characters are male, the symbolism reflects associations of masculinity with self-control and femininity with uncontrolled lust and passion (Foley 1990a:70, 79 n. 16). Topeng costume, masks, dance movements, and choreography are the same whether the dancer is a man or a woman, and historically the occupation of dalang topeng has always been open to both men and women.

Although discourse about participatory dance is less overtly focused on gender roles and behaviors, nevertheless issues of gender lie at the core of social dancing. The most attention is paid to the female performers, whose behavior is generally denigrated as morally corrupt. Raffles's oft-quoted statement in his 1811 *History of Java* that female performers' "conduct is generally so incorrect, as to render the title ronggèng and prostitute synonimous [*sic*]" (1965:1–342) still holds true in the twenty-first century. Ben Arcangel reports that some of his teachers at STSI Bandung still consider the term "ronggeng" to be an offensive label for female dancers (Arcangel 2006:54), and my own experience suggests that men who participate in social dancing are often viewed with contempt. The public transcript holds that their attraction to the female performers is unseemly, and that their time and money might be better spent on more profitable activities. Yet there is, at the same time, a private transcript of admiration (albeit grudging at times) for a man who is perceived to dance gracefully and cleverly.

Masculinity, *malu*, and Men's Dance

Although dance events inscribe an entire matrix of gender identities, their focus is on men and masculine behaviors. Audiences at dance events indulge in two main activities: (1) some, most, or all male audience members dance, and (2) all audience members, male and female, witness the goings-on whether they dance or not. The sole active female participants—the ronggeng—have a primarily professional interest in the events. They perform a role that requires them to deemphasize their own subjectivity and act as the object of desire for the male participants, who explore the extent of their own personal prowess by dancing to the accompaniment of drumming. Whether dancing or witnessing, each member of the audience is forced to confront the double bind of Sundanese masculinities.

Sundanese Masculinities

The complexity of gender identities is sometimes masked by the deceptively simple terms used to discuss them. Most people think they have such clear ideas about what "masculinity," "femininity," and other such

CHAPTER ONE

gender-related terms mean that they rarely define or question these terms. When they are challenged to do so, however, it becomes apparent that their definitions encompass a bewilderingly wide variety of topics and concepts. In his survey of anthropological investigations of masculinity, Gutman notes that the concept subsumes "related notions of male identity, manhood, manliness, and men's roles" (1997:386). Current theories of masculinity reject the notion that there is a single standard to which all men are held, but rather recognize multiple masculinities (Connell 1995). Little has been written specifically about Sundanese masculinities. The anthropologist Joshua Barker's dissertation on Sundanese notions of crime and security (Barker 1999) is a notable exception, and I follow his practice of making use of analytical writings about masculinities in comparable communities (such as central Java and Malaysia) or in Indonesia as a whole that resonate with my own experiences of men and masculinity in West Java, even though they do not address specifically Sundanese communities.

Dede Oetomo describes masculinity as an "unmarked category" in Indonesia, by which he means that the criteria for acceptable masculine behavior are rarely articulated (2000:46). He infers a broad picture of Indonesians standards for men "from the criticisms voiced of inequalities between women and men":

The portrait that emerges is of men always acting as heads of families and as breadwinners, operating in the public sphere, and not being responsible for the upbringing of children or the sharing of household work. In the area of sexuality, one would infer a thinly disguised "legendary" heterosexual promiscuity of men and a consistent role of men as initiators and dominators in heterosexual intercourse.   (OETOMO 2000:57 N. 1)

R. W. Connell would characterize what Oetomo describes above as a hegemonic masculinity—the "configuration of gender practices" that represents the "one form of masculinity . . . that is culturally exalted" at a particular time in a given place (Connell 1995:77).

Of course, other configurations of masculine practices—alternative masculinities—are possible as well. The specific time and place of which Oetomo speaks is Indonesia in the final years of Soeharto's New Order regime (1965–98). An older masculine ideal—the courtly central Javanese ideal of manliness—still carries a great deal of prestige in modern Indonesia. Exemplars of this approach to manliness are refined (*alus* in Javanese and Sundanese, *halus* in Indonesian), emotionally restrained, modest, slight of body but powerful as a result of spiritual exercise and

DISCOURSES OF SUNDANESE DANCE

ascetic practice, sexually potent but in control of sexual urges, and capable of wielding great influence without undue physical effort. This refined masculinity is exemplified in many ways by the characters Rama and Arjuna, the respective heroes of the Indian epics *Ramayana* and *Mahabharata*, which are familiar to most Javanese, Sundanese, and Balinese individuals, even those whose pedigrees are far removed from the aristocracy, through the medium of wayang (puppet theater). It seems likely that some aspects of this approach to masculinity are uniquely Malay-Indonesian and predate the cultural influences of Hinduism in Indonesia, because the autochthonous Indian versions of Rama and Arjuna are much more extroverted than their Indonesian counterparts (Narawati 2003a:150).

Under the influence of Javanese culture, Sundanese ideals of masculinity paralleled those of the Javanese in the nineteenth and early twentieth centuries (Narawati 2003a:149). Tati Narawati cites a Sundanese-language poem that describes the ideal Sundanese man (Narawati 2003a:140):[6]

Kewes gandes tandang gandang	How is, at first sight, a *satria* [knight]
sinatria pilih tanding	who has no match?
Handap asor pamakena	Modest is his behavior
Titih rintih tur nastiti	Polite and well-mannered with complete control
Mun nyaur diukur-ukur	He speaks with complete measure
Nyabda diungang-ungang	He says what needs to be said
Ciciren teu ieu aing	His character is not conceited
Panatana satria tedak Pasundan	Such is the behavior of a Sundanese satria

This refined masculinity remained the dominant masculine ideal over a large swath of Indonesian time and territory, yet other masculinities have always coexisted with it (Clark 1994:115). Javanese society regarded a wide variety of behaviors as "properly masculine"—from "he-man to rather . . . 'effeminate,' " according to James Peacock (1968:204 n. 3). Keeler makes the case that other masculine sensibilities have an important role to play in social interactions:

While the quality of alus is idealized as a virtue, other qualities are available to counterbalance it. A person may command respect for his ability to get things done, even if that ability depends precisely on his willingness to act more forthrightly than is usually considered proper. Or he may be appreciated for his straightforwardness and a sense of humor that depends on that undauntable frankness   (KEELER 1975:92)

CHAPTER ONE

Although Arjuna and other refined characters were models for ideal rulers before Indonesian independence, the armed struggle for independence made way for Indonesia's first president, Sukarno, to identify with a more aggressive wayang hero—Arjuna's large-bodied and crude but heroic brother Bima (Pausacker 2004:217). During the Sukarno era, Jabang Tutuka (the young Gatotkaca, Bima's son), whose weak body was reborn as a strong warrior, came to be seen as a metaphor for the emergence of a strong, independent Indonesia from its colonial roots (Anderson 1965; Weintraub 2004b:110). Masculine ideals are always in flux; even though a hands-off, alus approach may have been the Javanese aristocracy's preferred means of wielding their power, one of the chief legacies of Soeharto's New Order was establishing "violence as a legitimate mechanism of domination" (Clark 1994:128).

Non-Javanese ethnic groups have generally cultivated their own hegemonic masculinities. Many Sundanese, for example, have regarded Bima's gruff son Gatotkaca to be the "ideal hero," and Sundanese *dalang* dwell on scenes where Gatotkaca corrects the refined Arjuna, the ideal hero for central Javanese wayang fans, when he strays from the straight and narrow (Rosidi 1984a:149), perhaps to reflect the fans' own assessment of a Sundanese ethnic character in relation to the Javanese. According to Benedict Anderson, "the proverbially hot-headed, impetuous Madurese (from the nearby island of Madura) are known to have a special fondness for Bålådéwa" (Anderson 1965:24).

The varied role models presented by these traditional characters are supplemented by a host of additional masculinities visible in contemporary Indonesia's advertising and entertainment media. They present a hodgepodge of traits perceived to be masculine—wanderlust, reasonableness, and sexual passion, among others—that are not necessarily quite consistent with one another.

At all turns, then, a Sundanese man is met with contradictory expectations. As a lover, a man's wife expects him to be a skillful, experienced, and passionate sexual partner. Men are expected to acquire these skills somewhere other than the marital bed. Although public discourse encourages them to be chaste before marriage, and women demand fidelity from their husbands, private discourse tells another story: nobody truly expects the men in their lives to live up to the standards of public discourse (cf. Hatley 1990). Likewise, a man's duty, as head of a household, is to provide financially for his family, yet wife and children are genuinely (if pleasantly) surprised if he is not lazy and profligate. Sundanese men are introduced to a double standard of masculinity early in life. As boys, they are waited on and doted on by their parents and older siblings, but these same people also constantly subject the boys to many little humiliations to impart a proper sense of malu.

Malu

A complex emotional state, central to Southeast Asian concepts of sociality, is known in Indonesian as malu.[7] It is problematic to translate malu into a single English word because the usual glosses, including shame, embarrassment, shyness, bashfulness, humility, and modesty, do not quite capture the subtleties of this important cultural concept. One feels malu when dressed inappropriately, or when asked to do something in public, or when observed making an error. Malu also describes a self-administered instrument of social control—a potent superego force carefully inculcated into individuals when they are children that governs their actions and reactions and pressures them to conform to prescribed social conventions. A proper sense of malu keeps one from behaving inappropriately toward one's equals, the opposite sex, or one's social superiors.

Writing on *lek* (the Balinese equivalent of malu), Clifford Geertz proposed "stage fright" as a better English equivalent than shame or modesty. According to Geertz, individuals find themselves playing the role of people who behave properly, and malu is the self-conscious awareness that proper behavior is at odds with the genuine self as well as the fear that the genuine self might shine through any carefully constructed social persona (Geertz 1973b:402).

Ward Keeler objects to this characterization, pointing out that it puts an artificial distance between the individual's inner self and his outer social persona. Rather than a fear of the genuine self's shining through the social persona, Keeler asserts that *isin* (the Javanese equivalent of malu) is the danger that the relative status and power of individuals will not be clear (1983:161–62). Malu, then, is more accurately described as an awareness of one's "vulnerability in interactions" (1983:158). In other words, malu is a tool for constructing, negotiating, and maintaining social status and power and as such is a key facet of Sundanese masculinities. According to Keeler, status is "the outward manifestation of an immaterial but impressive power" (Keeler 1983:159). There has been considerable ethnological discussion of Javanese concepts of power, most famously by Benedict Anderson in his essay "The Idea of Power in Javanese Culture" (1972). Robert Wessing's *Cosmology and Social Behavior in a West Javanese Settlement* provides a detailed analysis of Sundanese notions of power and status, which he believes represent an approach common in

CHAPTER ONE

other Indonesian and Southeast Asian cultures as well (1978:166–67). Following Anderson's axioms about Javanese concepts of power (1972), Wessing asserts that a Sundanese worldview holds that everything (and everybody) is imbued with power, and that the sum total of power in the cosmos is finite. Power flows to the cosmic center, which redistributes it back through the cosmos; this flow is what maintains the vitality of the system. Uncontained power is dangerous. How much power something (or someone) contains is determined by how much it is capable of holding, which can vary depending on a number of circumstances. One way to increase one's capacity for power is to acquire esoteric knowledge, through the study of traditional practices and/or Islam.

Another means is to demonstrate one's capacity for power by redistributing it to others, creating dependency relationships that increase one's status and, consequently, one's capacity for containing power (Wessing 1977:297–98; 1978:157–58). Keeler provides essentially the same explanation from a slightly different angle: although power may be acquired in ascetic activities, he states, ultimately it "is manifest primarily in encounter." A person's power can be discerned only by the way others treat him, "the deference he elicits from others." A man with status "should be able, by virtue of his impressive presence, to exert control over other people." Others should feel malu in the presence of this power and status; a man who does not induce a feeling of malu in others feels malu himself over his failure (Keeler 1983:160).

Daniel Fessler, in an examination of attitudes about malu in a community in southwestern Sumatra (1999), concludes that it is associated with two rather different situations: (1) when a person is in the presence of a superior, she or he feels malu; and (2) when a person violates a norm, malu is the aversive emotion felt in response to the fear that others might find the failure reprehensible. In other words, malu is an emotional response either to inferiority or to public failure. The opposite of malu is sometimes identified as *bangga* ("rightful pride") (Fessler 1999). It is important to note that the negative implications of arrogance and conceit that adhere to the English word "pride" are expressed with an entirely different Indonesian word, *sombong*; bangga is always positive (Heider 1991:67).

Standing out in a crowd—being somehow prominent, through appearance or behavior—can cause feelings of either malu or bangga, depending on the circumstances. Standing out for doing something inappropriate is likely to lead to a feeling of malu, while standing out because of something that is customarily lauded creates bangga. Standing out in general results in a reaffirmation or a change in others' opinions of an individual, and the judgment of others is the crucial factor that determines whether one's actions engender a feeling of shame or one of pride. Keeler, again speaking of the Javanese equivalent of malu, concludes that an individual's mastery of isin involves "understanding the full range of situations in which one's dignity and status are on the line" (Keeler 1983:160).

What is at stake in such situations? Fessler explores malu as an example of how humans parlay basic emotions into more complex engagements with their social environments. He sees as human universals two "primitive" emotions, which he calls protoshame and protopride, that developed in response to "the quest for social dominance." They provide a foundation for "second-order emotions" that "motivate conformity rather than rivalry" (1999:75–76). Protoshame and protopride govern the interactions of an individual with others based on the assessment of whether he or she is superior or inferior (1999:87). Second-order shame or pride involves a complex comparison of one's own self-evaluation to the perceived evaluations of multiple others, with whom one shares expectations for proper social behavior, in order to facilitate inclusion in the cooperative efforts of the larger group. This second-order shame or pride "became the foundation for a system of social control premised on conformity to cultural understandings" (1999:102), but one that still allows for adjustments in rank and status. Fessler points out that displays of dominance or subordinance within dyadic interactions with another individual serve to articulate relative status—a relationship of rivalry. The same displays in larger group situations, however, can signal instead one's understanding of the mechanisms of cooperation; they can allow others to assess one's potential contribution to the cooperative effort (Fessler 1999:87). This double function—rivalry and conformity—provides an explanation of the contradictory expectations for men's behavior.

Eve Kosofsky Sedgwick and Adam Frank have discussed the psychologist Silvan Tomkins's opposition of shame to a different affect—interest:

Tomkins considers shame, along with interest, surprise, joy, anger, fear, distress, disgust, and in his later writing contempt ("dissmell"), to be the basic set of affects. He places shame, in fact, at one end of the affect polarity shame-interest: suggesting that the pulsations of cathexis around shame, of all things, are what either enable or disenable so basic a function as the ability to be interested in the world.
(SEDGWICK AND FRANK 1995:5)

Tomkins's word "interest" reinforces the notion that those behaviors restricted by feelings of malu are not necessarily behaviors that should never be enacted. Displays of dominance, which typically are limited by

CHAPTER ONE

one's own sense of malu as well as by the judgments of others based on their understanding of malu, can become sources of rightful pride if others perceive such displays as appropriate. Sometimes overcoming malu and being *berani*—the Indonesian word for "daring" or "brave"[8]— has rewards, in the form of increased status. I am unaware of instances in which malu and berani are used as direct opposites; *takut* ("afraid"), however, often is clustered with malu in Indonesian landscapes of emotion (Heider 1991:77). The term bravado is another possible opposition, but it places too much emphasis on the elements of bluster and swagger that indeed sometimes, but not always, characterize non-malu actions. The term boldness is another useful opposition to malu in that it suggests not only shamelessness and bravery but also "prominence" in the sense of interest and pride in standing out in a crowd.

Although the phrase "standing out" here is intended to be interpreted in its widest sense, its relationship to malu and bangga can be quite literal. Physical expressions of shame and pride involve the whole body (Lazarus 1991). In a nutshell, individuals feeling malu express it by attempting to appear small, while those expressing bangga adopt postures that make them seem big. Fessler contrasts the types of bodily comportment associated with malu—averted gaze, stooped shoulders, bent-kneed shuffle—and relates them to submissive gestures common to all mammals. He likewise relates bangga's physical expressions—eye contact, erect posture, squared shoulders, stiff-legged gait—with animal gestures that communicate confidence or threat (1999:84–87). Benjamin Kilborne suggests that the association of bigness with pride and smallness with shame is a widespread pattern in many cultures (Kilborne 2002:9).

One of the rare Malay-language terms that have taken a firm hold in English is *amok*; the *Oxford English Dictionary* defines "running amok" as "a murderous frenzy." Tom Boellstorff asserts that amok is a "masculine and often collective enraged violence" that is a "normative male response to malu" (Boellstorff 2004:469). He suggests that extreme aggression addresses men's feeling of malu by countering "a sense of vulnerability in interaction with *invulnerability in action*" (2004:476)—in other words, by allowing men to imagine themselves outside of the constraints of social norms and empowered to act without regard to them. While society as a whole might view amok as a normative response, it is not considered positive in view of its use of force and its uncontrolled rage; this assessment of amok is simply one example of the double standards of masculinity with which Sundanese men (like men in most other cultures) are faced.

The actions prohibited by malu are ones in which people would indeed engage, presumably to the detriment of society as a whole, if there were no prohibitions against them. As Sedgwick and Frank point out, "without positive affect, there can be no shame; only a scene that offers you enjoyment or engages your interest can make you blush" (Sedgwick and Frank 1995:22). Such actions promise rewards for those who can get away with pursuing them. Malu's function is to mediate the constant negotiation of the size of each individual's "share" of the rewards, with input from society as a whole, based not only on how well one conforms to social conventions, but also on how gracefully one manipulates social conventions to one's advantage. Malu, then is a measure of how much power an individual can hold, or at least is proportional to the individual's capacity for power.

It is not a simple matter to negotiate one's position within this contradictory maze of social conventions. Individuals must somehow impart the impression that they are conduits of power, yet they have to do so without using undue force. They must make their own relative status clear without compromising their suitability for cooperative efforts. They should not stand out except when others deem standing out to be appropriate—a collective judgment difficult for the individual to gauge in advance.

Sundanese ideals of masculinity call for an optimal balance that takes into account malu, power, and status. Such a delicate balance depends on many situational factors and individual characteristics. It would be impossible to set in stone one particular set of qualities and behaviors that define an ideal man. Perhaps such double standards are the inevitable consequence of a society's investing the basic emotion of shame with two demonstrably parallel, but often contradictory, functions, those of rivalry and conformity. It is up to each individual man to craft a masculine identity that makes sense for him within this contradictory territory.

Men's Dance

Resorting to violence—running amok—presents an incontrovertible demonstration of actual physical power and as such leaves little ambiguity about the perpetrator's status or potential for contributing to cooperative efforts. Fessler suggests that it is always "cheaper" to signal superiority or inferiority through a display than actually to "demonstrate it in a contest" (Fessler 1999:106 n. 20). Barker establishes that for Sundanese men, for example, tattoos signal that their wearer is a powerful person without any need to demonstrate it. Tattoos are, in effect, a source as well as a symbol of power (Barker 1999:274). To appear powerful is to be powerful; to act manly is to be manly. Keeler points out that Javanese

CHAPTER ONE

demonstrate how alus they are through their bodily comportment: "Alus movement should be effortless, apparently (and in larger towns, often) unthinkingly elegant, with no sudden, jerky motion to interrupt the impression of calm" (Keeler 1975:89).

In West Java, dancing in public, usually with professional female dance partners to the accompaniment of drumming, is another normative male response to malu. Like running amok, men's dancing represents a social context that allows men to step outside the constraints of normal behavior. Dance—a whole-body activity—provides a particularly expressive medium for enacting malu and boldness, which are emotional states that involve whole-body displays. Through subtle displays combining dominance and submission, men can negotiate their relative status and signal their conformance with accepted norms of behavior. Their choice of gestures and styles of moving demonstrate their individual strengths and encapsulate their own approach to masculinity.

In his rebuttal of Geertz's equation of malu with stage fright, Keeler points out that a Javanese dancer's enacting a character onstage does not induce stage fright because the rubrics of Javanese dance conventionally associate particular styles of movement with particular characters and character traits. A dancer need only quite literally "go through the motions," and in such a context there is little risk of exposing one's true self (Keeler 1983:163). In West Java, the conventions surrounding men's dancing additionally provide a framework of external motivators—"excuses"—that allow men to act non-malu without violating the constraints of proper behavior. Excuses such as *kaul* (putting one's self on display to honor another), sexual desire for the female performer, and the notion that drum patterns can uncontrollably animate one's body combine to get men onstage and keep them dancing.

Without the excuses, however, malu quickly returns. A wedding I attended in 1999 provided a stark demonstration. Male guests were dancing onstage with a provocatively dressed dangdut singer to the accompaniment of a small band. Suddenly the electricity went out, rendering the band eerily silent. The men who were dancing, suddenly stripped of their excuses, momentarily looked confused, then squatted on the sides of the stage until the sound system was again operational. It was as if they were suddenly and keenly reminded of their sense of malu and responded accordingly by quite literally making themselves small and inconspicuous until the electricity returned, and with it, their cover—the music and the drumming, their excuses to act not malu.

Anybody observing a man dancing is forced to question whether the dancer is truly being himself or simply going through the motions—

acting a part. The context of the performance provides male dancers with plausible deniability. If their performance is not convincing, they need not claim that it represents their true, authentic self. If it is convincing, they have acquired power and status by virtue of appearing to have it already. This deniability enables men to challenge the established pecking order as well as to confirm it. Men make social conventions work in their favor to accrue status and prestige by creating large effects with little physical effort.

Discourses of Masculinity: Terms for Male Dancers

Benedict Anderson stresses that the successful reconciliation of opposites is a sign of power (Anderson 1972:14–15). I argue that performing—onstage—the contradictions in which Sundanese masculinities are embroiled is nothing less than a demonstration of power. The plausible deniability provided by the context of a dance event enables participants to experience the contradictions of Sundanese masculinities by going through the motions of them onstage. One of the terms applied to male dancers at dance events—*jawara* (e.g., Fajaria 1996:42; Sumiati 1996a:208)—captures the contradictions of masculinity in a single word. The Sundanese word *jawara* (roughly equivalent to the Indonesian *juara*) means "champion" or "winner," but also carries the connotation of "thug" or "shady character." The jawara that Barker describes as a petty criminal who exacts a tribute from those who live and do business in the area he claims as his territory in Bandung is indeed a powerful individual. Although the jawara consolidated their power through one-on-one fights with other jawara, they display their power through tattoos that mark them as *kebal* ("thick-skinned," that is, impenetrable and invincible) characters. They redistribute the power that cycles through them by providing protection to and patronage of the individuals who pay them tribute (Barker 1999:66–77).

It is as if the very notion of winning were tainted with inherent visibility and unacceptability, and (conversely) that the desire to win is a dubious one. Certainly the means by which jawara (in the sense of "thugs") acquire power—through blatant intimidation and threat—are socially unacceptable. And yet, their benevolent acts toward their lieges go a long way to temper people's negative attitudes toward them (Barker 1999:66–77).

Indonesians, including Sundanese, are fond of examining the philosophical implications of a word by constructing an acronymic etymology for it called a *kirata*. It is important to note that kirata are retroactive—

they do not represent the true origin of a term, but rather explicate the term's current meaning and significance. Because they are presented as etymology rather than exegesis, however, kirata disingenuously lend the weight of history and precedence to modern interpretations of labels (see Rosidi 1984a:157–58). Barker reports that one kirata for the term jawara includes syllables from Sundanese words that capture some of the qualities that have come to be associated with street toughs—strutting cockiness (from *JAgo*, rooster), bravery (from *WAni*), and the disaster and suffering they can cause (perhaps *sangsaRA*, sufferings) (Barker 1999:273 n. 42).

The ambiguity of the term jawara emphasizes that the boundary between laudable and reprehensible behavior for Sundanese men is extremely vague. It is by simultaneously conforming to society's standards (malu) while violating them (boldness)—maintaining an alus appearance while engaging in non-alus behavior—that Sundanese male dancers demonstrate their possession of status and power. Another term applied to male dancers, *jago* or *jagoan*, similarly captures the contradictions of masculinity. At its simplest, *jago* means "cock" or "rooster" and conjures up an image of strutting, aggressive masculine displays. A related meaning of jago is "champion"—somebody who has demonstrated power and prowess in a positive way. Among Sundanese people, the term jago or jagoan also is applied to an individual who has acquired a great deal of esoteric knowledge through ascetic and physical practices and is capable of "phenomenal feats of invincibility" (Wessing 1978:84).

In recent years, the term *bajidor* has become a popular designation for Sundanese men who like to dance.[9] Mas Nanu Muda provides a kirata for bajidor—*BArisan JIwa DORaka* ("a row of sinners")—that addresses the double standards of masculinity. He relates that it was originally used as a joke among bajidor themselves but eventually came to be applied to an entire musical genre, *kliningan-bajidoran*, in which a cadre of devoted fans interacts with female performers (Muda 1999; see also Suganda 1998).[10]

The word *bajidor* is curiously assonant with the term *bajing* ("squirrel"), which is a common euphemism for misbehaving men in Sundanese (the derivative *bajingan* actually means "scoundrel"). American English has a comparable idiom: Americans use the name of another rodent—a rat—to designate somebody, especially a misbehaving man, who lies or cheats. Objectively, a squirrel is little more than a rat with a bushy tail, but that tail makes a big difference in the way Americans regard the animal. That Sundanese equate their misbehaving men with a "cute" rodent may be yet another reflection of their double standard of masculinity: such behavior may be unacceptable, but it is "cute" (and covertly accepted, expected, and even admired) nevertheless. The popular song "Bajing Luncat" (literally, Jumping Squirrel), which is associated with men's dancing, capitalizes on this association.

Although public dancing articulates masculine status and power through demonstrations of rivalry versus conformity and malu versus bangga, there is another aspect to dancing that looms large in the imaginations of the participants and even seems at times to take precedence over the pursuit of power: sexual desire. In West Java, as in most places, attitudes about sexual desire represent one of the key sites of masculine contradiction. Some of the measure of a person's manliness is bound up with his sexual prowess, fertility, and ability to attract and satisfy the sexual urges of women. At the same time, however, he is expected to control his own urges, and abstaining from sex is a means of accumulating power. In the public transcript, sexual fidelity in marriage is valued, but in the private transcript, few people believe that men are actually capable of such control.

Collins and Bahar point out that malu is an important operative in regulating sexual behavior: "As with the English concept of shame, malu is closely associated with sexuality. The Indonesian word for genitals (kemaluan) echoes the English expression 'private parts.' Furthermore, sexually provocative behavior by self or others should elicit malu" (Collins and Bahar 2000:42). One of the attractions of Sundanese dancing for male participants is the presence of a female object of desire, in the form of a singer-dancer. The protocols of dance events give men permission to interact with these provocative females without the usual strictures on their behavior. In effect, they temporarily suspend the usual feelings of malu that bold sexual behavior might otherwise engender. Once again, the setting grants men plausible deniability for their actions. These female performers' reputation for sexual availability outside of the ordinary economy of marital relations, coupled with the covert approval for casual sexual relationships with them embedded in the protocols of dance events, provides men an opportunity to face the contradictory sexual norms of Sundanese masculinity both onstage and off.

Freedom

A key property of men's dancing is the perception that it is "free" (*bebas* in Indonesian). When participants and observers say free, they mean that men's movements proceed instinctively and naturally from the feelings stirred up by the event and the sexual desires aroused by the ronggeng. The term freedom generally suggests the capacity to behave

CHAPTER ONE

in whatever ways one wants. It is a state in which one feels unrestricted by rules or constraints imposed by others, a state where one's own will, and only one's own will, controls one's thoughts and actions. In his book *Myths of Freedom*, Stephen L. Gardner makes a convincing philosophical case that this kind of freedom "is an object of imagination, an object of desire, a 'metaphysical' passion for an exemplary state of being. . . . Its primary mood is discontent; its primary emotion, at bottom, envy" (Gardner 1998:1). In other words, the objects, experiences, and feelings that individuals imagine that they "freely" desire are, in fact, suggested to them—even imposed upon them—by others, who are not only dictating what to desire, but also competing for the same objects of desire. What freedom amounts to, then, is a way of masking the reality that one's desires are motivated by others and convincing oneself that desire comes from within rather than from without.

Thus, dance events provide a context for competing with other men for power and influence, both directly and in the form of sexual desire represented by the ronggeng. By dancing in the company of ronggeng, the participants imagine that they are responding freely to natural impulses rather than conforming to the norms of behavior imposed by society and regulated by strictures of malu.

A Dance Triangle

In West Java, dancing is a masculine pursuit in much the way that sports are in the Western world (cf. Connell 1995:54). The discursive struggle between presentational and participatory dancing discussed earlier in the chapter encapsulates dialogues about gender roles in twenty-first-century Sundanese society, and men's improvised dance, as a site of masculine display, has an important role to play in these negotiations. Dancing continues to loom quite large in the lives of Sundanese men. Events at which men dance have been and continue to be important sites for learning, practicing, and negotiating what it means to be a man in contemporary Sundanese society. At first glance, it may seem that men's dancing is a fringe activity in present-day West Java. However, the protocols of dancing are common cultural capital; virtually every Sundanese man, woman, and child takes them for granted. Almost all Sundanese, furthermore, are routinely involved in such productions as witnesses, assessing and validating the meanings produced by more active participants. My conversations with passive Sundanese participants have convinced me that they experience vicarious engagements with these events. Furthermore, I contend that what Sundanese audiences find most interesting and attractive about *any* dancing is the references it makes to the kind of dancing that has the potential for masculine display and gender articulation. Presentational dances that manage to evoke the sensations of men's improvisational dance are more exciting and interesting than those that do not.

Anthony Seeger has observed wisely that, far from being an objective mirror of the past, "history is the subjective understanding of the past from the perspective of the present" (Seeger 1991:23). Sundanese dance histories, like all histories, are as much self-conscious efforts to enforce a particular vision of contemporary Sundanese dance as they are explications of it. Despite the efforts of historians to write the men at the side of the stage out of history, men's dancing remains an integral part of Sundanese life. In the dance performances I attended in the 1990s, audience members resisted merely watching dance performances by injecting their own bodies and sensations into the events. Incidents such as the wedding described at the beginning of the chapter, in which a guest unilaterally joined a rehearsed presentational dance, serve to reblur the boundary between audience and performer and resist the discourses that turn dance into a presentational, rather than a participatory, activity.

Ironically, one manifestation of this resistance is the increasing popularity of dangdut music and dance as a medium for participatory dance in situations where, in the past, more traditional Sundanese participatory dance forms might have been included. Dangdut is characterized by music that utilizes an "international" instrumentation—guitars, keyboards, and the like—playing diatonic melodies and pop harmonies. In other words, dangdut's sonic signature is quite different from that of traditional Sundanese music, which emphasizes gongs and gong chimes playing nondiatonic melodies. It is relatively easy to graft the protocols of dance events onto new styles of music and movement. In doing so, Sundanese participants salvage the persistent meanings that are lost when traditional music and dance are coopted for staged, presentational dances (cf. Spiller 2004:256–58; 2006). Some dangdut songs feature overtly Sundanese-sounding musical features, such as melodies cast in the Sundanese *pelog* or *sorog* mode (both of which can be approximated convincingly with Western tempered tunings). Many dangdut music videos make the recontextualization even more explicit by intercutting images of dancers in traditional costumes with scenes of dangdut performers outfitted in the latest fashions.

CHAPTER ONE

The song "Goyang Karawang" (composed by Bobby S. and Muchtar B.), as performed by the dangdut diva Lilis Karlina (*Best of the Best* 2000), is only one example of a dangdut song whose lyrics explicitly situate the practice of participatory dancing as an everyday activity that, although firmly rooted in the Sundanese past, is nowadays associated with modern popular music rather than with traditional music. The karaoke video for the song is set at an outdoor dance party. A large group of men stand in a circle, and several flaming torches light the scene—nostalgic references to traditional dance events. Lilis Karlina sings and dances in the center of the circle; she is dressed not in traditional ronggeng garb, however, but in a sexy red sequined evening gown. The words specifically suggest that the musical accompaniments are now modern—dangdut and jaipongan—but these new sounds, like the traditional ones, always compel listeners to dance. Although the first several verses of the song are cast in a traditional Sundanese melodic mode—the hemitonic pentatonic *pelog degung*—the text that describes these new musical styles is set to a clearly diatonic scale, driving home sonically the lyrics' contention that the sounds of the music change over time, but the invitation to dance provided by the drums and the music remains constant. By juxtaposing traditional elements (the torches, the singer-dancer, and the pelog degung melody) with new elements (the evening gown and the diatonic melody), the song effectively superimposes traditional Sundanese dance events onto dangdut. The overt recontextualization of participatory dancing with non-Sundanese-sounding music suggests that the sonic signature of traditional music has come to represent a presentational approach to dance, and that traditional dance is now a visual icon of Sundanese identity in an Indonesian context. Sundanese men must turn elsewhere—to dangdut, in this case—to satisfy their urge to dance in traditional fashion.

What are the persistent protocols that characterize this traditional approach to dance? It is clear they are independent of style and genre. Rather, in my approach to understanding Sundanese men's dance, there are three clusters of Sundanese dance practice that go together:

1. female singer-dancers, which I call by the common Sundanese term ronggeng, who are visual and aural objects of desire for men;
2. drumming, which provides standard rhythmic motifs that participants recognize as being associated with particular kinds of movement; and
3. men who engage in dancing that they perceive to be "free."

Each of these clusters encapsulates a contradiction of masculinity as well. The ronggeng is both a goddess, by virtue of her association with

Nyi Pohaci/Dewi Sri, and a whore, through her association with prostitution, and thus she embodies the contradictions and double standards of men's desires. The drum patterns are both regulative—leading—in that they limit the kinds of dance movements that are appropriate, and liberating—following—in that the drummer's choice of which patterns to play can be coerced by clever dancing. The men who are dancing are empowered to act malu or bold—submissive or dominant—or both simultaneously if they can manage it.[11]

Threeness permeates Sundanese men's dance traditions. The name associated with men's improvisational dance—ketuk tilu—means "three ketuk" and refers to one of the instruments in the ensemble, a chime with three small gongs called ketuk. There are also three flames on the standing oil lamp (*oncor*) around which outdoor ketuk tilu performances take place, and the instruments in the ensemble (ketuk, goong, kendang, and rebab) are typically played by three men (a single musician can play both goong and ketuk at the same time). Gugum Gumbira Tirasondjaja notes this threeness as well, but he declines to interpret its significance; he only suggests that further research might provide a philosophical explanation (Tirasondjaja 1979–80).

Edi S. Ekadjati's research into the roots of Sundanese culture cites an important three-part model of the working of the world, called *tri tangtu* (three truths), in early Sundanese manuscripts (Kropak 630 and 632) from the Hindu-Javanese era. In this model, three forces, represented by three social roles, create a balanced society: *raja* (king), *rama* (priest), and *resi* (ascetic). Raja is the source of authority and power and is responsible for governing, rama is the source of truth and wisdom and provides wisdom and guidance, and resi is the source of the kind of dogged determination that leads to prosperity (Ekadjati 1995:79). Jakob Sumardjo sees reflections of tri tangtu, in the form of three heterogeneous things combining to make a whole, as an organizing principle in the three levels of pre-Hindu Sundanese cosmology as well: the world above where the gods live, the world below represented by the rice goddess Dewi Sri, and the world between where people live. The notion of realms above and below the middle world occupied by people is evident in Sundanese houses, which have a roof above and a space below the middle area occupied by the family (Sumardjo 2005a). In more recent times, this three-part principle has been transformed into a catchy aphorism: "silih asah, silih asih, silih asuh" (educate one another, love one another, care for one another) (Iskandar 2005; Sumardjo 2005b).[12] Sumardjo posits tri tangtu as a fundamental ordering principle in Sundanese philosophy that persists from era to era and transcends political and religious change; in his view, these

CHAPTER ONE

three heterogeneous roles complement one another to create a society that is truly Sundanese (Sumardjo 2005b).

Popular song videos reference these three elements when invoking Sundanese dance events. The song's female singer often is costumed to suggest a ronggeng. The video images frequently include a kendang player, and drums are the only musical instruments depicted in the videos. Videos often include a group of men who actively participate in dancing. The interactions of these three elements in dance and representations of dance model gender identities and provide a context for negotiating and defining gender roles, among other things. The rules of engagement are initially set by the norms of these three roles.

Triangles and Gender

Triangular models frequently emerge in discussions of gender differentiation and identity. Often gender identities involve contradictions that must be made to seem natural for these identities to seem coherent. Each side of the triangle in my model schematizes a contradiction enacted by the participants whom the sides represent. I was initially inspired in this direction by Eve Kosofsky Sedgwick's development of the notion of erotic triangles. In her influential book *Between Men* (1985), Sedgwick analyzes how European novels construct notions of sexuality and patriarchy through narratives involving two men transforming their coveting of each other's power into desire for a third, female party. Nancy Cooper has argued persuasively for a similar dynamic between female singers and their male admirers in Central Java: "Although men may appear to be competing for the women, more significant is their jousting with other men for prestige" (Cooper 2000:617). This provides another triangular perspective from which to view the persistent set of conditions that comprises Sundanese dance events.

The erotic triangle of Sundanese dance that emerges over the next few chapters is, in effect, a theoretical representation of a structure that shapes the way Sundanese men and women practice both dance and gender. My use of the term structure here is not strictly structuralist. Rather, I am guided by the nuanced ideas of structure that William H. Sewell lays out in his article "A Theory of Structure: Duality, Agency, and Transformation" (1992). Sewell, building on Anthony Giddens's theories, sees structures as comprising mutually sustaining schemas, which are transposable, "generalizable procedures applied in the enactment/reproduction of social life" (1992:8), and resources, which are "manifestations and consequences of the enactment of cultural schemas" (1992:11). Unlike

40

many structuralist models, Sewell's acknowledges the agency of individuals in transposing and applying structures to meet their own needs and to produce new kinds of resources, which in turn can account for modifying the structures that helped to generate them. Structures, then, do not simply determine behavior, but rather "empower and constrain social action and . . . tend to be reproduced by that social action" (1992:19).

No single theory provides a magic bullet for thoroughly understanding cultural practices. J. M. Balkin argues that human culture is a jury-rigged "cumulative marshaling of existing capacities to form new ones" (Balkin 1998:31). He applies Lévi-Strauss's term bricolage to express how the unintended uses and unintended consequences of cultural schemas result in a messy, inconsistent, thoroughly unsystematic system of beliefs and behaviors. Balkin suggests further that the best way to study human culture is to apply a bricolage of theory—a "metabricolage" of sorts that "cobbles together different ways of understanding human understanding in the hope of providing a more powerful and unified account" (Balkin 1998:175). Joe L. Kincheloe asserts that such an approach moves beyond reductionist, monological knowledge that stems from a "rationalist quest for order and certainty" (Kincheloe 2005:326).

In subsequent chapters, I develop the triangular model by juxtaposing various theoretical approaches to acknowledge that each illuminates a different facet of the issues at hand. My goal is to understand the processes by which the inherent contradictions with which Sundanese men and women live (as do the rest of us) are reconciled. None of the theoretical models can claim to expose the whole truth, but each can perhaps provide a glimpse of part of the truth.

In a spirit of theoretical bricolage, I take the underlying current of threeness a bit further and literally give form to the discussion by applying Euclidian geometry. Imagining the three clusters outlined above as a three-sided geometric figure suggests several ways of analyzing the conventions, interactions, and transformations. For example, if I imagine that what the guest saw at the wedding I described at the beginning of this chapter can be represented by two sides of a triangle and the angle they create, then following one of Euclid's triangle congruence theorems,[13] I theorize that the guest was able to interpret the incomplete triangle he encountered as congruent to a complete dance-event triangle. By entering the performance space and dancing, he was, in effect, "drawing in" the implied third side to complete the triangle (see fig. 1.5). The two sides he encountered were female dancers along with female vocals (side C) and recognizable drum patterns (side B), meeting to form an angle (angle a)—an accompaniment that features animating drum

CHAPTER ONE

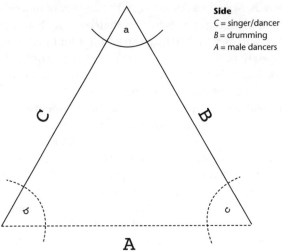

1.5   Triangle model for wedding dance event.

patterns and female vocals. The implied third side was amateur male dancers (side *A*), who form the other two angles by coordinating their movements with the drum accompaniment (angle *c*) and interacting with the female dancers in some fashion (angle *b*).

The structure that the erotic triangle of Sundanese dance attempts to represent functions more subtly and more widely than any individual model might predict. Casting this amorphous cluster of ideas in the certain sense of plane geometric terms may lead to insights inspired by a Euclidean vision of reality, but it is important that triangularity not be put forward as a realistic picture. It provides, rather, a common framework for my examination of the ideas, practices, and implications of a large array of dance events that on their surface may seem to have very little in common, but that I hope to demonstrate point to a very persistent and very powerful structure for regulating gender identities.

Men's dancing, and the long-standing protocols and conventions that surround it, continue to be an integral part of the negotiation of Sundanese masculine identities and gender identities in general. Examining these protocols as a flexible but stable triangle of ronggeng, drumming, and free dance leads to a clearer understanding not only of the aesthetics of Sundanese, dance but of the performance of gender ideologies throughout the world as well.

TWO

Drumming and Power

For Sundanese listeners, drumming is at once liberating and regulative—liberating in that it inspires them to dance in a way they feel is free, but regulative in how it compels, controls, and induces conformity. This chapter explores this contradiction in Sundanese concepts of drumming and its relationship to movement. I argue that the liberating and regulative qualities of drumming represent paradoxes in Sundanese and Javanese ideas of power in a form that is tangible—or at least audible.

Drumming and Movement

Cul dogdog tinggal igel is a Sundanese saying that means literally "without drums all that is left is dancing." For Sundanese, the proverb suggests that one has given up something of value in favor of something less important (Eringa 1984:170; Zanten 1989:83). A free translation might be "dance, without drumming, is nothing but [empty] gestures." The metaphor has several implications for understanding the quality of the relationship between sound and movement in Sundanese music and dance. Implicit in this proverb is the assumption that Sundanese dancing and drumming always go together—that dance movements require an aural analog to be whole. It suggests that dance is somehow incomplete without the sound of drums, and furthermore that the sonic element of dance performance—drumming—has more value than the visual elements.

CHAPTER TWO

Scholarly commentary on Sundanese performance genres frequently makes special mention of the close association of drumming to dance movement and affords this relationship a fundamental importance. Enoch Atmadibrata identifies prominent drumming as "characteristic of all current Sundanese dance" (Atmadibrata 1980:121). Soedarsono describes drums as "eminently suited" to the "gay energetic and dynamic" spirit of Sundanese dance (Soedarsono 1974:123). Soepandi and Atmadibrata cite this close association as a primary difference between Javanese and Sundanese dance (Soepandi and Atmadibrata 1976:66–67).

This chapter investigates the interaction between dancing and drumming. I argue that drum sounds have come to represent simultaneously and paradoxically both a cause and an effect of movement. The ambiguity about whether movement makes sounds or sounds animate dancers allows both explanations to be "true." In large part because of this ambiguity, drumming emerges as a potent metaphor for power in Sundanese performance. With regard to Javanese drumming for gamelan music, Keeler notes that drumming, like Javanese power, is "an invisible presence," with considerable influence on the actions of others (Keeler 1975:106). Since the control of invisible power is part and parcel of the creation and maintenance of gender identities, and because masculinity is measured by assessing how individuals accumulate, maintain, and display power, an awareness of how drumming models power is a key to understanding this element of erotic triangles in Sundanese dance.

Drum Patterns: Tepak

Put a group of Americans in a place where there is a musical performance that features a steady pulse, and most of them will likely begin to move subtly to the beat—most typically by tapping their feet. In contrast, Sundanese men and women tend *not* to tap their feet to the beat when they hear music. Sundanese audiences strike me as eerily still when they listen to music, even music with what I perceive as a driving beat. This is not to suggest that Sundanese audiences are quiet when they are not listening closely, for there are few proscriptions against talking loudly and moving about during any kind of performance, whether formal or informal.

One Sundanese musician told me that the Sundanese's sense of malu inhibits the movements of the audiences; even toe tapping might seem too daring for some. Braver audience members are more likely to dance in place by moving their arms and heads according to the drum patterns than to tap their toes (Ade Komaran, personal communications, April 7, 1999, and May 19, 1999). The bravest participants get up onstage and

44

dance with complete abandon. My impression is that many Sundanese take an all-or-nothing approach to embodying the rhythms they hear. They either remain still or else allow the rhythm to animate them completely and dance. The preference for dancing, onstage or in place, with complete movement units rather than toe tapping to the beat suggests also that it is not the pulse that Sundanese apprehend as driving, but larger units of rhythmic organization—drum patterns—that suggest particular types of movement, even particular choreographic units.

The journalist Her Suganda implies that people make drumlike sounds when involved in certain natural activities, such as being surprised or rocking a baby (Suganda n.d.:9). Sunarto believes that when people are overcome by happiness, "they spontaneously dance around while vocalizing the sounds of the kendang or clapping their hands in an imitation of kendang rhythms. In an unconscious way they have played the role of a drummer" (1990:1).[1]

Drummers and nondrummers alike internalize movement sequences and the drum patterns that accompany them by associating spoken phrases with them as mnemonic devices; these phrases, in turn, come to suggest the movements they accompany. Dancers, when practicing or demonstrating, typically provide their own "accompaniment" in the absence of a drummer by singing onomatopoeic representations of drum patterns—*kendang mulut* ("mouth drumming"), as one dancer jokingly described it (Abay Subardja, personal communication, 1981). The tendency of dancers to sing the appropriate drum patterns when performing dance movements without drum accompaniment suggests that movement is conceptualized partly in terms of its accompanying pattern, and that the accompanying pattern is an integral part of the dance movement. Movements have an audible component, without which they are incomplete.

The Sundanese word tepak onomatopoeically describes percussive sounds. The sound of swatting an insect, for example, may be verbalized as "tepak." The word has several more specific meanings as a musical term. It describes general approaches to rhythm: *tepak Indonesia* refers to Indonesian rhythms, as opposed to, say, *tepak barat* (Western rhythms). It also describes Indonesian drumming traditions: for example, *tepak Sunda* (Sundanese drumming) compared to *tepak Jawa* (central Javanese drumming). In penca silat (self-defense dance), the five ostinato patterns and the dances they accompany are called tepak. The term tepak also applies to the basic phrase units of dancing and drumming, which might be realized as clusters of movements, drum patterns, or mnemonic imitations of drum patterns. These units often have names, which typically describe the associated dance movement. For example, the tepak name

CHAPTER TWO

engkeg gigir means "stepping sideways," which describes the dance movement. Some patterns, however, are known by names that clearly derive from mnemonic syllables and have nothing to do with the movement they accompany, such as *pakbang*. A tepak name such as *aduh bapa* likely derives from the drum sounds that accompany it, but it carries semantic meaning ("Oh! Father!") as well.

Tepak kocak

Drum syllables are not the exclusive domain of performers. Ordinary people as well as musicians and dancers imitate the sounds of kendang patterns vocally, and the potential for gleaning semantic meaning from drum sounds is also widely acknowledged. Several Sundanese musicians told me about patterns, dubbed *tepak kocak* (humorous drum patterns) by one of them, that suggest a certain movement by actually saying it. For example, the drum pattern notated in figure 2.1 is heard to say "kadupak pingping, gulingkeun (goong)," which means in Sundanese "rub thighs, roll around (ending on the stroke of the goong)" (Tosin Mochtar, personal communication, January 28, 1999). Her Suganda reports a similar, perhaps even more suggestive interpretation of essentially the same drum pattern: "tumpak pingping . . . dedetkeun"—in Sundanese, something like "mount the thighs, force it in" (Suganda n.d.).

The cause-and-effect relationship here is vague. It is unlikely that these particular drum sounds are specific enough to mimic the words unambiguously. Nevertheless, Tosin told me, this linguistic interpretation is clear to most listeners (personal communication, January 30, 1999). There is a circularity inherent in this kind of joke: listeners need to be expecting the drum sounds to suggest words in order for any lexically meaningful phrases to emerge; it is then relatively easy to hear any words one wants to.

An analogous circularity underlies the entire dance-drum relationship in Sundanese music: one must expect drum patterns to suggest movement, and at the same time the coordination of movements to drum patterns reinforces this expectation. The ambiguity about whether drumming leads or follows dance movements is built into the very foundation of the Sundanese dance-drum connection.

Drum sounds and patterns have the power to index movement at many levels of organization. Onomatopoeic imitations of drum sounds characterize even entire genres. The terms jaipongan and dangdut, for example, are generally acknowledged to be imitations of drum sounds (e.g., Amilia 2001:96; Hardjana 1996:129; Hatch 1985:218; Soeharto 1992:27–28; Soepandi, Sukanda, and Kubarsah 1996:49; Tirasonjaya

2.1   *Tepak kocak* (from Tosin Mochtar, personal communication, January 28, 1999).

1988:293). In the course of popularization these genres acquired names that characterize their distinctive rhythmic groove and the movement style associated with it by essentializing it in a catchy vocal imitation of the drum accompaniment.

The connection between rhythmic patterns and movement is demonstrated to Sundanese children early and often. I took the following notes watching the audience at a performance at the Bandung Zoo on April 18, 1999:

> I noticed three separate occasions of inculcating young boys with the notions of dancing. The first was a 40ish man there with a group of kids (presumably his), one of whom was a four- or five-year old. The father would dance around his son, encouraging him to move. The boy would do a move now and then and was already pretty good at responding to drum patterns. The things the boy had were a posture (sort of bent forward at the waist) and hand oppositions, as well as the idea of a "body stop" at the ends of patterns. The father kept encouraging his son to dance. One of the things the father did was make his own "body stop" at the end of a phrase end with an affectionate grab at the boy's crotch, which made the boy giggle appreciatively. The boy's older sisters would giggle and laugh every time the boy danced (as would the father). The second occasion was a young father carrying a baby while jaipongan music was going on. He "manipulated" the baby along with the characteristic jaipongan drum pattern (which the father clearly knew). Again, this was on the sidelines and never entered the actual "arena" of action. In the third occasion, a small boy was watching the ketuk tilu dancing intently from near the stage. Several people gently urged him to move. Finally, one of the old ronggeng actually bent down over him and manipulated his arms and shoulders along with the music.

Juju Masunah, a dance education scholar at the teacher's college in Bandung (IKIP Bandung), once showed me a video of young Sundanese children experimenting with music and dance. Some of the children were told to make up dance movements that imitated various animals, such as a rabbit. The other children were instructed to sing something to accompany the dance movements. The children sang "ning—nong—ning [rest] plak tuk." These vocalizations suggest the sound of bronze instrument

CHAPTER TWO

ostinati ("ning—nong—ning") and drums ("plak tuk"). The drum (i.e., the "plak tuk") part of the phrase coincided with the most distinctive part of the movement, namely the rabbit's hop.

All of these examples demonstrate how the connection between drums and movement is literally drummed into the bodies of Sundanese individuals at an early stage, and that particular kinds of movement are appropriate for responding to music, especially music with drumming. In her book *Deep Listeners: Music, Emotion and Trancing*, Judith Becker suggests that individuals learn particular ways of engaging with music that lead to specific emotional and physical responses. An extreme example is trance, but Becker addresses more moderate modes of reacting, called deep listening. Riffing on Pierre Bourdieu's notion of habitus (acquired and persistent patterns of thought, behavior, and taste), she develops the concept of a habitus of listening, which she defines as "a disposition to listen with a particular kind of focus, to expect to experience particular kinds of emotion, to move with certain stylized gestures, and to interpret the meaning of the sounds and one's emotional response to the musical event in somewhat . . . predictable ways" (Becker 2004:71). Becker's terminology is useful in for describing a generalized Sundanese habitus of listening that associates drumming and movement.

Connections between Drumming and Movement

Drumming and movement relate in several ways in Sundanese performing arts. In the following discussion, I first consider cadential patterns played on drums and how they suggest movement. Next, I describe drum patterns that accompany walking movements. Finally, I analyze how these basic units of drumming are combined into more complex choreographies that imply specific movement combinations to those who hear them. Throughout the discussion I will refer to the circularity of cause and effect—how dancers and drummers maintain an ambiguity about whether drumming causes movement or vice versa. It is this ongoing slippage between cause and effect that makes Sundanese drumming an effective representation of more abstract Sundanese notions of power, and it makes drumming an important component of the erotic triangle.

Sundanese Drums and Drumming

Three drum types are common in West Java: dogdog, *terbang*, and kendang. Dogdog are single-head conical drums struck with sticks or bare

2.2 *Dogdog* (photo: Michael Ewing, 1978).

hands (see fig. 2.2) and are associated with harvest ceremonies and with the comic genre *reog*. The name is apparently onomatopoeic and imitates the sound of a low-pitched drum. Ensembles typically include four dogdog of different sizes, each of which is played by a different musician (Kubarsah 1996:77–80). Terbang, also called *rebana*, are single-head frame drums, played with the hands only; based on Middle Eastern models, they are associated with Islamic music such as *qasidah* (see fig. 2.3). Like dogdog, terbang typically are played in ensembles with four or more drums, each played by a different musician.

Kendang are double-head barrel-shaped drums. Sundanese kendang players perform with a set of drums. Each individual drum as well as the whole set is called kendang, sometimes rendered as *gendang* in Sundanese. The set consists of one large drum, called kendang indung ("mother drum"), and one or more (typically two or three) small drums called kulanter. Drums of both sizes share the same general appearance and construction.[2] Usually one performer plays several kendang, and as a general rule there is only one kendang player in an ensemble.[3]

Kendang parts lead and coordinate rhythmic activity in a variety of Sundanese ensembles, including most varieties of gamelan. The kendang player provides the tempo for the other players. Special drumstroke patterns lead to and enhance cadences. Drum signals indicate to the other musicians form, tempo, dynamic levels, and points of starting, transition, and ending. In addition to setting the tempo for the ensemble and

CHAPTER TWO

indicating changes in rhythmic treatment, the kendang's timbres and rhythmic patterns are part of the overall sound of the ensemble. If the ensemble accompanies dance or other movement, the drummer has the additional responsibility of supplying for each dance movement the drum pattern associated with it. He incorporates cues for the rest of the ensemble into these patterns, thus coordinating dance and music activity. When accompanying dance, drum parts are more closely aligned with dance phrases, which do not always correspond neatly to musical phrases, than they are with musical structure.

Jaap Kunst's remark about central Javanese drumming, "which, at first sight, looks hopelessly difficult to learn, (but) nevertheless employs only a relatively small number of primary varieties of beating" (1973:204), is equally appropriate for Sundanese drumming. A good drummer, armed with a few basic techniques and an assortment of different drums, can produce a dazzling array of timbre and pitch variations.

DRUMMING NOTATION At heart, Sundanese drumming is an aural tradition. The practices most akin to "notation" in discourse about drumming historically were pattern names and drum mnemonics. Drummers and dancers could communicate about their performances by using conventional names that described large chunks of material, and they could use drum mnemonics to specify details in their descriptions. One obvious

2.3   *Terbang/rebana* (photo: Henry Spiller, 1988).

BKN JLKPR CP2x PRG KPT :

Key:
BKN = bukaan   PRG = pring
JLKPR = jalak pengkor   KPT = cindek kepret
CP = capang (2x means 2 times)   : (colon) = goong

2.4 Aep Diana's notation for standard *jaipongan* pattern (from personal communication, August 9, 1999).

approach to notating drumming is simply to write down pattern names and/or short strings of drum mnemonics.

Jaipongan drummers are obligated to perform upon request the drumming sequences from a large collection of commercially released cassettes of jaipongan songs. Some drummers maintain notebooks with notation routines. The drummer Aep Diana, for example, learns the *pola* (sequence of drum patterns) from cassettes and transcribes them using his own idiosyncratic system. According to Aep, a lot of drummers use notation, but there is no standardized notational system.

Aep's notation provides a window into understanding how he and other drummers conceive these accompaniments. He uses abbreviated pattern names to recall which patterns occur in a particular goong phrase; a few letters represent an entire drum pattern or sequence of patterns. Figure 2.4 shows a sample line in Aep's notation of the standard phrase of jaipongan drumming (see fig. 2.12 for the same phrase in conventional notation). Sometimes his abbreviations refer to a named dance or drum pattern (for example, *jalak pengkor* or *capang* in fig. 2.4). Others might refer to unnamed drumming patterns by suggesting the important sounds or strokes (for example, "pring" in fig. 2.4). There is no systematic indication of rhythm, and the different mnemonics occupy different numbers of beats.

In the 1980s Atik Soepandi and Maman Suaman developed a kendang notation system for use in government-sponsored schools of music and dance. Although this notational system has been featured in a number of publications and reports promulgated by STSI, it has not achieved widespread usage outside academic circles.[4] As noted in the preface, in this book I use a sort of modified staff notation to represent kendang patterns.

Cadential Patterns

It is my contention that movement, broadly construed, is encoded into drumming at every level. Even the drumming's musical level of articulating cadences implies a kind of movement. Explaining how Sundanese

CHAPTER TWO

drum patterns give motion to the musical phrases they shape provides a good foundation for understanding how drumming can motivate dance movements.

Sundanese music theorists, when discussing the functions that various instruments in ensembles play, typically assign to the drums the role of coordinator or leader the music's rhythmic dimension.[5] Soepandi and Atmadibrata differentiate the role of kendang in nondance music from that in dance music: in nondance music, "the kendang's function is only to regulate the flow of the piece and guard the rhythm," while in dance music, "various types of kendang sounds always must fill the dance movements" (Soepandi and Atmadibrata 1976:66–67).[6]

The significance of the goong strokes that occur in the midst of sound streams cannot be overstated. The goong strokes represent the beginnings and endings of musical cycles, i.e., important points of cadence. David Goldsworthy postulates that the goong's rich tonal spectrum and undifferentiated pitch provide a background "to which the other instruments give a specific direction in sound and space." He also notes that goong strokes mark the moments in time when all the parts come together in "harmonious agreement" (Goldsworthy 2005:313). The goong's importance to Indonesian listeners is often expressed metaphorically. Otong Rasta told me that the "meaning" of gamelan music is the working together of the various musicians toward a common goal, namely the stroke of the goong. He sees the goong stroke as the payoff, the reward for working hard and cooperating—it is *enak* ("delicious"; personal communication, June 19, 1999). According to Kathy Foley, "players say that the sounding of the deep-toned goong is as necessary and inevitable as death is to life" (Foley 1979:55). The aesthetic sense of all music, dance, and drum phrases depends on their relationship to goong strokes.

The goong stroke's release of musical tension is also comparable to an orgasmic release of sexual tension. The mapping between sexual and musical tension and release is always an undercurrent; my earlier observation of a father teaching his son to dance at the Bandung Zoo by touching the boy's crotch at the goong strokes suggests one means by which this mapping of sexual gratification to goong strokes is made. Returning for a moment to tepak kocak, Entis Sutisna suggested that some were *porno* (pornographic); Otong Rasta disagreed that they were pornographic, but did admit they were all about sex. Another tepak kocak—"domba nini domba nini kencar kencar"—makes sense only with a sexual subtext. Its literal meaning is "the old goat has escaped," but most Sundanese interpret "domba nini" to mean a she-goat in heat, which they equate

DRUMMING AND POWER

2.5   "Trundling" *kendang* motive (transnotated from Cook 1992:81).

with a woman eager for sex, and "kencar kencar" to mean "out looking for sex" (Tati Haryatin, personal communication, April 30, 1999). Otong further pointed out that tepak kocak would not be particularly amusing if they did not end with goong strokes (personal communication, April 30, 1999). What is funny about the ending gong strokes, I believe, is the way they suggest sexual release coming at the end of the activities alluded to in the tepak kocak without making it explicit. The patterns usually stop just before the actual goong stroke, as if the sexual association remains implied—undrummed, but made obvious by the cadential goong stroke. It is no surprise, then, that some of the simplest Sundanese drumming has as its function the setting up of rhythmic tension to be released by the goong stroke. In nondance music, one of the drummer's activities is to cue or signal cadences marked by strokes of the large goong.[7]

DEGUNG DRUMMING   Among the least complex drumming in the current Sundanese instrumental repertoire is that for so-called classical (*klasik*) degung pieces (Harrell 1974:148). This drumming utilizes three strokes: (1) a low sound ("gedug" or "dong") played with a stick on the large drum, (2) a higher-pitched sound ("kempring" or "peung") played with a stick on the small drum, and (3) a slapped sound ("tepak" or "pak") played with a hand on the small drum. In his primer for playing gamelan, Simon Cook describes two basic motives built from these three strokes for degung drum patterns (which Cook calls *kendangan*): "a very simple kendangan . . . consists essentially of two motives. The first is for trundling along . . . and the second is a closing pattern to mark the goong" (Cook 1992:81; see also Harrell 1974:157). Cook's "trundling" pattern, notated in fig. 2.5, has a number of small variations as well.

The pattern leading to a goong stroke appears to have nine pulses in it rather than eight, "borrowing" one from the preceding measure (see fig. 2.6). A pitch/timbre contour neatly divides the nine pulses into three groups of three in a common variation of the goong pattern, as shown in figure 2.7 (the groups of three are indicated with brackets in the figure). According to Cook, if the "trundling" pattern in figure 2.5 is leading to the goong pattern, "it is often preceded by the following more rapid syncopation" (see fig. 2.8).

CHAPTER TWO

I interpret these drum patterns as rhythmic groupings of three in anticipation of the cadence, rather than as syncopations. Harrell also notes that approaches to cadences in degung include patterns "with strokes on every third beat" (Harrell 1974:153). The sixteenth-note figures fall into 3 three-(sixteenth-note)-pulse groupings (indicated with brackets in fig. 2.8), each of which begins with a stroke followed by two sixteenth-note rests. They lead to the three (eighth-note) strokes of the usual "trundling" pattern, followed by the usual three-groups-of-three-eighth-notes cadential pattern.

Cooper and Meyer might call such a rhythmic treatment "shifting groups," a kind of "noncongruent" rhythmic treatment; the term refers to the noncongruence of the groupings of three with the unrelenting duple meter of gamelan pieces. About noncongruence, Cooper and Meyer say that it "welds the whole phrase into a single dynamic impulse toward a goal" (Cooper and Meyer 1960:93–94). In gamelan music, these noncongruent rhythmic groupings create the sense of acceleration toward the goong stroke while a steady pulse is maintained. Goldsworthy notes that many instrumental parts in gamelan music increase in activity up to the goong stroke to help emphasize the goong stroke's importance as a phrase marker (2005:313). With regard to drumming, Judith Becker calls such patterns with increased activity "configurative" drum patterns because they help shape a sense of musical direction; she identifies configurative drum patterns as a musical feature common throughout Southeast Asia (Becker 1968:178–80).

2.6   Variation of *kendang* motive that leads to a *goong* stroke (transnotated from Cook 1992:82).

2.7   *Kendang* motive that leads to a *goong* stroke (transnotated from Cook 1992:82).

2.8　Syncopated pattern leading to *goong* pattern (transnotated from Cook 1992:82).

It is this drive toward a cadence or goal that gives Sundanese gamelan music much of its sense of movement, and it is specifically the drum that provides the impulse. The association of noncongruent rhythmic groupings or configurative patterns and drumming is not limited to gamelan music; similar motives, with groupings of three, are played on the *kacapi indung* (large zither) when accompanying *panambih* (fixed-meter songs with gamelan-like accompaniment). Kacapi players acknowledge the drumlike role of these left-hand patterns by calling them kendangan (Ashworth 1996:28) or *pukulan kendang* (Zanten 1989:182). Harrell points out that similar patterns are played on cellos in Sundanese ensembles of Western instruments (Harrell 1974:25), and *kroncong* (a song genre featuring Indonesian or Malay lyrics and European instrumental accompaniment) style features drumlike patterns played pizzicato on the cello (Hardjana 1996:129; see also Kornhauser 1978; Kunst 1973:382; Natapradja 1971:105). Zanten echoes Cooper and Meyer when he says that the "strict four-beat metre is 'counteracted' by the many syncopated patterns of this left hand playing" (Zanten 1989:181). Such patterns contribute to the perception of goong-like cadences even in ensembles where there is no goong with which to mark them explicitly.

TEPAK MELEM　Simple drumming of the type described above for degung is rarely heard in other gamelan music. Tosin Mochtar, who was one of Bandung's most respected drummers from the 1970s until his death in 2000, told me that he believed that similar stick drumming and simple kendang parts (consisting of "trundling" and cadential patterns) were much more commonly played for other types of gamelan music before the 1950s (personal communication, January 29, 1999). Since that time, some drummers developed a more florid style of hand drumming for use in gamelan salendro music for listening, both for the long, grand pieces in the *sekar ageung* (large piece) repertoire and especially for *rerenggongan* (medium-length piece with a prominent vocal melody). A standardized version of this new style of drumming, called *tepak melem*,[8] was pioneered by Entjar Tjarmedi (Upandi 1997:18–21) and further developed by his

2.9 One of Tosin Mochtar's *tepak melem* cadential patterns (from personal communication, June 17, 1996).

disciple Tosin Mochtar. Tepak melem patterns are based on dance drumming patterns, with most of the rubato and dynamic contrasts smoothed out (Tosin Mochtar, personal communication, March 11, 1999; Ade Komaran, personal communication, March 17, 1999), and are tied to the formal structure of the pieces (i.e., to the regularly timed structural pitches, often marked by strokes of a large gong chime such as kenong or jengglong) rather than to dance structure.

In my drumming lessons, Tosin taught me to play particular tepak melem patterns that "ask for" goong strokes (*minta goong*). Leaving these out might not necessarily result in the goong player's failure to strike the goong, but it would make for dull drumming (personal communication, March 12, 1999). These tepak melem cadential patterns also feature noncongruent three-beat groups (delineated again by pitch and timbre contours) leading to the cadence. One such tepak melem pattern that leads to the goong stroke is notated in fig. 2.9; the noncongruent groupings of three are indicated with brackets.

Walking Patterns: Mincid

Configurative drum patterns, by contradicting the established meter of a piece of music, contribute to the creation of a sense of movement and motion by driving toward cadences. A more direct connection between movement and drumming is a common feature of Sundanese ensembles that include a cadre of dogdog.

DOGDOG PATTERNS Atmadibrata (Atmadibrata 1980:212; Atmadibrata, Dunumiharja, and Sunarya 2006:2–3) and Soepandi and Atmadibrata (Soepandi and Atmadibrata 1976:71–75) describe a situation where rhythmic sound is the direct result of movement during rural harvest festivals, when farmers transform bundles of rice, tied to either end of a pole and carried on the shoulders, into a musical instrument called *rengkong* that makes a rhythmic squeaking sound when carried. Several dogdog, each played by a dancer, provide a rhythmic accompaniment that interlocks with the sound of the rengkong.

In the comic entertainment genre called *ogel* or reog, four performers provide their own accompaniment on dogdog while they dance and tell jokes. Specific interlocking patterns of dogdog strokes are associated with specific movement patterns (Soepandi and Atmadibrata 1976:49), such as walking, circling, and the like. In this case, the dogdog accompaniment not only provides an aural analog to movement patterns, but also serves as a means for communication and signaling between the performers.

The use of particular rhythmic patterns as signals is not limited to the performing arts. Joshua Barker describes how residents of rural and urban neighborhoods alike rely on the sound of a *kentongan* (large slit gong) to keep them informed of their territory's status. Some kentongan calls are quite elaborate and elicit various responses from the people who hear them: "A particular pattern of strokes might bring people out with particular tools, or might indicate the presence of a specific threat" (Barker 1999:48–49).

In his report on reog drumming, Asep Solihin provides a detailed description of the three main interlocking patterns that the four dogdog players in the Reog Mitra Siliwangi troupe from Bandung perform.[9] The first dogdog player leads the tempo, rhythm, and movements. The second dogdog is pitched lower than the first and is played on offbeats. The third dogdog is pitched lower than the second and plays on the beat. The fourth dogdog is pitched the lowest and plays rhythmic variations (Solihin 1986:14–15).

The two patterns that accompany walking movements, called *takol kendor* and *takol gancang*, have one crucial feature in common: the ostinati played on the second and third dogdog. These ostinati are the same in each of the patterns, although the tempo is different (*kendor* means slow, *gancang* means moderately fast). Each ostinato is a simple pulse— each drummer plays an absolutely steady rhythm. The pattern on the higher-pitched drum is 𝅘𝅥 𝅘𝅥 𝅘𝅥 𝅘𝅥, while the lower-pitched drum's pattern is 𝅘𝅥𝅮 𝅘𝅥𝅮 (n.b. the strong beat falls on the last note of these in-text notations). The two pulses are offset from one another so that they interlock, creating a recurring composite ostinato: 𝅘𝅥 𝅘𝅥𝅮 𝅘𝅥 𝅘𝅥𝅮 (which can be approximated as "high–rest–high–low–high–rest–high–low"). It ends on the strong beat of the music. The silent beats in the composite ostinato contribute to the apprehension of a shorter pattern as well; the interlocking parts also can be parsed as a repeating motive (𝅘𝅥𝅮𝅘𝅥, i.e., high–low–high), separated by the rests, that is offset from the strong beats. The sound of

CHAPTER TWO

the shorter composite motive becomes part of his physical process of taking a step, and the pitch contour reflects the weight changes involved in taking the steps. The result signifies, in some sense, the sound of a body walking (but not necessarily the sound a body *makes* when walking).

In sum, interlocking dogdog patterns are an aural side effect of physical movement, comparable to a rongkeng's squeaking sounds, in contrast to the degung cadential patterns, which create a sense of movement. The other parts (the first and fourth dogdog) play patterns reminiscent of those in degung drumming, especially with regard to the groupings of three leading to cadences. Here, however, there is a slightly different approach to the groupings of three. Whereas the degung drumming groupings were positioned so that the end of the final grouping coincided with the goong stroke, here the groupings of three end with two eighth notes before the goong stroke. The first dogdog rhythm is ♪♪ ♪♪ ♪♪ ♪ ♪(G). The fourth dogdog plays a more ornate version of the same pattern: ♪♪ ♪♪ ♪♪ ♪♪ ♪♪(G). The two eighth notes at the end of the pattern suggest even greater quickening of the impulse toward cadential release; the offbeat sixteenth notes in the fourth dogdog version exaggerate this quickening, that is, acceleration toward a goong stroke while maintaining a steady beat.

The interlocking figurations of dogdog playing are iconic of the egalitarian nature of small Sundanese agricultural communities. Performers are generalists—dancers who provide their own musical accompaniment. Power and authority are distributed among the players rather than concentrated in a single individual. Yet even in this egalitarian setting, drumming's power eludes complete human control. Dogdog are also part of most angklung ensembles, including those that accompany *kuda lumping* (hobbyhorse trance dancing). Randal Baier notates essentially the same parts for the two middle drums of the *angklung buncis* ensemble in Ujungberung except that the pattern is offset so that the rests, rather than strokes on the lower drum, fall on the ends of phrases (Baier 1986:16). Jaap Kunst provides a compelling description of a kuda lumping performance he saw in Cimahi (near Bandung) in 1923:

The drums persist in their rhythm; their ever more penetrating sound becomes an obsession; the tarompèt yells like mad; we sense a growing tension in the atmosphere. . . . And then, all of a sudden, . . . the horse-men break loose, foaming at the mouth and with rolling eye-balls. . . . Then the leader removes the white cloth from the head of the dancers, who are still wringing themselves, to the rhythm of the music . . . and at last they are induced to sit down.   (KUNST 1973:286)

Here we see that the rhythms of the drums might be thought quite literally to animate those hearers who are open to entrancement. Baier describes a situation where the drum's power to induce trance is thought to be so powerful that musicians employ another drum imbued with special power that prevents entrancement from occurring (Baier 1988).

Performance genres featuring dogdog typically rely on interlocking figurations between the dogdog drums and on a division of labor among them to provide the drumming that makes audible the movements they perform and, at the same time, animates the movement activity. The lead dogdog player uses particular patterns to signal changes in tempo and choreography to the rest of the group. The repeated ostinato patterns echo and embody the movements coordinated with them. And the drums themselves may be perceived to have powers to entrance (or not entrance) willing subjects. However, as a reog performer pointed out to me, there are only a few patterns in the repertoire, and these suggest movement rather unspecifically, giving the performers considerable freedom of choice. Besides, he said, they are able to choose movements only for their feet and legs, because their hands and arms are otherwise occupied with playing the drums (Ade Komaran, personal communication, July 13, 1999). Thus, these patterns suggest ideas of moving through time in a coordinated but individual manner.

KENDANG MINCID PATTERNS   Dogdog patterns—short ostinati of two or three drum sounds, possibly enriched with a syncopated, variable part—have come to stand for the sound of walking, and Sundanese listeners, upon hearing them, respond by imagining or performing walking movements. A kendang player has at his disposal a set of sound resources similar to that of four dancers playing dogdog, and the patterns he plays to accompany walking movements are reminiscent of interlocking dogdog patterns.

The several renditions of the drum pattern *keupat kendor*, transcribed in figure 2.10 (each iteration in the figure is bracketed and numbered), for example, appear to have four "voices" analogous to those provided by four dogdog: the first dogdog role is in the top voice (the "tepak" or "pak" sound, notated above the top line of the staff, with x-shaped noteheads). Strokes notated in the top space of the staff ("kempring" or "peung") are equivalent to the second dogdog role, while strokes notated in the space second from the top ("kempring" or "pong") correspond to third dogdog strokes. The kendang player produced all three dogdog players' strokes with one hand. The strokes he played with the other hand, notated in

CHAPTER TWO

2.10   *Keupat kendor* (from Spiller 1996:37).

the bottom line and spaces of the staff, correspond to fourth dogdog strokes.

The "peung" and "pong" sounds on kendang combine to form an ostinato similar to that created by the combination of the second and third dogdog, that is, high–low–high. The low-pitched strokes have the same variety of timbre and syncopated delivery that characterizes the fourth dogdog part. The "pak" sounds, like the first dogdog part, often double the fourth dogdog part.

In genres that feature dogdog, each dancer who plays a dogdog provides a part of his own accompaniment while he dances. When dance is accompanied by kendang, a single specialist sits and provides all the drumming, while the dancers only dance. The nature of the kendang parts, however, is still dance oriented in that particular drum patterns suggest specific kinds of movements and a specific drum pattern accentuates and supports each dance movement.

Several Sundanese terms often are applied to these kinds of drum patterns and dance movements: mincid (and variants *incid* and *pincid*) or *mincig* (and variant *pincig*) and *keupat*.[10] These walking movements and the drum patterns that accompany them illustrate circularity and ambiguity with regard to cause and effect. The drum patterns can be explained either as being caused by the walking movement—resulting from the very steps that the dancer-musicians take—or as actually causing, or at least signaling, the walking movements.

Drumming as Power

Drumming's capacity to motivate others into action with minimal effort on the drummer's part and simultaneously to allow the perception that those moving are creating, rather than responding to, the sound is an apt metaphor for Javanese and Sundanese notions of power. Benedict Anderson characterizes the Javanese conception of power as "something concrete, homogeneous, constant in total quantity, and without inherent moral implications as such" (Anderson 1972:8)—in other words, a real and divine universal force. One who possesses power "should have to exert himself as little as possible in any action. The slightest lifting of his finger should be able to set a chain of actions in motion" (Anderson 1972:42–43). This description unintentionally relates to the topic at hand quite well, both because the sounds of drumming are literally produced by the lifting and lowering of fingers and because they can make an individual who is dancing convincingly appear to be a source of power.

Drum sounds provide a neat metaphor for the cosmic power that fills the Sundanese universe. It is intangible, yet capable of motivating significant physical effects. It flows from a central place to the various participants, who can take advantage of as much of it as they can contain by dancing well. It manifests itself in the dancers visibly because containing power is a means whereby men can accumulate status, which they accrue when others judge favorably the skill with which they transform the drumming into movement. Yet, at the same time, dancing to drumming is something over which the men believe they have control, even if that control is limited. The drumming provides a convenient excuse to justify dancing in the face of embarrassment or shame at the thought of getting up and performing in public, or in the face of the disapproval that dancing with ronggeng invites. The power of the drums to animate men overcomes their feelings of malu and empowers them to be bold; in this way, it contributes to the dance event's plausible deniability.

The power of drum sounds to animate people provides these people with a convincing excuse for abrogating any responsibility for their actions. The plot of a *sandiwara* (a kind of semi-improvised theatrical production) I attended in 1981 hinged on the power of sounds to animate people against their will. In the play, two musical instruments had magical effects on anybody who heard them. A magic ketuk caused uncontrollable itching, and a magic kendang caused involuntary and frenetic jaipongan dancing. These sounds caused the protagonists to act inappropriately and get into all sorts of trouble, but at the end of the

CHAPTER TWO

play the heroes were redeemed when it was revealed that the magical instruments, not the heroes themselves, were responsible for all their bad behavior.

A similar plot twist occurs in the Rawit Group's *lawakan* (stand-up comedy) act. During a mock news broadcast at a performance in 1999, one of the comedians, Oman, shows the other one, Caca, how to sign the news for the hard of hearing. Caca gets so carried away with the gestures that they become a sort of dance, and Oman stops reading the news to admonish him simply to sign, not to dance. When they try again, Oman starts to read an introduction to the news to the accompaniment of music. At this point, the drums begin to play, and Caca begins to move dancingly again.

Oman: *Make jeung kikituan atuh kawas . . . kawas nu rek nyeuseuhan. Wartos-wartos anu penting diantawisna. . . . kalahka ngahajakeun! Lain ngigel gelo!*
Caca: *Pake kendang belegug, hihih . . .*

—————

Oman: Just do the signing, yikes, you look like . . . like somebody doing the wash. [*Reading the news*] The news that's important, among other things . . . [*Music begins, and Caca begins dancing again*] You're doing that on purpose! Don't dance, idiot!
Caca: But they played a drum, stupid. Ha-ha!

Caca justifies his dancing in defiance of Oman's explicit prohibition by blaming it on the drums—he cannot help dancing when the drums play.

In order to be animated by drums, a dancer must have an understanding of the conventions of drumming and the combination of drum patterns into choreographies. Over the years, and between the various types of men's improvisational dance, there has been considerable variation in whether the dancer or the drummer takes the initiative for combining patterns into choreographies. These different models of leading and following reflect changes in social institutions and fluctuations in the relative valuation of individuals and community in twentieth-century West Java.

Concentrating all the authority and power in the hands of a single individual departs from the egalitarian model of dogdog playing. The drummer becomes a specialist, rather than a generalist, with a particular role to play. His relationships with dancers, however, are imbued with ambiguity. In some contexts he interacts with the dancer he accompanies as a servant, responding to the dancer's needs and whims and evoking a feudal relationship. This type of connection has characterized aristocratic men's dancing. Ketuk tilu and jaipongan drumming also involve a single specialist drummer, but he plays patterns well-known to all the participants, either through convention or via mass mediation, who respond in coordinated but individualized ways. The dancers balance conformity and personality to carve out a space for themselves within a community framework that reflects modern, post-independence Indonesian social ideals.

Combining *mincid* and Cadential Patterns

At its most basic, drumming for dance accompaniment can be thought of as combining the two kinds of drumming described above: mincid (stepping or walking) patterns and cadential patterns. The oldest existing recording of Sundanese music for dance accompaniment provides a particularly interesting illustration. Benjamin Ives Gilman recorded the (mostly) Sundanese musicians and dancers who performed daily in the Java Village exhibit at the 1893 World's Columbian Exposition in Chicago (for more information about music and dance in the fair's Java Village, see DeVale 1977; Johnson 1998; Spiller 1996). These cylinder recordings include a section that Gilman describes as "Tandak (performed by dancing girls from West Java)" (Lee 1984:7). Several sources suggest that performances by the "dancing girls" preceded a dance drama, which Gilman called "Sundanese wayang" (Burnham 1894:304–5; Truman 1893:568–69).

An 1893 Dance Accompaniment

It is difficult to say with any certainty precisely what kind of dance Gilman's recording represents. Presumably Gilman obtained the title *tandak* from a printed program or a reliable informant. The term tandak clearly has been related to ronggeng dancing for a long time, and it seems likely that the music and dance performed at the Village under the rubric "tandak" were related in some broad fashion to ronggeng dancing.[11]

The music in the recorded performance comprises two separate pieces. The first piece has a "regular" structure, that is, two alternating sections, each of which consists of 4 sixteen-beat phrases. The end of each section is marked by a goong stroke (inaudible on the recording, but implied by the pattern of audible kempul strokes). Dance-related events, such as the entrance of the dancers (announced by Gilman on the recording) and

CHAPTER TWO

the transition to the new piece (marked by a dramatic speedup), occur in the fourth phrase of a section and are marked with special drum patterns that also herald the coming of goong strokes. The second piece consists of three phrases of variable length. The first part of each of these phrases consists of a variable number of four-beat rhythmic units, each of which ends with a particular goal pitch. The drumming for this first part of each phrase consists of repetitions of a short mincid-like pattern.

I imagine that the dancing girls performed short, repetitive gestures while maintaining some sort of formation to the accompaniment of these mincid-like drum patterns. The second part of each phrase is always 4 four-beat units long. I speculate that upon hearing a drum signal, the musicians begin the process of bringing the phrase to an end by playing triplet patterns anticipating the next goal pitch, at which there will be a goong cadence. During the time leading to the cadence, the dancers probably move around the stage, only to coalesce into a new formation at the stroke of the goong. The drum cue to change is quite short and subtle, but it precipitates a complex chain of events. After the goong a new phrase, with a new mincid-like drum pattern accompanying a new set of gestures performed in a different formation, begins. The overall choreographic scheme is presented in figure 2.11.

In short, the structure of the dance determines the form of the accompanying music in this example. Such flexible pieces are almost never used for contemporary Sundanese dance accompaniments.[12] For modern dance pieces, in contrast, the choreography is fitted into a piece's predetermined phrase structure. Gestures are repeated to make dance cadences coincide with musical ones. A piece's structure might involve phrases of different lengths, but the phrase lengths do not change each time the song is repeated.[13] The 1893 example, in contrast, represents dance accompaniment music in which the musical structure is entirely dependent on the choreography. Each goong phrase appears to be of an arbitrary length, dictated by circumstances other than some sort of regular structure, and iterations of the same phrase vary in length. Nevertheless, like modern dances, the 1893 accompaniment alternates mincid and cadential phrases.

Ketuk tilu Accompaniment

Ketuk tilu drum accompaniments are constructed similarly to the 1893 "Tandak," except that the structures of the accompanying pieces are regular and there is no dance-generated variability of the kind described above. As explained to me by Tosin Mochtar, ketuk tilu pieces usually

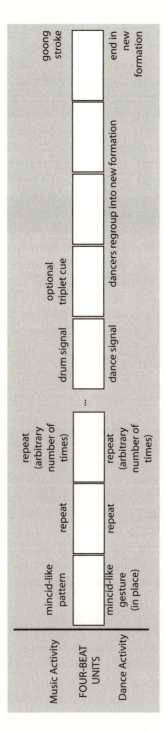

2.11 Dance accompaniment scheme from 1893.

CHAPTER TWO

begin with a special section called *nyered* ("dragged forward") or *nyorong* ("pushed forward"), which does not vary from piece to piece.[14] After the *nyered*, the *lagu* (main song) begins, consisting of a repeated cycle that may consist of one or more goong phrases. The drumming for the lagu can be thought of as having two main sections. In the first, the drumming for each goong phrase of the lagu usually begins with a "stationary" pattern, followed by a "moving" pattern; leading to the end of the goong phrase is a cadential pattern. At some point, after a few repetitions of the lagu cycle, there is a signal to change to the second main section, the mincid section. The change may be initiated by one of the male dancers (in which case the drummer changes the drumming appropriately) or by the drummer (in which case the dancers follow suit). In mincid, walking patterns of the kind described previously are repeated without break. Although there may be special cadential figures leading to the goong strokes, there are no "stationary" patterns following the goong stroke. After several repetitions of the lagu, the pulse quickens a bit to the goong, and nyered is tacked on as a sort of coda (to end) or bridge (to another lagu). Participants do not dance to the nyered sections. This standard outline of a ketuk tilu piece can be represented formulaically (brackets indicate that the material they contain may be repeated ad libitum):

nyered [: lagu [: stepping/waiting—cadential pattern :] [: mincid :] :] nyered

The two main sections combine serially the two sorts of organization discussed previously—moving or cadences and mincid. This two-part choreographic structure is a pervasive pattern in Sundanese dancing. Penca silat dances, for example, have a similar structure (Atmadibrata 1980:212; Harrell 1977). Drumming and dancing within a piece have two alternating sections: a stationary part and a mincid part. Drumming in the stationary sections usually fits into a fixed song structure, with special drum patterns and movements to mark the ends of phrases.[15] The mincid sections feature repeating patterns without any release of tension except for optional cadential figures leading to the goong.

Jaipongan

Ketuk tilu lost popularity in the mid-twentieth century, but a reinvigorated version surged to popularity in the 1970s and 1980s with a new name: jaipongan. Jaipongan achieved its popularity in part through the dissemination of cassette recordings. The influence of cassette culture on

Indonesian popular music has been described and analyzed in several places (see Hellwig 1993; Hugh-Jones 1982; Manuel 1988; Manuel and Baier 1986; Myers 1992; Yampolsky 1995). In a nutshell, cassette players and prerecorded cassette tapes became cheaply and widely available throughout Java in the 1970s (Manuel and Baier 1986:99). In West Java in the 1980s, cassettes became the medium for a phenomenal explosion of popular innovations in traditional Sundanese music. Several companies churned out releases by the dozens, and accomplished musicians found frequent work in recording studios. Some of these musicians now look back fondly on the *zaman kaset* (era of the cassette), when they were able to pick up significant extra income by playing for recordings. Many of the cassettes produced in the 1980s are still available for purchase, but not very many new cassettes of traditional music are being produced in Bandung, and those that are appear to be much more conservative in the choice of repertoire (perhaps being aimed at the tourist or export CD market rather than the local cassette market).[16]

Through cassettes, predetermined, fixed choreographies, as manifested in the drum accompaniments on the tapes, became widely available. Cassette owners could listen to these tapes over and over again to memorize the sequence of drum patterns that made up the choreographies and then put moves together to go with the drum patterns. In this manner, the most popular jaipongan tunes, along with their choreographies, became canonized.

The journalist Her Suganda quotes the drummer Mang Ijun as saying that, under the influence of cassettes, the kendang assumed the role of the leader of dances. It is obviously impossible to have the same kind of give-and-take relationship with a recording that one can forge with a living, breathing drummer, so dancers had little choice but to follow the drum accompaniments cast in stone on the cassettes (Suganda n.d.:9). Abun Somawijaya reflected the sentiments of many people I spoke with when he wrote, "With a cassette, each person can dance ketuk tilu/jaipongan based on/following the drum's patterns and/or the song's melody" (1990).[17] Somawijaya goes on to suggest that cassettes encourage people to dance who might not otherwise be brave enough to get up onstage. They can turn on the tape recorder and find an outlet for their desires, trying out the moves they see other people do and moving according to the drum patterns, all in the privacy of their own homes (Somawijaya 1990:59).

The hosts and guests at *hajat* (life cycle celebrations) strongly prefer live musicians to canned music. At some of the celebrations I attended in 1999, the sound system operator did indeed play taped music during

CHAPTER TWO

the musicians' breaks, but typically it was the tape he had recorded moments before of the group performing at the hajat—not a commercial or prerecorded tape. Dancers who hone their routines to the accompaniment of commercial cassettes expect their live accompanists to provide the same (or at least recognizably similar) music and drumming. Thus, the choreographies, that is, the fixed sequence of drum patterns (pola or *runtuyan*), have become canonized as well. Jaipongan drummers learn the pola from cassettes, too. Some jaipongan drummers have developed a shorthand notation system that enables them to reproduce a wide selection of jaipongan sequences without having to memorize them all (Tosin Mochtar, personal communication, June 8, 1999).

In figure 2.4 we saw a sample of the jaipongan drummer Aep Diana's shorthand. The main units into which Aep divides the choreographies are goong phrases—musical units whose ends are marked by the stroke of the large gong. Each line of his notation represents a goong phrase, and the goong stroke itself is represented by a colon (:). Filling up most of this goong phrase are a few named drum patterns that I will describe shortly: *bukaan*, jalak pengkor, and capang. The last three symbols specify how the goong phrase will end. *Pring* here is shorthand for the pattern that typically signals the coming of a goong cadence. *Cindek kepret* specifies exactly how the pattern will approach the goong stroke, and the colon indicates the goong stroke itself. The rhythmic placement of these patterns in the music is governed by convention, so no special notational symbols are needed. From this compact sequence of abbreviations, coupled with his extensive understanding of the conventions of jaipongan choreographies, Aep can reconstruct almost a full minute of drumming.

When hajat guests *kaul* (perform onstage to honor someone else), the drummer is supposed to follow them in the sense that the dancer will determine the progress of the performance (although, as we have seen, the drummer often leads dancers as well). Aep describes two approaches to such performances: freestyle (bebas or bajidor) and pola (literally "pattern"; a fixed order of movements). For the freestyle people, Aep says he follows the dancers. If there are multiple dancers onstage, he follows whoever is dominating the stage or whoever is the best dancer. For the pola people, he leads; first he finds out what cassette they learned from, and then he reproduces the pola, either from memory or from the appropriate page in his little book of notation (personal communication, August 9, 1999).

The particulars of Aep's notation are consistent with the way in which jaipongan choreographies are put together. Dahlan identifies three general categories of movements and drum patterns that make up the complete "standard phrase" (which Dahlan calls *pola ibing*): bukaan (opening) is the opening movement, *pencugan* (deep diggings) are stepping movements of various sorts, and *nibakeun* (cause to fall) is the closing movement, in which a dramatic drum accent occurs one beat before the goong stroke (Dahlan 1996:74). The dancer and choreographer Ana Mulyana provided me with slightly different terms for the sections of the standard phrase (personal communication, December 4, 1998). Like Dahlan, he calls the opening movement "bukaan." He provides names for the stepping movements: jalak pengkor (lame bird) and capang (sticking out sideways with upward points). The final movement, which Ana calls *ngala genah* (look for deliciousness), is prepared by a short movement he calls *cindek* (a punctuation mark in Sundanese script indicating the end of a phrase or sentence). The entire standard phrase occupies a gong phrase with thirty-two slow beats (approximately one beat per second), subdivided into 4 eight-beat subphrases.

Figure 2.12 is a transcription of this standard dance phrase for jaipongan, as taught to me by Ade Komaran. The phrase comprises six separate flurries of activity (notated with larger noteheads) separated by short periods of inactivity. The drum part for the inactive periods is a simple ostinato (indicated with smaller noteheads), played very quietly. Ade Komaran calls these strokes *ketukan*, meaning "pulse" or "beat" (personal communication, March 4, 1999), suggesting that its function is merely to keep the beat going and fill the empty space. This ostinato could be carried out for the entire phrase if it were not interrupted by the flurries of activity, which the drummer plays very loudly. The first flurry is bukaan (in the first line), and the second is jalak pengkor (in the second line). The two flurries in the third line are capang (iterated twice), the first flurry in the last line is cindek, and the final flurry is ngala genah.

Bukaan, jalak pengkor, and capang all end with a characteristic drum motive in which an accented, low-pitched drum sound in a weak rhythmic position is followed by an unaccented, higher-pitched drum sound on the strong beat. Cindek ends with a definitive accented stroke on a strong beat. Ngala genah's ending is emblematic of ketuk tilu and jaipongan drumming in general; it is characterized by a very strongly accented stroke on a weak beat before the goong stroke, followed by a conspicuous silence on the goong stroke. I have already discussed drumming for mincid in ketuk tilu, and it is essentially the same in jaipongan and bajidoran. There is considerable leeway on the drummer's part with regard to both the right-hand ostinato and the left-hand variations he plays.

2.12 Standard phrase (*pola ibing*) for *jaipongan* (from Ade Komaran, personal communication, March 4, 1999).

Tosin Mochtar characterized jaipongan songs as having two sections, as far as the drumming was concerned: a *bubukaan* (opening) section, followed by a mincid section. Jaipongan songs typically alternate between the two (Tosin Mochtar, personal communication, June 8, 1999). The standard phrase described above is only one of the phrases that occur in the opening section. In most choreographies it recurs toward the end of the dance as well.

Jaipongan songs begin with a fast section, then slow down to the song part. Most jaipongan songs have a unique fast section; the drumming depends on the section's character. The introductory sections feature lively drumming and special orchestration. Each introductory section is unique and features a hook of some sort that immediately identifies the song (to an experienced listener). "Adumanis," for example, opens with an a cappella chorus singing the words "adu manis" (literally "sweet conflict," a reference to a beautiful combination of dissimilar things) in two-part harmony. Once the slow part begins, the drums usually stay quiet for most of the first phrase, allowing the pasinden to dominate; they enter strongly only when approaching the first goong stroke of the slow section (Manuel 1988; Manuel and Baier 1986).

With regard to the sequence of drum patterns that comprise the choreography of a jaipongan tune, my examination of several jaipongan hits points toward a slightly more complex model than those described either by Tosin or by Manuel and Baier. Figure 2.13 represents the choreographic outline of three popular jaipongan songs, "Banda Urang/Rendeng Bojong," "Daun Pulus/Keser Bojong," and "Adumanis."

The details of the fast opening sections are not provided in the figure; their presence is acknowledged simply with a box labeled "intro." In the figure, each segment bounded by a double line represents a goong phrase; each segment may be broken into four equal subphrases. The standard jaipongan phrase, which takes up an entire goong phrase, is indicated in the figure with the notation STA. The notation MIN represents mincid. The letter "x" represents transitional phases; the letter "c" represents cadential drum patterns leading (usually) to a goong stroke. These jaipongan songs include a third kind of choreographic phrase, which I characterize as a "standing" phrase. These are relatively complex drum patterns that repeat several times. Repetitions of a standing phrase typically occupy an entire goong phrase, ending with a special cadential pattern that accentuates the goong stroke. The repeated units of the standing phrases are represented by capital letters; a lower-case "c" is appended to the capital letter if the phrase is modified to end with a cadential pattern.

The choreographies usually begin with one or more quiet goong phrases, in which the drummer quietly plays a mincid-like pattern, labeled a holding pattern in the figure. The first several full goong phrases of drumming are invariably some version of the jaipongan standard phrase. After two or three goong phrases of the standard phrase, there is a transition to some kind of mincid, which may occupy one or more goong phrases. Sometimes special cadential material leads up to a goong stroke, sometimes not. Following mincid, there may be a standing phrase or phrases. These three kinds of sections—standard phrase, mincid, and standing phrase—are alternated, usually ending with a *rangkep* (fast doubletime) version of mincid. The final goong phrase ends with a special ending drum signal, which slows down to the final stroke of the goong.

The choreographies as represented by these jaipongan hits are fairly complicated and include quite a bit of material that is neither the standard phrase nor mincid. According to Tosin Mochtar (personal communication, June 8, 1999), in the early days of jaipongan (i.e., the 1980s), dancers were able to improvise and expected to be followed by drummers as

"Banda Urang/Rendeng Bojong"

intro				

1		2		3		4			
holding pattern		holding pattern		STA		STA			

5		6			7		8		
STA		x	MIN		MIN		A1	A2	A1	Ac

9				10			11		12
B	B	B	Bc	x	MIN	c	MIN	c	STA

13		14				15		16	
STA		x	C	C	Cc	x	MINR	MINR	c

17	
MINR	end

2.13a Choreographic scheme for "Banda Urang" (based on the Jugala recording on the cassette *Serat Salira* [n.d.; see also Sunarto 1990]).

"Daun Pulus/Keser Bojong"

Intro				

1		2		3		4		
holding patterns		STA		STA		STA		

5			6		7		8		
x	MIN	c	STA		STA		x	MIN	c

9				10				11			12			
A	A	A	Ac	B	B	B	Bc	x	MIN	c	x	C	C	Cc

13			14			15				16			
MIN	c	x	MIN		D	D	D	Dc	x	E	E	Ec

17			18		19		
x	MIN	c	STA	out	MINR	End

2.13b Choreographic scheme for "Daun Pulus/Keser Bojong" (based on the Jugala recording on the cassette *Daun Pulus/Keser Bojong* [n.d.]. The same track has been released in the United States on the album *Tonggeret/Idjah Hadidjah* [Elektra Nonesuch 79173-2, 1987]).

"Adumanis"

intro				

1		2		3		4		
holding pattern		holding patterns		STA		STA		

5		6				7		8			
STA		A	Ac	A	Ac	x	MIN	B	Bc	B	Bc

9			10				11			12			
x	MIN	c	C	Cc	C	Cc	D	D	D	Dc	x	E	E	Ec

13		14		
MINR	c	MINR	end

2.13c Choreographic scheme for "Adumanis" (based on the Gita recording on the cassette *Adumanis* [n.d.]).

well as to improvise along the lines of whatever a drummer played. The late tayuban expert R. Bidin Suryagunawan provided a slightly different explanation to me: according to his understanding at the time, drummers fitted the jaipongan drum patterns to the music according to their own tastes, and the dancers followed along (personal communication, May 30, 1981). As the cassettes became more popular, people memorized the pola on the cassettes and expected drummers to play them for live performances. While the pola include piece-specific drumming (in the form of standing phrases), quite a bit of any choreography is conventional in that it consists of alternating standard phrases and mincid. When drumming for well-known jaipongan songs, a drummer usually assesses whether or not the dancers are following the pola and drums accordingly. Thus, despite the apparent fixity of jaipongan choreographies, in which recorded drumming eliminates give-and-take between dancers and accompaniment, jaipongan still creates some ambiguity with regard to who leads and who follows.

Leading and Following

It should be clear by now that Sundanese drumming and dance paradoxically lead *and* follow one another simultaneously. In ketuk tilu, for example, most people agree that there are not a great many drum patterns, that sequences of ketuk tilu drum patterns are relatively fixed, and that many different dance movements could fit the same drum pattern. Yet the dancers are said to compete for the drummer's attention, and drummers are expected to bring out the best in the dancer they are following by making their movements come alive.

The rhetoric around tayuban usually states unequivocally that the dancer is in charge, and that the drummer's job is to follow the dancer's every movement. The social relationship between dancer and drummer— an aristocrat and a hired servant, respectively—has no doubt contributed to this characterization of the relationship. The best tayub dancers, however, always bring their own drummers along, and it is generally acknowledged that a good drummer can lead a dancer through difficult musical situations. In many cases, the drummer surreptitiously leads his social superior (in collusion with that superior). It is never clear, despite occasional unequivocal discourse, exactly who is in charge in dancer-drummer relationships.

CHAPTER TWO

Movement, Drumming, and Power

Drum sounds and movement are connected in Sundanese practice on several levels. Contrametric rhythmic groupings of threes, played on drums, motivate musical lines and propel them to cadences. Certain drum ostinati suggest the motions involved in stepping and walking. A seated kendang player's patterns are rooted in the interlocking patterns that dancer-drummers might play to accompany and coordinate their own movements. The sounds made on drums can even imitate language to dictate movements. Sundanese listeners are taught from an early age to interpret these sounds as movement cues, so that the impulse to move in particular ways seems a natural accompaniment to particular drum sounds and patterns. It often appears that the dominant paradigm for Sundanese drumming and dancing is that drum sounds animate people, and particular patterns suggest particular kinds of movement. As Somawijaya sums it up, "The presentation of music, especially the dynamic drum patterns, stimulates everybody to dance and ultimately to enjoy it" (Somawijaya 1990:64).[18]

I have stressed that there is ambiguity with regard to whether the drummer causes the dance or vice versa. This ambiguity emerges whenever the dominant paradigm is probed. For example, that Sundanese proverb—*cul dogdog tinggal igel* ("without drums there is only dancing")—which opened this chapter is a reminder that it is "foolish to give up valuable things for matters of less importance" (Zanten 1989:83). This suggests that the drum sounds are the primary focus in dancing, and that the physical movements are, in effect, a realization of the drum sounds' implications. At the same time, however, it suggests that movement is independent of (although less significant than, perhaps) drumming. Certainly the drum sounds impart *semangat* (zest or spirit) to movement (Soepandi and Suaman 1980:9), and without drumming the dance would appear awkward and inexpressive (Sunarto 1990:10).[19] The oft-encountered "joke" of garbling or omitting the requisite drum sound for a movement in comedy routines is similarly ambiguous. Elsewhere I have described the laughter evoked when a clownish dancer's *goyang* (swaying of the hips and buttocks) was accompanied by a quacking squawk from the ensemble's bowed string instrument rather than by the expected drum strokes (Spiller 1999). Andrew Weintraub describes how the "audience roars with laughter" when the drummer makes the clown puppet Cepot's dancing look "awkward and timed incorrectly" by omitting the appropriate drum patterns (Sunarya 1998:67).[20]

These different models of leading and following paralleled changing social relationships and the relative values placed on individuals and community in West Java over the course of the twentieth century. Dogdog drumming, in which the emergence of the drum patterns themselves relies on the cooperation of several individual dogdog players, evokes egalitarian village organization. Accompaniment for upper-class men's dance, in which all the drumming is delegated to a single specialist who responds appropriately to the whims of his aristocratic master's dance movements, is more feudal. The single specialist drummers for ketuk tilu and jaipongan enable male dancers to imagine a sense of exhilarating freedom while conforming to general norms imposed by the fixed drum patterns, reflecting modern, post-independence ideologies.

In none of these models, however, is it ever completely clear who leads and who follows, and there always are ways for a clever dancer to usurp the power of the drums, to surreptitiously seize it and take control of which patterns get played. And if he does, the other men are obliged to follow him. Although the participants are not self-conscious about such takeovers, they can alternate claiming and abrogating responsibility. Drumming provides a mechanism and a set of conventions for overriding social restrictions and enabling participants both to take credit and to deflect blame. It is precisely this ambiguity, this give-and-take relationship between dancer and drummer, that makes drumming an appropriate icon of power, and dance events a flexible context in which to explore masculine contradictions.

THREE

Ronggeng and Desire

Although drumming for dance—especially in its ambiguity with regard to who leads and who follows—models the contradictions that characterize ideologies of masculinity, female performers embody a contradiction of their own: their nature is simultaneously both divine and profane. The professional female entertainers known as ronggeng create a representation of this vital goddess-whore contradiction in dance events by the performance styles that they adopt.

Myths and Triangles

Myth is one cultural strategy for coping with irreconcilable contradictions and for making arbitrary cultural constructs seem inescapable. In West Java, the myth of Sangkuriang weaves together many of the contradictions that characterize Sundanese gender ideologies. Reading the myth, we see some of the ways in which triangulation contributes to smoothing over irreconcilable contradictions and provides a way to begin discussing the female performers who play a central role in the erotic triangle of Sundanese dance.

Sangkuriang

In its barest telling,[1] Sangkuriang's father is a god who has been condemned to live on earth as a dog named Tumang. His mother is the beautiful Dayang Sumbi, whose own mother was a goddess condemned to live on earth as a pig. Dayang Sumbi was conceived as a result of her mother's drinking the urine of a human king. Sangkuriang regarded Tumang as a faithful hunting dog and did not know that he was the young man's father. During a hunting trip, Tumang prevented Sangkuriang from killing a pig that Tumang recognized as Dayang Sumbi's mother and a fellow deity. In anger, Sangkuriang killed Tumang. Dayang Sumbi, appalled that Sangkuriang had killed his own father, struck Sangkuriang in anger, leaving a scar on her son's head, and banished him.

Sangkuriang and Dayang Sumbi met again many years later, did not recognize one another, and fell in love. Dayang Sumbi agreed to marry Sangkuriang. When she discovered the scar on his head, however, she was horrified that she was about to commit incest. So, to prevent the marriage from taking place, she set an impossible task for Sangkuriang to complete before the wedding could take place. She ordered him to dam the Citarum River and build a boat for her to sail on the resulting lake—all before the cock announced the dawn of the next morning. Sangkuriang, who was superhumanly capable, was well on his way to completing the task when Dayang Sumbi, fearing his success, tricked the cock into crowing early by simulating the dawn. Sangkuriang, enraged by his failure, hurled his partially completed boat at the dam he had built, draining the lake. The myth is connected to the geography of Bandung, which is situated on a prehistoric lakebed. Legend has it that the dramatic volcanic peak that towers over the northern end of the city, called Tangkuban Prahu (overturned boat), is the remains of the unfinished boat that Sangkuriang threw.

Sangkuriang's pedigree is a curious mixture of creatures with both divine and profane natures. Both his father and grandmother are deities who were condemned to live as animals, and Sangkuriang, as their offspring, thus mediates the divine and the profane—the world above and the world below. Sangkuriang's relationship to his father has a dual nature. In his capacity as a hunting dog, Tumang both guides Sangkuriang (to prey) and follows behind him. This ambiguity of authority mirrors the ambiguous relationship in Sundanese dance events to the role of drumming in leading and following men's dance movements. As an object of desire for Sangkuriang, Dayang Sumbi has her own ambiguity. She is both divine (as the descendant of a god and as his mother) and profane (as a lover), reflecting the dual nature of women in general and ronggeng in particular as objects of men's desire.

The story of Sangkuriang enjoys enduring popularity in West Java. In the past, it was a *pantun* story (pantun is all-night storytelling related in song and speech by a single performer who accompanies himself on a small zither called *kacapi*). In recent years, the tale has been given literary

CHAPTER THREE

treatments, adapted for film and stage, and mined as a plot for modern Sundanese dance dramas (cf. Aveling 1996:116; Aveling and Sontani 1979:26; Rosidi 1961; Sedyawati 1983:163; Sontani 1962). The ongoing fascination with the story confirms its continuing mythic relevance for Sundanese people. For them, the Sangkuriang myth not only reconciles the contradiction of humankind's divine and profane nature, it relates this paradox to two other fundamental contradictions: desire for both the sacred and the profane, and desire for both power and freedom—the same binary contrasts that participants explore in the erotic triangle of Sundanese dance.

Oedipal Triangles

Different tellings of the Sangkuriang story vary in details, but the overall shape of the legend is remarkably similar to that of the Greek story of Oedipus. There is considerable controversy over whether the Oedipus myth is universal (see Edmunds and Dundes 1983). Although it is clear that comparable stories are present in many different mythologies around the world, the details—and thus, presumably, the meanings—are different. This Sundanese version has some striking resemblances to the Greek myth in that Sangkuriang killed his father and tried to marry his mother, and in the erotic triangle formed by its three main characters. It will shed light on both the Sangkuriang myth and the erotic triangle of Sundanese dance, then, to examine the theoretical explications of the Oedipus story.

Sigmund Freud famously related the triangle formed in the Greek version by Oedipus himself, his mother Jocasta, and his father Laius to the psychological development of sexual drives. He concluded that a desire to have sexual relationships with one's parents was inevitable and that overcoming this desire was part of the normal individual's psychological development. Freud believed that male children experience desire for their mothers and resentment of their fathers; suppressing the desire and overcoming the resentment are critical hurdles that the boy must clear to develop the conscience necessary for a normal sexual drive (Freud 1955:261).

In *Structural Anthropology* (1967), Claude Lévi-Strauss used the Oedipus story to demonstrate how myths operate to mitigate irreconcilable binary contrasts.[2] He began by bundling together similar events that take place at different points during the narrative and essentializing their similarities. For example, he grouped together events such as Oedipus's marrying his mother and Antigone's burying her brother, despite prohibitions against these actions, and characterized them as "overrating blood relations." Another group of events (including Oedipus's murder of his own father) he characterized as "underrating blood relations." These two mythemes (as Lévi-Strauss called them) represent a contradiction in how people regard their kinship ties. Lévi-Strauss identified a second pair of mythemes, and a second binary contrast, between the "denial of the authochthonous origin of man" (in events where a human overcomes an undeniably autochthonous creature, such as the sphinx) and the "persistence of the authochthonous origin of man" (in events where humans display physical handicaps, which Lévi-Strauss argued are symbolic of being born from the earth). In Lévi-Strauss's view, equating a set of binary opposites that has no resolution with another set that has some mediating term provides a basic mechanism in myth for resolving contradictions. This process does not result in an actual solution to the initial binary opposition, but by iteratively associating the opposition with other oppositions that are solvable, the initial opposition becomes acceptable.[3]

The simultaneously divine and subhuman nature of Sangkuriang's progenitors provides a striking parallel to the Greek myths. By iterating these contradictions and relating them to cosmological "truths," Lévi-Strauss concluded, the myth mitigates a contradiction inherent in Greek, and by extension, Sundanese cosmology—that man is authochthonous despite experiential evidence to the contrary (Lévi-Strauss 1967:212; see also Peradotto 1983:186).

Lévi-Strauss interprets Freud's use of the Oedipus myth to explain a single individual's psychological development as a variation of his own interpretation (Lévi-Strauss 1967:212–13). Gayle Rubin clarifies the relationship between Lévi-Strauss's cultural and Freud's psychological approaches by putting them into a dialectical relationship. She argues that, taken together, Lévi-Strauss and Freud explain the mechanisms that construct and maintain gender ideologies:

Kinship systems require a division of the sexes. The Oedipal phase divides the sexes. Kinship systems include sets of rules governing sexuality. The Oedipal crisis is the assimilation of these rules and taboos. Compulsory heterosexuality is the product of kinship. The Oedipal phase constitutes heterosexual desire. Kinship rests on a radical difference between the rights of men and women. The Oedipal complex confers male rights upon the boy, and forces the girl to accommodate herself to her lesser rights. (RUBIN 1975:198)

The cultural component, as explicated in myth, lays out and naturalizes the laws, such as kinship systems, exogamy rules, and incest taboos,

CHAPTER THREE

that undergird culture. The psychological component inculcates the law into each individual's psyche. In other words, what Freud calls developing a normal sexual drive is, in Rubin's wider perspective, learning to behave in ways that perpetuate the kinship structures based on exogamy that underlie human cultures and societies—ways that normalize a particular sexual drive.

Taken together, the interpretations of Lévi-Strauss and Freud suggest that the Oedipus myth's "meaning" is to inscribe and reinforce arbitrary kinship and exogamy rules as natural laws to which humans are subject. To enforce these laws, individuals learn that some forms of sexuality (e.g., intercourse with one's close relations) are prohibited. To keep track of who may marry whom without compromising kinship rules, cultures exaggerate the biological differences between sexes to establish distinct gender groups, one of which (usually the masculine group) holds power that it controls and manipulates through the exchange of members of the other (usually the feminine group).

Jacques Lacan's reinterpretation of Freud and the Oedipal triangle provides a more refined, but still triangular, approach to gender, sexuality, and desire. Lacan theorizes that subjectivity itself is predicated on the individual's mastery of symbolic systems (such as language), and that an individual's learning to manipulate symbolic systems requires coming to understand human reality as divided into two genders. In Lacan's view, human infants are born into a register of existence he terms the "Real," in which the child is a fragmented aggregate of organs, needs, and impulses with no overall unifying consciousness. The child's needs are predictably and completely satisfied by tangible objects (e.g., milk). At some point, the child enters what Lacan calls the "mirror stage," in which it comes to understand itself as separate from the world around it and begins to categorize things as either part of itself or not part of itself—*other*. It forms a notion of self, as reflected in another, and learns to control this image by conceiving of itself as a corporeal body that interacts with that other. Lacan calls this register the "Imaginary."

In the Imaginary, the child recognizes that its needs can be satisfied only through the intercession of the other and so begins to frame its needs as demands addressed to the other. Demands have two objects: the thing that can satisfy the need, and access to the other. The two-term relationship between self and other that characterizes the Imaginary provides for only two equally unpleasant outcomes: being overwhelmed by the other, or being abandoned by the other. Needs, and the objects that satisfy them, become excuses—symbols—for demands that cannot be satisfied. The part of the demand that remains unsatisfied, which Lacan calls desire, is repressed. The child generalizes desire as a wish for the other to return the same desire, but it then encounters something that interrupts any two-way exchange of desire. This third term is an authority figure that prevents the fulfillment of the self's desires and competes for the attentions of the other.

The third term, in effect, imposes rules that govern the relationship between self and other. Since the "other" in the Imaginary relationship is typically the child's mother, Lacan calls the third term the "Father." To emphasize, however, that the third term is not necessarily the child's biological father (or even a single individual), Lacan sometimes uses the term "Name-of-the-Father" instead. The father's name, as passed onto his descendants, stands for the rules (i.e., kinship laws) that provide the subject a position within the world of culture. The term Other (with a capital "O") also refers to this third term outside the self-other duality.

Engaging with the third term marks the child's entry into a third register, the "Symbolic." Key to this transformation is developing a relationship to the phallus—that which the third term possesses and which satisfies the desire of the (m)other, and so it becomes that which the child seeks to acquire in its own quest to win the desire of the other. The way a subject relates to the phallus determines its position in the Symbolic order. The subject maps the notion of the phallus onto an organ—the penis—that only some bodies have. In the Real, female sex organs have a functional utility equal to that of the male sex organs. In the Symbolic, however, they become a lack, and differences between genitals are reconceptualized as the presence or absence of a penis.[4] Lacan's version of the Oedipal triangle then, like Freud's, involves a child, a mother, and a father, but the roles are much more generalized. The child is a subject, and the subject's desire is always split. The mother is the other, through whom desire is satisfied. The third term regulates the mother's capacity to return the subject's desire, however, so the subject always desires that which the third term desires (Grosz 1990:80).

If we map Lacan's triangle onto Sundanese men's dance events, the dancing men become the subjects, the ronggeng the desired other, and the drumming the Other. Lévi-Strauss's structuralist approach to myth and Lacan's structuralist rendering, built on Freud's psychoanalytic work, of the Oedipus myth provide a perennially compelling explanation for the fundamental division of humans into two genders of unequal status and power. Although Lacan, Freud, Lévi-Strauss, and Rubin all use different language, terminology, and reasoning to explain gender, sexuality, and desire, their models all create gender distinctions through the interaction of three terms. The third term functions to enable the subject's

CHAPTER THREE

desire to be redirected to some object other than its real object, effecting a reversal of cause and effect that masks the arbitrariness of gender distinctions.

Ronggeng and Dance Events

Ronggeng—professional female singer-dancers, whose duties are generally assumed to include sexual services as well—exhibit many of the characteristics of Lacan's other/mother. They are objects of desire through which a man's cravings might be satisfied, provided he can mobilize the power of the Other (in the form of movement-regulating drumming) to get it. Like the mother figure in the Sangkuriang myth, ronggeng are perceived to be both divine (through their connection to the rice goddess) and profane (through their association with sexual behaviors that transgress conventional morality).

Professional female performers who sing and/or dance with male patrons have been called by various names in different times and places in Java.[5] The designation ronggeng is typical in many parts of West Java. In addition to singing and dancing, ronggeng are usually assumed to engage in sexual acts for pay with their male customers. Ronggeng simultaneously portray two irreconcilable sides of Sundanese femininity. On the one hand, they are goddesses—sacred because of their fertility, both literally as childbearers and figuratively as symbols of the earth, agriculture, and creative energy. On the other hand, making people aware of these feminine qualities, whether through flaunting or merely advertising, is considered deviant.

Each of Lia Amelia's two possible etymologies for the word ronggeng emphasizes one term of this contradiction. She cites the scholar S. Dloyana Kusuma, who believes the term ronggeng derives from the Sanskrit *renggana*—a female idol. Another etymology is *wara anggana*, Kawi (old Javanese) for "woman alone" (Amelia 1996:82–83; see also Cooper 2000:614). Rengganis also is the name taken by the legendary first *ronggeng gunung* (a style of female performance in southern West Java), Siti Samboja, when she assumed her role as a female entertainer (Djadja 1998; Suganda 2002). Some additional terms for male dance fans emphasize the possibility of illicit sexual relationships with ronggeng. For example, *pamogoran* is a man who sleeps with loose women (Amelia 1996:23; Fajaria 1996:13), and *palacuran* is a man who engages in an immoral lifestyle (Turyati 1996:5).

82

Men find the feminine presence of ronggeng to be compelling and express their desire for ronggeng by dancing. The paragraphs that follow explore the rich history and variety of the professional female performers who, with voice and movement, tempt their male partners to get up and dance. They also explore how ronggeng function as a crucial element in the erotic triangle of Sundanese dance.

The Origins of Ronggeng

Events at which men dance to the accompaniment of music that features drumming while they partner with professional female entertainers have been a fixture in the lives of many Southeast Asians for millennia. Referring to carvings on the ninth-century Buddhist monument near Yogyakarta in central Java, Claire Holt sees reflections of modern men's dancing in "the lively attitudes of the dancing boys on the Barabudur relief" (1967:111; see also Murgiyanto 1998:502). Clara Brakel-Papenhuyzen states that "ronggèng dancing is an ancient and indigenous Indonesian 'entertainment'" (1995:545). R. Anderson Sutton and David Goldsworthy both provide excellent summaries of some old references to dance events in Java, including Theodore Pigeaud's annotation of a fourteenth-century Javanese poem, *Nagara Kertagama*, that describes a singer-dancer who danced and sang for various audiences; she provided more personal entertainment for noblemen as well (Goldsworthy 1979:365–72; Sutton 1984:121).

Legends and myths describing the origins of men's dance events point to roots in agricultural and fertility rituals honoring the rice goddess, known by her Sundanese name, Nyi Pohaci, as well as her Indic name, Dewi Sri. According to Gandamihardja, dance events grew out of agricultural rituals in which a girl was chosen to represent the goddess while the village men danced around her. Over the course of history, the girl herself began to dance and became a ronggeng (Gandamihardja 1978–79:33). Erotic dance movements and sexual activity between the men and the ronggeng are personifications of these forces of nature and were meant to imitate and influence them.

Robert Hefner asserts that men's dance events (called *tayuban*) in east Java still have a sacral role (1987:85–86). Brakel-Papenhuyzen quotes the Javanese aristocrat R. M. Suwandi's 1937 treatise on tayuban: "For the Javanese the tayub dance is held to ensure the continuation of the world" (1995:568). Ben Suharto provides more insight into the continuing ritual aspects of tayuban dancing; he reports that the name of the first dance

CHAPTER THREE

involving a man following the solo ronggeng dance is *bedhah bumi*—"plowing the earth" (Suharto 1980:71). The conflation of agricultural and sexual imagery, with the shared theme of fertility and continuity, is striking and suggests that dance events are a ritual enactment of human interactions with the cycles of nature.

The protocols of dance events thus suggest indigenous agricultural roots, but it is possible to ascribe Indic roots to dance events as well. Stutterheim postulates a sacred Hindu origin for ronggeng in Indian *devadasi*, the female "servants of god" in Hindu temples who sing and dance for temple rituals (1956:100). Dance events that involve ronggeng may also have a relation to tantric ritual. Tantric thought involves a syncretic combination of "mother goddess" worship (such as the Dewi Sri cult described above) with Hindu theology, in which *shakti* (creative energies) that come from a god are imagined as female deities, such as the spouse of Shiva (Becker 1988:388).

A folk tale related by Claire Holt describes how three men—a carpenter, a tailor, and a goldsmith—create and dress a wooden statue of a woman which comes to life through divine intervention.[6] Each of the men recognizes his contribution to the living woman and claims her as his own, but the three men are doomed instead to wander around with the woman and accompany her singing and dancing. Each man's assigned musical instrument recalls the material with which he works professionally. The carpenter is to play the rebab (two-string spike fiddle), the tailor the drum, and the goldsmith the ketuk (small gong; Holt 1967:113; Pleyte 1916). Brakel-Papenhuyzen suggests that this tale can be traced to a Hindu-Javanese myth "in which the three main Hindu gods transform themselves into a group of roaming artists" (1995:545–546), but most modern versions are Islamicized. For example, Probonegoro situates a version of the story as a plot outline for a *topeng Betawi* (a north-coast theatrical genre that involves female singer-dancers) play entitled "Jaka Pertaka," in which the statue is brought to life by an Islamic holy man named Kaki Jugil. In this version, all the characters then formed an itinerant troupe in which Kaki Jugil made the three young villagers the musicians, while he himself became the dalang (narrator), and Jaka Pertaka herself became the leader of the group (Probonegoro 1987:24).[7]

Modern Sundanese, like many other Muslims, understand themselves to have a wild inner essence—*nafsu* (passion)—which can be controlled by *akal* (reason). Islamic notions about reason and passion (cf. Peletz 1996) dovetail in some ways with indigenous Sundanese agricultural mythology. The same divine source that gave birth to Nyi Pohaci, who, as the rice goddess, is the source of all useful plants, also begat two wild animals, Kakabuat and Budug Basu, whose purpose is to ruin these useful materials if they are left unattended and uncontrolled by humans (Sumardjo 2005a). Collectively, the men in the troupe can control the potentially destructive passion ignited by women, as personified by Jaka Pertaka, in a way that as individuals they could not (cf. Foley 1989).

In southern West Java, around the city of Ciamis, a local version of men's dance events called *ronggeng gunung* is structured around the telling of its own origin myth. A princess, Siti Samboja, made a daring escape into the mountains after her husband, the king, was killed by pirates. She was told in a vision to disguise herself as a performer and change her name to Dewi Rengganis to escape the same fate. Grieving her husband's death and wanting to elude her pursuers, she wandered from place to place, gaining protection by surrounding herself with the hardiest youths in each community to which she came. The youths competed with one another to show their strength and prove their worthiness to guard her. In ronggeng gunung performances, the ronggeng's songs relate the various episodes in Siti Samboja's adventure, and some of the dance movements echo the actions taken by the mythic characters. For example, the words of the song "Manangis" (Tears) relate the story of her sorrow. The dance movements that involve covering the face with a *sarung* commemorate an episode in the story in which Siti Samboja encounters the rotting corpse of a friend (Djadja 1998; Suganda 2002).

These diverse origin stories accommodate various cultural and religious movements in Javanese history, maintaining a few common themes throughout. Ronggeng represent femininity, which is portrayed as a complement to masculine energy. Ronggeng are sources or catalysts for power that can be harnessed and used by men. Regardless of the mythical ideology, the relationship between female performers and the men with whom they dance remains the same. It is not a personal relationship. Ronggeng are not individuals—spouses or mates—but objects. It is as if they, too, were agricultural resources to be shared among men. Holt paraphrases the folk tale: "And thus it was shown that the dance girl does not belong to one but to many" (1967:113).

Kathy Foley concludes that the many contemporary music, dance, and theater forms centered on female entertainers have roots in goddess-centered religious rites. She points out structural similarities in a variety of modern dance and theatrical genres that are centered on ronggeng or ronggeng-like female performers. Such genres usually include a solo dance performed by the ronggeng, followed by a couple dance performed by the ronggeng and a male partner (often a clown or pimp figure associated with the troupe), followed by general dancing or a play. Ronggeng

CHAPTER THREE

assume the role of Dewi Sri (the rice goddess), so interacting with the ronggeng through dance or sexual intercourse is a metaphor for plowing the earth (symbolized by Dewi Sri) and planting rice (Foley 1989).

Ronggeng performance operates in two media—song and dance—that intersect with the two elements of the erotic triangle that are gendered male. With the men who dance, the ronggeng intersects in the dimension of movement. With the musical accompaniment, including the drumming, the ronggeng intersects by providing the important components of song, melody, and words. Together, a ronggeng's free-flowing voice and her rhythmically constrained movements translate the contradictions of femininity into an aesthetic realm of music and dance. When combined with suggestions of drumming and free dancing, the ronggeng image provides an entry into the rich symbolic world of men's dance events. The following discussions of historical and modern female performers show how the role and image of ronggeng persist through time and cut across many different musical and dance expressions.

Historical ronggeng

The "exotic dancing girl" is a common trope in Western accounts of visits to Asia in general and to the East Indies in particular. One possible explanation is the apparent congruence of Asian dancing customs with European ones. Travelogue descriptions provide valuable information about the female entertainers of the past. European writers often make note of the physical beauty, or at least the extraordinary dress and grooming, of female performers. Christopher Fryke, who traveled to Java in 1680–86 as a surgeon in the employ of the Dutch East Indies Company, wrote in 1700 that the female performers he saw "are of an extraordinary small size, but of the most exquisite Form and perfect Shape . . . besides their natural Beauty, there is all the artificial Dress that can be contrived" (Fryke and Schweitzer 1700:105–6). Sir Thomas Stamford Raffles, the governor of Java during the brief period of British control (1811–15), thought the visual image of ronggeng worthy of a full-page engraving, along with voluminous description, in his monumental *History of Java* (1965:342–44).

Descriptions generally mention that ronggeng frankly demand recompense for their services. It is a common stereotype of Sundanese women that they are demanding, and that men must somehow give something—support, family, status—in return for their continued attentions. Sundanese women are criticized if they are perceived to be greedy. Ronggeng, on the other hand, are not afraid to appear greedy; they cut to the chase

86

and simply demand a cash fee in exchange for a limited period of attention.

Many writers report that ronggeng not only dance for recompense, but often are prostitutes as well. Given the large number of single Dutch men in nineteenth-century Java, prostitution was viewed as a necessary evil requiring government intervention and control and hence was a matter of much public discourse among European colonials (Jones, Sulistyaningsih, and Hull 1998). The naturalist J. Beete Jukes noted that there was nothing in the dancing-girl performance he saw that was "indecorous . . . , although the girls themselves are, by their profession, considered as courtezans" (Jukes 1847:51). The Dutch scholar P. J. Veth reported that ronggeng live, work, and even learn their arts in houses of prostitution (Veth 1875:481). Although ronggeng were regarded as sex workers, government powers generally treated them differently from "ordinary" prostitutes. When prostitution was regulated in Java in 1852 (Ingleson 1986:127), ronggeng were subject to the mandatory medical examinations required for prostitutes but were not taxed like other prostitutes (Hesselink 1992:214).

European descriptions of the sexual aspect of the ronggeng's image often assume a sophomoric, smirking tone. J. Sarluy, a young Dutch adventurer who wrote an unpublished memoir in 1920, is wryly suggestive about the ronggeng's extracurricular activities. He hints that they provide a tempting opportunity: "[Ronggeng] are not famous as chaste virgins. . . . if there are ronggengs around, then [the boys] are there to seize their chance [*als de kippen*], better yet to "seize their chance" [*als de hanen*] (Sarluy 1920:51).[8] Here Sarluy does not directly accuse ronggeng of impropriety. He puns on the Dutch phrase *als de kippen* (which means literally "as the chickens," but as an idiom means "to seize an opportunity")—he suggests that the young men are out *als de hanen*—"as the roosters"—a twist on the idiom that conveys a strutting masculine sexuality and resonant with the common Indonesian use of the term jago (rooster) to describe men who affect such behavior.[9]

Kleden-Probonegoro, generalizing about female performance traditions, makes it clear that enabling masculine strutting through groping, pinching, and kissing is part of the public behavior in many of the modern forms that include female performers (1991:43). She is unwilling to rule out prostitution completely but suggests that for the most part it is the *appearance* of immorality, of looseness, of socially unacceptable behavior that has a function in these forms, rather than any physical consummation of it. She provides several case studies of ronggeng who are not prostitutes, but serial monogamists, who have been "married"

CHAPTER THREE

(i.e., cohabited with a man) as many as twenty times. Widodo likewise asserts that the image of immorality in central Javanese tayuban has "been constructed largely from gossip and newspaper coverage," although he does not rule prostitution out completely either (Widodo 1995:13). It is clear that an important part of the ronggeng's identity is the perception of easy virtue and sexual availability.

The importance of female entertainers' singing is suggested by the derivation of the Sundanese term *renggong* (and derivatives such as rerenggongan) to refer to a type of song characterized by a simple accompaniment and a prominent vocal melody. One possible etymology of the word renggong is that they are the songs sung by ronggeng (Panitia Kamus 1969:421–22). Raffles locates much of the local audience's artistic appreciation in the women's mastery of texts, which "sometimes possesses much humour and drollery; and in adapting their motions to the language, they frequently excite loud bursts of laughter, and obtain great applause from the native audience" (1965:343). Banner writes, "The words are generally improvized to the honour and glorification of the central figures of the festivity" (1927:96).

Europeans were often dismissive of ronggeng dancing. The caption for a 1597 engraving of Javanese dancers provides the uncomplimentary, if vivid, image of "arms and legs twisting, and the whole body turning, like dogs who come crawling out of their dens" (Rouffaer and Ijzerman 1915:plate 25).[10] The descriptions leave an overwhelming impression that ronggeng dance was relatively simple, even taking into account the likelihood that these images were perceived through filters of unfamiliarity and often disdain. Manipulation of a sash or scarf, twisting arm and torso movements, and simple foot patterns are frequent themes in European descriptions. Europeans typically characterized the dance style as "posing" or "attitudinizing," suggesting that the dancers frequently stopped moving and held poses. According to Turyati, a ronggeng named Bacih, who started dancing in 1950, summarized a ronggeng's movement vocabulary as "movements of the buttocks and stepping" (Turyati 1996).[11] Raffles (1965) suggested that dance movements somehow related to the texts, although there is little other corroborating evidence.

Europeans may have been disdainful of a ronggeng's artistic skills, but Javanese and Sundanese men often were quite taken with their voices and appearance. Present-day styles of female singing in West Java are characterized by a beguiling elasticity of rhythm. The accompaniment for much vocal music is cast in a quadruple meter, with a regular pulse, and characterized by cycles marked by binary subdivisions, but the vocal part floats over this rhythmically regular background. The poetic forms of the texts generally occupy only a portion of each musical cycle, and no analysis of that portion ever results in an explanation that involves a process of binary subdivision. It is as if a female singer deliberately resists the rhythmic constraints of the accompaniment. Her phrases spill provocatively over the edges of the rhythmic structures set up by the musicians. At the same time, however, a female performer's dance movements embody the very rhythmic structures her singing subverts. Ronggeng tread a line between rhythmically free, melody-oriented music, as exemplified by their singing, and strictly metered, percussion-oriented music, as exemplified by dance accompaniment (cf. Spiller 1999). This contrast is associated with, and perhaps a primary cause of, the ronggeng mystique that many men find irresistible.

The activities of female performers reinforce several "feminine" contradictions that are characteristic of Sundanese gender ideology. They at once embody both the divine goddess Dewi Sri and prostitutes. Their extraordinary beauty and dress appeal to men who are supposed to find virtue in modest women. Their frank greed for money flies in the face of ordinary standards of propriety and thrift. Their contradictory nature extends to their artistic idiom, in which free-metered singing is juxtaposed against dancing to rhythmically regular music. Over the centuries, the songs and movements of ronggeng have left an indelible impression on Sundanese sensibilities.

Modern ronggeng

In modern West Java, performers who identify themselves as ronggeng are rare. Comparable entertainers appear in a variety of contemporary guises, however. By embodying the same contradictions, these modern-day performers invoke the image of ronggeng, indexing the many associations the image has accrued over time. It is a common practice to try to downplay the image's many negative associations, however.

One of the ways in which female performers are afforded more respect is through the decoupling of the two artistic worlds—song and dance—that ronggeng occupy. Attempts in the first half of the twentieth century to bring tayuban (aristocratic men's social dance events) more into line with conservative sexual mores involved, for example, forbidding the female entertainers to dance and enjoining them to sit down while they sang. The prominent Sundanese singer Iyar Wiarsih told me that she began her career singing for tayuban in the 1940s. At that time, female performers were not allowed to dance—"nggak boleh!" ("it was not allowed!"), she once asserted forcefully to me (personal communication,

CHAPTER THREE

February 9, 1999). Etty Suhaeti notes that "ketuk tilu ronggeng nowadays no longer dance while singing, and the songs are sung by a special *pesinden*" (1986:57).[12]

The late musician Entis Sutisna discussed with me the notion of separating ronggeng *seni* (art) from the *cara* (manner of implementation). He believed the songs and the vocal style to have considerable intrinsic artistic value, which he thought could be salvaged from the *jelek* (bad) physical activities with which the songs were associated. He was applying the New Order cultural policy of "upgrading," controlling the moral content (see Yampolsky 1995:710) of ronggeng arts by extricating the songs and the vocal style from the sensual activities that went along with them. Entis himself was involved in one such government-sponsored effort in the 1970s with Entjar Tjarmedi, a prominent and versatile musician who led the traditional music section at RRI at that time, and Entjar's wife, the singer Imik Suwarsih. Together they spearheaded a revival of ketuk tilu music for RRI broadcasts.

They learned, performed, and aired the song repertoire of ketuk tilu without ever actually accompanying any dancing. The intention was to maintain what the cultural bureaucracy regarded as both "good" and *khas Sunda* (authentically Sundanese) while excising the "bad" behavior. This effort may have succeeded in partially severing the ketuk tilu song repertoire from the ronggeng image, but whether their radio listeners' attitudes were changed by these broadcasts is uncertain. Even when deprived by the medium of radio of any real visual stimulation, listeners enculturated to associate singing and drumming with sensual dancing likely used their imaginations to fill in the dancing—a practice which is arguably even more khas Sunda.

Susan Pratt Walton, examining a similar evolution in central Java, points out that new performing conventions for female performers—remaining seated, wearing tight clothes—quite literally restricted their ability to move (Walton 1996:375–79). The use of amplification probably contributed to the separation of singing and dancing roles. The tether of a microphone limits a performer's mobility and ability to dance.[13] Before such technology became available, singers developed a voice that could be heard over the sound of their accompaniment (Weintraub 2004a:65). The ketuk tilu expert Salam Mulyadi remarked that spaces in which ronggeng performed were typically small so that the ronggeng could be easily heard. Entis was convinced that singing could be easily heard over the gamelan because the atmosphere was different back then—without the overwhelming noise pollution we encounter today. It is likely that the focused vocal timbre singers cultivated before the 1960s enabled their voices to be heard over gamelan accompaniment without amplification.

There has been much change in the discourse about female performers over the past few decades. The most common term for female entertainers today is *sinden* or *pasinden*, which usually implies a singer in a gamelan salendro ensemble. Most typically, the designation pasinden implies a woman who sings and does not dance. Some Sundanese people, however, regard the terms pasinden and ronggeng to be more or less synonymous. Proponents of sanitizing the arts for national and international consumption argue that there is little difference between the two terms—that the ronggeng's primary job is to sing, and that the dancing part is not important. Entis Sutisna and Salam Mulyadi regarded ronggeng dancing as a sideline and cited as evidence the simplicity of ronggeng dance movements. The continued association of female singing with dancing and with other connotations of the ronggeng image, however, belies this claim.

In the past thirty years or so, a very polite synonym for pasinden—*juru kawih* (song artisan)—has come to be used in formal situations. This is the term most often applied to star pasinden and to pasinden who study and teach in academic settings. K. S. Kost has traced changes in the status and role of female singers in West Java and concluded that patrons of Sundanese arts should insist on more respectful names such as juru kawih or *juru sekar* (melody artisan) to raise the level of Sundanese arts in general (see Kost n.d.; for a discussion of Sundanese terms for singing and singers, see Zanten 1989:13–21). A similarly "upgraded" term for female singers, *waranggana*, is gaining currency in central Java (cf. Cooper 2000).

Regardless of terminology, and regardless of whether a female entertainer sings, dances, or both, the ronggeng image is projected onto any female performer who sings or dances. In the following sections I briefly introduce some modern-day "ronggeng" and discuss how they continue to evoke the ronggeng image.

TAYUBAN SINGERS Aristocratic tayuban events evidently included female singer-dancers around the turn of the twentieth century. Some writers apply the term ronggeng to these performers (e.g., Lubis 1998:244–45). However, P. A. A. Djajadiningrat, a prominent aristocratic *bupati* (regional bureaucrat) and a participant in early twentieth-century tayuban, does not; although he discusses ronggeng at several points in his massive memoir, he avoids the term when describing the women who performed at tayuban. It is clear, however, that he enjoyed both their voices and their dancing. He describes one performer as "the most beautiful little

CHAPTER THREE

dancer in the whole district, . . . who furthermore had a beautiful voice" (1936:145).[14]

Aristocratic dance parties (tayuban), like their underclass equivalents (ketuk tilu parties), were reputed to be sites for drinking and womanizing as well as for dance. A movement in the early twentieth century by Sundanese aristocrats attempted to redeem tayuban in the face of moral opposition to them. Muslim aristocrats who enjoyed dancing, such as R. Gandakusumah of Sumedang, revised the protocol for tayuban to eliminate both the alcohol and the female dancers (Natapradja 1975:105). As previously mentioned, ronggeng were admonished to stay seated and to sing only, not to dance. Clever aristocratic dancers developed the improvisatory aspects of the men's dancing to shift attention away from interaction with the female performers to solo dancing.

But female performers found ways to "bend" the rules. Iyar Wiarsih, whom I already have quoted as asserting adamantly that female performers at tayuban were forbidden to dance, also admitted with a wink that she and other singers circumvented the prohibition by performing upper-body dance gestures while remaining seated (personal communication, February 9, 1999). Abay Subardja told me that tayuban did not feature ronggeng, only pasinden; he then added that the pasinden might get up and dance (personal communication, November 17, 1999).

These anecdotes suggest that any elimination of ronggeng from tayuban was largely rhetorical. A more direct approach would have been to eliminate all traces of ronggeng from the events. This tack was not taken, however, probably because female performers were an integral part of the events. By being seated with the gamelan, female performers could still promise hints of their sexual availability. The beguiling sound of their voices, singing in free rhythm over the quadruple-meter gamelan accompaniment, evokes the complete ronggeng image.

WAYANG   Foley discusses a similar evolution for the pasinden in Sundanese *wayang golek* (rod puppet theater) accompaniment. She postulates that dalang (puppeteers) coopted ronggeng performers who might compete for their audience at celebrations and seated them with the gamelan accompanying the puppet show (Foley 1979:89–92). This view is corroborated by Kost (n.d.). According to Entis Sutisna, such female singers were called *ronggeng wayang* when they first appeared (personal communication, April 6, 1999; see also Kost n.d.).

Ruth Fryer reports that the Sundanese dalang Otong Rasta first included a female singer for wayang in 1951; at that time, he claims, only a few wayang troupes had pasinden. The addition, according to Otong, was in response to the popularity of ketuk tilu groups, who took advantage of the crowds that gathered at wayang performances to secure their own audience. Dalang began to include similar entertainment—a female performer singing in the style of ketuk tilu—to keep their audiences from defecting (Fryer 1989:245).

In her discussion of wayang golek, Lubis (citing R. Danoeredja's 1929 Sundanese-language publication, *Serat-Sinerat Djaman Djoemenengna Raden Hadji Moehamad Moesa*), mentions some famous pasinden (whom she defines as women who sing kawih to accompany wayang golek), namely Iti Narem from Ujungberung, Nyi Mas Warnasari, and Nyi Dasimah, from the beginning of the twentieth century (1998:247). The widespread use of amplification, beginning in the 1950s, contributed to the increased prominence of pasinden in wayang golek (Weintraub 1997:175).

Otong Rasta suggested to me that the incorporation of female singers into wayang had far-reaching ramifications. He retuned his own heirloom gamelan from *pelog jawar* (seven-tone hemitonic tuning system) to salendro (five-tone anhemitonic tuning system) in 1958 because the pasinden preferred to sing to salendro accompaniment (personal communication, June 11, 1999). The salendro tuning system is compatible with a variety of vocal modes such as sorog and pelog degung, while pelog jawar is less versatile from the pasinden's point of view (for more information on gamelan and vocal tunings in wayang golek, see Weintraub 1997:89–97).

Quoting K. S. Kostaman (among others), Andrew Weintraub characterizes the period of 1959–64 as the *krisis sinden* (pasinden crisis) (Weintraub 2004a:58). He recounts what amounted to a struggle between pasinden and wayang golek dalang for the attention of wayang audiences during the years of Sukarno's presidency and his policy of "Guided Democracy" and relates it to profound changes to attitudes about gender, politics, and memory during the period. Weintraub points to homologies between the female singer's popularity and the situation of the rank-and-file populace, and between the dalang's high status and the government's authority. The rising status of the female singer and the grafting of dance-event protocols into wayang performances, along with the concomitant lessening of the dalang's authority, represented a form of resistance to Guided Democracy's excesses and an expression of the populace's desires in the domain of culture. It is little wonder, then, that government authorities implemented draconian policies aimed at maintaining the status quo by restricting how female performers could appear and act at wayang performances. Once again, the primary strategy for tempering the ronggeng

CHAPTER THREE

image was to immobilize the female performers. In particular, the practice of placing the female performers on high tables, where spectators could easily see them, was discouraged in an attempt to rein in the collapse of government authority (Weintraub 2004a).

JAIPONGAN   In jaipongan, the roles of singer and dancer both are highlighted, but they are performed by separate individuals. Jaipongan dancing is rather athletic, and the singing is virtuosic; it would be difficult to perform both simultaneously. One often sees, however, a predilection for performers who can do both. One of the original star jaipongan performers in the early 1980s was Tati Saleh (see Amilia 2001), who was equally famous for her singing and dancing. However, she rarely did both at the same time. In Subang, the popular jaipongan and bajidoran groups feature lineups of as many as fifteen female performers, most of whom both sing and dance, but not simultaneously. The star female performer at these performances only sings and does not dance at all.

The singer on most of the most famous jaipongan hits, Hajah Idjah Hadidjah, never dances at all. In fact, she never even performs jaipongan music for live dance events—only during recording sessions and performances of wayang golek. Nevertheless, she is well-known all over West Java for her sirenlike voice. When she performs in public (most typically as a pasinden for the wayang performances of her husband, the dalang Tjetjep Supriadi), her male fans turn out in great numbers.

The individual female performer's subjectivity lurks below the surface of her stage persona. Men rely on a ronggeng's complicity, trusting that she will act in accordance with convention and pretend to be attentive to her partner's desires. They suspend disbelief while dancing, but they never truly believe that the individual ronggeng *is* the role she plays. Even a "star" orientation, in which the individual performer is granted individual subjectivity, does not enable pasinden to transcend the ronggeng image. The ronggeng image and the men's dance-event triangle of which it is an important component are so persistent that they are applied to female performers of all sorts.

ARTIS DANGDUT   Dangdut is Indonesia's most popular music (Weintraub 2006:414), with a large following throughout the country. Hit songs are recorded by a small number of star performers and promulgated via radio and television. However, as Philip Yampolsky points out, "The live performance scene is sustained . . . by innumerable minor singers who have not a prayer of stardom" (Yampolsky 1994:38). In and around Band-

94

ung, such singers are known as *artis dangdut* (dangdut artists), and they are typically young women. The moniker *artis*—derived from the English word "artist"—has a modern connotation and is used mainly to describe non-gamelan, nontraditional performers. At Sundanese hajat (life-cycle milestone celebrations), the entertainment might include an afternoon or evening dangdut performance, with one or several artis dangdut singing onstage to the accompaniment of a dangdut combo featuring transverse bamboo flute, keyboard, bass, and drums, or a more modest accompaniment of electronic keyboard and drum machine.

At many weddings I attended, the artis dangdut usually chose a man from the audience to be the central male dancer onstage for each song. She interviewed him, or gave him a goyang lesson—goyang refers to a sensual rolling hip-and-buttocks movement—before beginning to sing and dance. Several friends and relatives typically joined this central male dancer, and they danced with each other while the artis dangdut performed. The artis dangdut also provided amusing or titillating patter between songs.

Artis dangdut at Sundanese hajat display many of the identifying characteristics of ronggeng. Although their style of dress is modern—typically low-cut dresses or pantsuits made from shiny fabrics in flamboyant colors, with revealing cutouts at the midriff and thighs, high platform shoes, heavy makeup, and long straight hair—they conform to the ronggeng image in that their clothing and demeanor are quite sexually suggestive. In addition, they sing, dance, and interact with male guests. Despite the profound difference in the sound of the songs, in this hajat context an artis dangdut reproduces many characteristics of ronggeng performances (cf. Foley 1989:60–61).

FICTIONAL RONGGENG The ronggeng image is frequently cited in other cultural productions. As a multivalent symbol of masculine desire and feminine desirability and of the contradictions of gender identities, it provides considerable grist for the artistic mill. The singer-songwriter Doel Sumbang's Indonesian-language pop song "Ronggeng," for example, casts the battle between reason and passion inspired by a man's interaction with a ronggeng that the song's words describe in idiomatic gestures of global popular music (see Spiller 2007). Other modern Sundanese media often portray ronggeng images as well. The central character of Alam Surawidjaya's 1969 film *Nyi Ronggeng* (directed by Alam Surawidjaya, based on a short story by Kurnaen Suhardiman) is a ronggeng. David Hanan writes about *Nyi Ronggeng* that "the film as a whole im-

CHAPTER THREE

plies that the social position of the ronggeng dancer stems from the fact that these dancers externalize and allegorize what often are unadmitted dimensions of sexuality in Javanese Muslim society" (1992:197). The film relies on its viewers' understanding of the contradictions that a ronggeng exemplifies to make its point. *Nyi Ronggeng* was shot on location, featuring Tati Saleh, then an up-and-coming star performer, in the role of the ronggeng (Amilia 2001:130–32), and Hanan claims that the traditional arts in the film give it "a documentary relevance" (1992:161). Jen Harjantho points out, however, that some of the performing arts sequences, particularly the penca silat (martial arts) routines, are wooden and uninspiring, which he attributes to the difficulties of filming on location and in color (1970). Although Tati Saleh was a gifted dancer, she represented that she learned the ronggeng dance moves especially for the film (Amilia 2001:132). Vanessa Richardson rightly points out that the "folk traditions have been 'modified' or 'amplified' for the purposes of the plot" (1994:37). According to Hanan, the director claimed that "the dance in its precise form was invented especially for the film" (Hanan 1992:175–76).

In *Nyi Ronggeng*, the dance event's structure involves the ronggeng's dancing with a man, who tries to touch her hair bun while she fends him off with martial arts moves. If the man succeeds in touching her hair, she must kiss him. If he fails, he must pay. This particular structure is set up as a competition, with a winner and a loser, between a ronggeng and a male dancer. In real life, a man pays regardless of whether he "wins" or "loses," and from a monetary point of view, he always loses. This fabrication of a protocol to suit the film's own themes testifies to the persistence and flexibility of the ronggeng image. The filmmakers index the network of contradictions inherent in the model, nuanced to make their own particular point.

Ahmad Tohari's trilogy of novels, *Ronggeng Dukuh Paruk* (Tohari 1982–86),[15] tells the story of a ronggeng from the small village of Dukuh Paruk who becomes embroiled in the large national political movements of the 1960s (cf. Tohari 2003). Nancy Cooper analyzes how Tohari takes advantage of the ronggeng image as "a polysemic icon" (2004:548), both divine and profane (2004:532), to personify many of the contradictions and binary contrasts—local versus national, rural versus urban, backward versus progressive, and traditional versus modern—that encapsulate the complex political and social struggles of the time. The novels' power stems in large part from readers' understanding of how the ronggeng image indexes the long-standing Javanese view of femininity and masculinity as complementary, and of the ability of the ronggeng's "powerful yet contained femininity" and its tempering and balancing effect on masculinity (Cooper 2004:550) to serve as a metaphor for the Javanese struggle between tradition and modernity.

Evocations of ronggeng are not limited to textual media. The Sundanese composer and conductor Yazeed Djamin wrote an orchestral work, *Nyi Ronggeng*, for the Third International Music Festival in Leningrad (Planasari 2005); it subsequently won first prize at the International Music Festival in Sydney (Raden 2008). Several orchestras in Southeast Asia and Europe have since performed it, and a transcription for concert band has also been widely distributed and performed. The composer evokes men's dance events by incorporating its emblematic musical forces—Sundanese female vocalists and Sundanese drumming—into the orchestra. Some performances even include traditional Sundanese dancers (Colombant 1997). Here, the ronggeng image is a sonic image that imparts a sense of Sundaneseness to Western orchestral textures. Yazeed's intention was to Indonesianize the Western classical tradition by "quoting" from "folk" music (STE 1999) along the lines of European nationalist composers of the late nineteenth and early twentieth centuries. For one critic, Sita Planasari, the piece's dramatic contrasts evoke the many different emotions that a ronggeng might experience as she faces her fate (Planasari 2005).

The ronggeng *Image*

The ronggeng image persists, in myriad manifestations, into a present in which few actual ronggeng are found. A few characteristics of female performers are particularly emblematic of ronggeng and make up what I call the ronggeng image. The tropes of objectifying beauty, sexual availability, and free-meter singing with fixed-meter dancing provide a common background over which these various types of contemporary female performers operate.

A female performer's visual presence is an important part of her appeal, and her appearance, according to Nano S., is at least as important as her musical ability (personal communication, June 6, 1999). Cicih Muda, the leader of a bajidoran troupe in Subang, is quoted as saying that when choosing female performers for her ensemble, "talent can be molded; what's important is a beautiful appearance" (HERS/NAR 2002).[16] All is not lost, however, for women with exceptional voices and less-than-exceptional faces (Euis Komariah, personal communication, April 19, 2007). Performers can compensate for a dearth of conventional beauty

CHAPTER THREE

with exceptional clothes and makeup. It is these visual cues of femininity, more than raw beauty, that play a significant role in a female performer's popularity.

A conversation I once had with several Sundanese men epitomized the masculine conception of the ronggeng double standard. I asked about their perceptions of ronggeng. One man's first reaction was to enumerate quite methodically their negative characteristics: they engage in inappropriate, extramarital sexual behavior and they always ask for money. Why then, I asked, do ronggeng continue to capture men's imaginations? This question did not elicit a methodical answer. Instead, the men shifted into a bantering mode, making vague statements about the charms of female bodies and the inescapable desires of all men, relating anecdotes of questionable veracity about ronggeng, and searching for double meanings in each other's statements that could be twisted to suggest an admission of sexual contact between the speaker and a ronggeng. There was nervous laughter after practically every exchange. The men agreed that ronggeng employ magic of various sorts, such as inserting a sliver of gold or diamond under the skin around their eyes, lips, or buttocks to make these areas irresistible. These inserts, called *susuk* (personal communication, June 16, 1999; Suhaenah 1996:14; Sumiati 1996b:20), are meant to cloud men's judgment (personal communication, June 16, 1999) and to provoke sexual urges.

Another conversation I had with a Sundanese man about ronggeng followed a similar trajectory. After first insisting that the reputation of ronggeng as prostitutes was undeserved and that the most generous sexual favor one could cajole from a ronggeng was a kiss on the cheek, my interlocutor recanted and admitted that outside of the context of performances, men could hook up sexually with ronggeng and then lie about their experiences. He took pains to imply that he himself might have gone further than a kiss with female entertainers. My attempts to elicit specifics resulted only in ambiguous statements and wicked smiles (personal communication, April 19, 2009).

By separating the roles of singer and dancer, women performers circumvent some of the assumptions of low morals associated with ronggeng. Nevertheless, the complex network of associations, implications, and meaning that make up the image of the ronggeng continues to determine how Sundanese men and women perceive and interpret any and all female performers. Many female singers endure (or enjoy) the ardent attention of their male fans. Female dancers, too, even those who bring their artistic expression to the fore, are often evaluated by their appearance and sexiness. Men who fall in love with and marry these performers in part because of their artistic skills often ask their new wives to forego further public performances.

But such marriages are notoriously prone to failure. A Sundanese proverb equates marrying a ronggeng (along with living in a house near the road and working under a general) as a sure way to ask for trouble (Zanten 1989:83). Ronggeng represent an exaggeration of everything that a man's desire says women ought to be (beautiful, sexually available, and responsive) and are thus irresistible despite—or perhaps because of—their being everything his reason says they should not be (promiscuous, greedy, vain, and uncontrollable).

RONGGENG AND POWER According to Benedict Anderson's explication of Javanese thought, power is something to be accumulated, concentrated, and preserved, not exercised (1972:8). One way to acquire power is through ascetic exercise and self-discipline. In a consistent world, people would accumulate power (and thus status) by transcending inappropriate sexual urges, not by gratifying them. However, Anderson suggests an alternate approach to accumulating power—through drunkenness and sexual excess: "the systematic indulgence of the sensual passions in their most extreme form was believed to exhaust these passions, and therefore allow a man's Power to be concentrated without further hindrance" (Anderson 1972:10). In dance events, the male participants do not view the ronggeng as a temptation to be overcome but as an opportunity not to be missed. Either way, they benefit—they can gain status both by gratifying *and* resisting their sexual urges toward the ronggeng, because she represents at once all aspects of Sundanese femininity.

In her analysis of why women find it more difficult to acquire power and status in Javanese society, despite the general acknowledgment by the Javanese (men and women alike) that "men find it more difficult to restrain their innate passions and desires . . . than do women," Brenner presents a way in which this seeming contradiction is reconciled (Brenner 1995:32). She explains that Javanese believe it is normal to experience desire; it is dangerous only when it is excessive. Despite the Javanese conviction that men have greater control over their instincts, most Javanese also take for granted the contradictory notion that men have innately greater sexual desires than women. These desires are seen as a sign of their sexual potency and virility, another manifestation of power (cf. Anderson 1972:18; Keeler 1990:130) and thus not to be completely overcome. Brenner suggests that "the positive associations of sexual potency and of generally 'manly' behavior offset any shame that might accompany their inability to exercise self-control" (1995:35).

CHAPTER THREE

The ronggeng's role is to provide a "safe" target for neutralizing these urges—a sort of electrical ground or heat sink for sexual tension—as well as a means for the men symbolically to display their sexual potency, and thus their power, to other men. Hefner points out that in East Java, the female dancers are itinerant women: "The relative social anonymity of the dance relationship allows them [the men] to regard the dance as outside the bounds of ordinary village behavior, giving them, on occasion, a sense of license" (1987:77). Sutton's comment about the female singer—that "there is something not quite real about her. She is not 'normal' in the way that a bathik saleswoman is, or a peasant rice farmer, or an urban housewife" (1984:132)—applies to the ronggeng as well.

In Notosusanto's short story "Tayuban," the mother tells her daughter of her husband's infidelity and drunkenness at a tayuban he attended with his boss. In her introduction to her English-language translation of the story, Sarah Weiss contrasts a "traditional" perspective with a more modern "moral" one: "The older perspective represents participation by men in tayuban activities of drinking, dancing, and sex as a duty; the more modern perspective regards these activities as immoral under any circumstances" (Notosusanto and Weiss 1995:119). Tayuban (and, by extension, other dance events) creates a context in which behavior that might otherwise be considered immoral becomes acceptable.

The image of ronggeng would seem on the surface to be antithetical to a religion such as Islam as it is practiced today. Anderson points out, however, that until the late nineteenth century, Javanese Islam linked existing conceptions of power to Islamic ideas without substantially affecting underlying traditional political or social paradigms (Anderson 1972:58–59). This reconciliation of Islam and dance events is exemplified by one devout Muslim male dancer's statement; he suggested that ronggeng are necessary because religion pairs men and women—without Eve, Adam would not be complete (Salam Mulyadi, personal communication, June 17, 1999). This statement harks back to Indic notions of balanced energy, but with a decidedly Islamic twist. It also reinforces the male focus of dance events; the female element is required to make the arena a "complete" site of male activity.

Ronggeng *Subjectivity*

What motivates a woman to choose an occupation of such checkered repute—a vocation that demands she conceal her own identity beneath a stereotype? There are a number of rewards for female entertainers that are denied to their more conventional sisters, including aesthetic satisfaction, remuneration, and the accrual of power.

There is no denying that many ronggeng find themselves inexplicably drawn to performing and cite as an important inspiration a desire selflessly to preserve traditional arts and develop an artistic sensibility. Female performers themselves often are drawn to what they regard as the purely aesthetic values of music and dance; they perform out of an artistic drive to do so. One of the ronggeng at the Bandung Zoo told me that her teacher's dedication to the art of ketuk tilu inspired her to perpetuate the art form as well (personal communication, March 7, 1999). Another dancer told me that she also derives satisfaction from the knowledge that she is successful at attracting lots of men (personal communication, April 18, 2009).

Aesthetic value, however, is a function of the complex interactions of power, politics, and status that emerge from artistic activities. The urge to sing and dance for art's sake can be a cover for more pragmatic incentives. The monetary rewards are another inducement. Female entertainers can easily earn more money from performing than the other occupations open to them would provide. They are also afforded license to be brutally frank about their recompense from their clients, without the ambiguity that surrounds the financial support men provide women under more conventional arrangements. Frankness about money is not the only way ronggeng get to flout social norms. They are expected to dress in an opulent, often outrageous way and to display behaviors that are demanding, petulant, flagrant, and others that typically are discouraged in females. Some women regard female entertainers as heroes and role models because of the strength and independence they show in the face of social disapproval.[17]

Access to power is another incentive. As ethnographic accounts of women's roles in Southeast Asia often relate, women in Java have considerable influence—"rule the roost," as Suzanne Brenner puts it—in the private sphere (Brenner 1995). Although men and women alike acknowledge that women are powerful, women are not accorded much status because of the perception that they lack self-control (Keeler 1990; Perlman 1998:56). As a result, according to Nancy Cooper, "women's power is usually expressed and used in ways that protect men's accumulations and uses of power" (Cooper 2000:609).

Although their role in dance events arguably guards "the spiritual and social potency of men" (Cooper 2000:609), while they are onstage ronggeng have the opportunity to accrue and display their own power

CHAPTER THREE

over the men with whom they dance. They can bask in the adulation of their male fans, who run the risk of being overcome by their own desire and becoming submissive to the ronggeng. Ronggeng may downplay their subjectivity to mediate the power struggles of their male partners, but they reap considerable rewards for their feigned subservience. Ultimately, women become ronggeng precisely because it affords them the kind of power they pretend not to have while performing.

Like ronggeng, the drummers I discussed in chapter 2 also self-consciously perform a role and are compensated for their efforts. In this sense, then, ronggeng and drummers may be considered "professionals," in contrast to the men who come to the events and pay to dance, who may be characterized as "amateurs." The terms professional and amateur have no standard meanings, although they usually describe sections of a continuum that describes the social status, economic reward, and motives of producers. Often, the adjective professional implies that the performer has a high standard of competence and receives remuneration in return for services rendered, while the term amateur suggests a noneconomic motive (such as dedication to "art") on the part of the performer and may hint at a lower standard of competence as well. Amin Sweeney, describing Malay storytellers, defines a professional performer as one

who, in the traditional context, is formally invited to perform at a specified place and time, and expects to be rewarded for his trouble. This definition of professional status thus includes not merely performers who derive a major part of their incomes from their art, but extends also to those who may perform perhaps only once in five years. (MALM AND SWEENEY 1974:54)

In Java, very few musicians survive entirely on their earnings from performing, but most expect to be paid for their efforts under certain circumstances. The determination of professionalism depends on "dual criteria of skill and income . . . to establish endpoints on [a] continuum" of professionalism (Benamou 1998:50–51).

In Sundanese dance events, the drummer and the ronggeng are likely to be considered "professional" by all participants. They meet the "dual criteria of skill and income" that Benamou mentions: both drummers and ronggeng are thought to bring specialized knowledge to the enactment of their parts in the events, and it is to these individuals that other participants make payments during the course of an event. Much of their status as professionals derives from a functional requirement that these two performers distinguish themselves from the main participants, that is, the men from the audience who dance. Identifying the drummer and

102

ronggeng as professionals draws a distinct boundary between them and the rest of the participants and emphasizes the audience's alignment with the amateur male dancers. Their professionalism ensconces the drummer and ronggeng in the role model and object positions, respectively, leaving the crucial subject position for the dancers and the audience members who watch them. Their professionalism endows drummers and ronggeng with a kind of subjectivity that relieves them from any compunction to behave normally. Ronggeng, like drummers, are empowered by their professional status to be masters of artifice—pretending to be things they are not—and thus they create an environment in which the performative twists of gender ideology can happen. They are at least partly aware of the artifice that their roles require, but an aspect of their professionalism is their complicity; they never acknowledge that their productions are fantasy.

The professional participants use their skill to construct a context in which amateur dancers can do the real work of creating, maintaining, and even contesting gender ideologies. Theoretical discussions in a variety of disciplines have put forward models to explain how people construct and maintain gender identities. These theoretical models are not always obviously complementary. Underlying many of them, however, are triangular patterns—triangles that somehow create and maintain this division of humanity into the masculine and the feminine. The professional participants provide the object of desire and the regulating power of authority. Amateur men complete an erotic triangle in which gender ideologies can be brought to life.

Amateur dancers and audiences regard the constructed environment produced by the professionals as completely natural. Using Pierre Bourdieu's words, professional status for drummers and ronggeng is a "misrecognition" of the artificial roles they must play in order literally to set the stage for the performance of gender ideology. They create a space in which male dancers and audiences can adopt a more conventional subjectivity. The space they create enables an aesthetic erasure of the staged quality of the event and allows the audience to regard it, and the gender ideology it produces, as reality. These professionals submerge their own subjectivity in service of the event's outcome—the performance of gender ideology.

FOUR

Dance Events and Freedom

Ronggeng embody the feminine contradiction between goddess and whore by performing flexible-rhythm singing while dancing to a metered accompaniment, and ideologies of power are modeled in the ambiguity of the drumming's leading and following the dancers. The third essential piece of a dance event is the potential for dancing by male participants who perceive themselves to be free of constraints. The male participants themselves dance the contradiction that regulates their daily lives: maintaining a sense of self, individual responsibility, and individual power in a social world that demands conformity. They must negotiate how to be bangga and malu at the same time.

Dance-Event Protocols

The protocols of dance events vary considerably from time to time and from place to place. After conducting an extensive survey of ronggeng-related performance genres throughout Indonesia, David Goldsworthy identifies seven basic variants to which most of them conform. Many, but not all, have a two-part form, in which the first section features entertainment, and the second section is social dancing with male audience members. Some genres include female entertainers who both sing and dance, while in others they only dance. Modern variants depart from their antecedents by using modern music, or by allowing for mixed couples, or by eliminating dancing altogether (Goldsworthy 1979:382–86).

Historical Protocols

The European historical record provides some clues about a comparable variety of dance-event protocols. Early travelogues provide descriptions of men's dancing events in Java for a variety of occasions. These works reveal considerable variety in the details of who was involved, who danced when, the relative status of the participants, and dance styles.

WHO DANCED WHEN   Charles Peter Thunberg, a Swedish physician who participated in an expedition to Java in 1773–75, reduces the protocol of the dance events he saw in or near Batavia (present-day Jakarta) to a serial progression of dancers who gave money for the privilege of dancing:

> There is always some well-dressed and decorated female, who begins the dance with one of the company, and afterwards continues, one at a time, with such of the others as find a pleasure in dancing; and these her partners always put a piece of money into her hand before the dance is over. . . . the money given is divided between her and the musicians.   (THUNBERG 1795: 307–8)

One hundred and fifty years later, J. Sarluy, who wrote an account of his amorous adventures or fantasies during his stay in Java between 1895 and 1920, described the same basic protocol of dance events in his journal:

> In turn the male spectators are invited, by the flinging of the slendang [scarf], to dance with one of [the ronggeng]. The remaining women dance and accompany with their song. When the male dancer has danced his part it is customary to throw a coin in the ring that the dancers have formed   (SARLUY 1920:51)[1]

Joseph Arnold, who found himself stranded in Java for a few months in 1815 and kept company with Stamford Raffles, describes dancing at the wedding (which he attended with Raffles) of the regent of Buitenzorg's daughter to the regent of Cianjur's son:[2]

> It is the custom here for the respectable women never to dance, but the principal men came forward and dance[d] a sort of minuet with one of the girls. This dance is very slow, and accompanied with great gesticulation of the hands. The Regent's son,

CHAPTER FOUR

magnificently dressed, first exhibited in this way. Then the Regent himself, and several
other men of rank. Between the dances the Governor's band played tunes.
(BASTIN 1973:51).

Arnold's statement suggests that it was the bridegroom who danced first,
then the man with the highest rank, followed by others in decreasing
order of rank, contradicting Raffles's generalization that the men danced,
"one after the other, commencing with the youngest" (Raffles 1965:342).
An alternate interpretation might be that the most honored guest danced
first. In modern protocols it is typically the highest-ranking or oldest man
who leads off the dancing.

George Windsor Earl's main interest was trade and commerce when
he visited Java in 1832–34. He describes a performance held for the entertainment of the Malay crew on his ship when docked in Cali Pujang.[3]
This was no aristocratic event. As Earl describes it, first there were ten
minutes of prelude music, then fifteen minutes of performance by the
first singer-dancer, followed by solos from the other two singer-dancers.
He continues: "After this prelude, however, the scene became more animated, for the musicians quickened the tune, and many of the seamen,
particularly those who had handsome dresses, joined in the dance" (Earl
1837:101). It is difficult to tell from Earl's description whether the men
are dancing all at once or serially, but is certainly comes across as quite
a spectacle.

OCCASIONS FOR DANCE EVENTS   Many writers mention that the performance they saw was held specifically in honor of a wedding or a circumcision. But even the arrival of a foreign dignitary apparently was
enough to warrant a dance party. Thomas Otto Travers visited various
Priangan regents' palaces between 1813 and 1820. He reports seeing
dancing girls in Sumedang, Bandung, and Cianjur, and specifically mentions that the men danced in Bandung: "In the evening we were amused
with Ronggengs [dancing girls], and as a particular compliment and mark
of respect to the Governor, the Regent's sons and all the members of the
family danced" (Travers 1960:74–75).

J. Sarluy reports that dance parties with ronggeng were popular among
both upper and lower classes for a variety of occasions.

They [ronggeng] are mobile and go from desa [village] to desa. Also they are asked to
dance at native parties, sometimes at parties of high-ranking native civil servants. Or
also they make their appearance at agricultural concerns, for example when the sugar

DANCE EVENTS AND FREEDOM

is ground, the coffee- or tea-picking is done and when a selametan [ritual feast] is given for the coolies for the good result of their industriousness. (SARLUY 1920:51)[4]

J. Th. Bik kept a journal on his trip through the Buitenzorg and Pre-anger (i.e., Priangan) areas in 1819. Bik notes three occasions that involved ronggeng and men dancing. His journal entry for September 15, 1819, describes a large celebration hosted by a local official in Tjibadas (presum-ably modern Cibodas) in honor of his three sons' circumcisions. In the evening, after an afternoon parade, there was a party at which all of the aristocratic guests danced (one at a time, it seems) with ronggeng. Even the three boys were brought to the ronggeng:

In the evening there was a frightful din from the gamelan and angklung. All the chiefs from the district and those from Garut were there and one and all they danced in a very stately manner with the ronggeng. The three children for whom the party mainly was sat beautifully dressed up on the side between the Kanduruan [a low-ranking aristocrat] of Selles and the Raden Patih [a high-ranking aristocrat] of Trogon from where their tondong [palanquin] was brought to the ronggeng. (BIK 1819:102)[5]

In his account of another dance party, this time in honor of the circum-cision of the son of the Raden Patih of Garut, Bik includes mention of a recurring theme at such parties, that is, the consumption of alcohol:

In the evening most of the chiefs danced with the ronggeng, which was very stately, [and] the chiefs who were sitting in the circle clapped their hands to the beat. The Raden Patih himself gave them the model/example, he was also one of the best danc-ers, and the others such silent, modest natives, so excited by him and so happy, that it was a pleasure to watch; the rank of each to the other was clear and although many of them, through the drinking of arak [a distilled alcoholic beverage], were no longer in their normal state, their respect for their superiors was not forgotten. (BIK 1819:106–7)[6]

This account also gives a sense of the vicarious thrill that watching other men dancing provides.

PARTICIPANTS   It would appear from most of the descriptions so far that the audiences are primarily men. A number of accounts include mention of female audience members as well. Raffles mentions that women (other than the ronggeng) do not participate in the dancing, but he also suggests that they do watch and enjoy as the men take part one at a time:

CHAPTER FOUR

Nobles of the highest class vie with each other. . . . So devoted are they to this exercise, that although their wives and daughters never dance, the happiness of a great occasion is considered incomplete, where an opportunity is not afforded to the chiefs themselves of introducing their favourite amusement. (RAFFLES 1965:342)

Although many pre-twentieth-century European descriptions of ronggeng make an issue of the female singer-dancers' reputation as prostitutes, they rarely address morals and illicit sexuality when discussing the male participants. This avoidance probably reflects both the European and the Javanese double standard about such matters. Earl's account of a shipboard celebration is a rare exception in that it relates a small drama of jealousy enacted by a wife:

Some of the young men from the shore also joined in the dance, and even the old pilot, who had come on board with his numerous family of children and grandchildren, commenced a pas-de-deux with one of the dancing-girls, and would doubtless have distinguished himself, had not his wife, annoyed by the bewitching glances which he sometimes cast at his partner, given him a smart tug behind, which brought him to the deck, and caused him to retire to his seat completely crest-fallen. (EARL 1837:101)

This account hints at an air of contentiousness that probably surrounded dance events as the participants danced a line between respectability and reprehensibility.

STATUS A number of sources suggest that men's dancing is associated with status in several ways. For one, the order in which men take turns dancing often relates to their status with respect to the other men involved. For another, an impressive display of dancing skill provides a means of establishing or increasing a man's status, and often the prize of increased status overshadows issues of jealousy or immorality. As we have seen, several authors comment on how the order in which dancers dance parallels their relative status. Raffles affirms that dancing at these occasions is a social skill: "The nobles of the highest rank are accustomed, on particular occasions of festivity, to join in the dance with a róng'geng. To dance gracefully, is an accomplishment expected in every Javan of rank" (Raffles 1965:342). J. C. Lamster, in a book about the East Indies published as a publicity gimmick by Droste's Cocoa and Chocolate Company, further develops the theme of status gained or lost through dancing skill:

As a rule, the Indonesian is a fairly good dancer, but sometimes it happens that one less proficient ventures upon the field of action. In such a case his clumsiness and awkward

DANCE EVENTS AND FREEDOM

movements cause open comment and candid criticism from the spectators, while if his achievement is too far below the average, there is general joy and hilarity. (LAMSTER 1929:64)

Earl's intriguing story of a sailor nicknamed "Gummok" (likely an Anglicized version of *gemuk*, which means "fat" in Malay), a chubby sailor from the mountains of "the interior of Java" (i.e., the Priangan), demonstrates how skillful dancing redeems a man who has been considered a bumpkin and made the butt of jokes:

Somebody called out from the crowd that Gummok, the jungle-man, wanted to dance, and he was pushed forward to the quarter-deck; but he cut so sorry a figure . . . that he was sent away to be dressed in a more becoming manner. In a short time he was again introduced, but his shipmates had made so complete a fright of him, that he afforded no little amusement. These wags had dressed him in all the colours of the rainbow, the costume being completed by a large black southwester, (a chapeau bearing a close resemblance to the coal-heaver's hat) placed upon his enormous bullet head. Gummok, however, commenced the dance with great confidence, and we were surprised to find that he was by far the most graceful performer in the ship, male or female, a discovery which contributed not a little to raise him in the estimates of his shipmates, for in Java, dancing forms an accomplishment in which lords and princes delight to excel. (EARL 1837:102)

In Louis Couperus's novel *The Hidden Force* (1900), the protagonist, van Oudijck, the Resident of Labuwangi, boasts that he is perceived as a "regular sport of a resident": instead of buying off his turn to dance, he actually dances:

He would actually take the scarf from the tandak-girl and tandak with her for a moment, very cleverly performing the lissom [*sic*] ritual movements of the hands and feet and hips, instead of buying himself off with a rijksdaalder [a Dutch coin] and leave her to dance with the wedono [local Javanese official]. (COUPERUS 1921:135)

In doing so, van Oudijck earns the respect of his Javanese subjects by coopting their own status-building behaviors.

DANCING STYLES Specific descriptions of dance movements and style are rare in European travelogues. Barrow's eighteenth-century description, for example, is tantalizing but vague: "The contortions of the body that are practised by the men may with more propriety be called posture-making than dancing" (Barrow, Truter, and Hill 1806:224). This description

109

CHAPTER FOUR

could easily apply to contemporary men's dancing. Modern dancers often strike a pose (or a "posture") at the end of a dance phrase, hold it for a moment, and then assume a nondance pose (i.e., they "just stand there") for a moment before reassuming a dance position. Raffles's conflation of "dance" and "posture"—"In the Súnda districts there are some individuals distinguished as regular posture or dancing-masters" (Raffles 1965:343)—echoes Barrow's evaluation of Sundanese dance style.

Earl's description of the men's dancing he saw lends more of a sense of motion to the activities:

> These amateur performers, with their hands resting on their hips, their elbows squared, and their heads bent downwards as they gazed upon their feet—a practice to which English rustics are much addicted when similarly engaged—chasséed to the right and left with a sort of hornpipe step, every performer deeming it necessary to assume the most funereal gravity of countenance. (EARL 1837:101)

He implies that most of the movement is in the stepping of the feet—upper bodies stiff and eyes focused on the feet—with less attention to the arms.

LEARNING TO DANCE Aside from Raffles's mention of dance masters for aristocratic courts, there are few mentions of learning to dance. Hubert Banner, who wrote many travel articles for British publications about his travels in "romantic Java," indicates that learning and practicing were ongoing activities for the common man in Java in the 1920s:

> it is of the tandak that I would write—the simple ordinary native dance of which every coolie, of however low degree, is master: the dance you will catch your servants practising when they should be washing dishes; the dance you may see being taught in the kampongs [neighborhood compounds] to mere babies scarcely yet able to keep their balance in an upright posture. (BANNER 1927:95)

The learning process described by Banner is informal and personal and gives the impression that particular ways of moving, and the social conventions surrounding dance events, were drummed into children at an early age.

COMMON FEATURES OF HISTORICAL DANCE PROTOCOLS These selected glimpses into the past provide only a fragmented and incomplete picture of men dancing in Java. There are a few important points to be drawn from them, however. First of all, the accounts suggest that both upper-

and lower-class men take part in dance parties, although probably not the same parties. The same singer-dancers, however, may have performed for aristocrats and commoners alike. Second, the ronggeng are the only women dancing. Wives and daughters might attend the parties, but they do not dance. Some reports (e.g., Raffles 1965) imply that the female audiences enjoy the events, but other sources (e.g., Earl 1837) state that they may become jealous of their husbands. There is an implication that once the female guests leave, the gatherings become increasingly wild (e.g., Brandts-Buys n.d.; Dyck 1922:65).

Details of various dance party protocols emerge from the descriptions. Some writers specify that the men pay the ronggeng, often in a very public manner. Quite a few of the descriptions mention drinking alcoholic beverages. Many of the late nineteenth- and twentieth-century descriptions mention the passing of a dance scarf as the means by which the next male dancer is nominated. In the aristocratic parties, the men typically dance one at a time. Raffles indicates that the lowest-ranking man danced first, but other descriptions reverse this order. The descriptions suggesting that men dance simultaneously rather than serially seem to describe events that are less aristocratic than the others. Some descriptions have the host choosing the male dancers (at least the first one); others give that role to the ronggeng.

Many of these European descriptions state or imply that dancing is a status-enhancing activity for men as well as a favorite activity, even though (or perhaps because) dance events involve elements that generally are frowned upon, such as drinking and womanizing. Raffles says that nobles are expected to be accomplished dancers. In Earl's story, the much-maligned Gummok gains status through his display of dancing skill. Banner indicates that hesitation or refusal to dance when nominated invites derision. Lamster goes so far as to suggest that clumsiness or awkwardness in dancing results in a loss in status.

Most of these historical protocols persist in modern versions of men's dance events. The following sections examine in more detail the conventions that enabled participants in twentieth-century Sundanese dance events to explore gender ideologies.

Ketuk tilu and *tayuban* Protocols

The received histories of Sundanese dance typically lump various participatory dance forms into two main categories: a version for the common people, usually characterized as ketuk tilu, and an aristocratic version,

CHAPTER FOUR

usually called *ibing tayub* or tayuban. Most Sundanese critics take pains to differentiate these two variants, although most recognize a fundamental kinship between them (e.g., Sugiharwati 1980:9). Modern readers label the events described in pre-twentieth-century sources anachronistically as ketuk tilu or tayuban, although neither term appears in print until the twentieth century.

Ketuk tilu

Gugum Gumbira Tirasonjaya suggests that the term ketuk tilu was originally applied only in parts of the Priangan area of West Java, where it referred to a common people's dance and music tradition involving female singer-dancers, a particular ensemble characterized by a three-gong chime, certain songs, and improvised men's dancing. The word ketuk usually refers to a small knobbed gong, and tilu means three in Sundanese, so the name ketuk tilu is generally thought to refer to one of the instruments in the musical ensemble—the gong chime with three ketuk (see fig. 4.1). Gugum points out that variants of this basic configuration are present in other parts of West Java as well and goes on to describe some of them—*banggreng* from Sumedang, ronggeng gunung from Ciamis, and bajidoran from Subang. He concludes that all types of men's social dances are basically similar, and that ketuk tilu is an appropriate term to apply to all of them (Tirasondjaja 1979–80:20).

Lia Amelia, too, argues that ketuk tilu is a generic category of people's dance. She analyzes three genres—banggreng, *doger*, and ronggeng gunung—and describes three points of similarity: the role of ronggeng as singer-dancers who dance with male participants, the presence of a simple musical accompaniment, and audience participation in free dancing based on the rhythm of drumming (Amelia 1996). Sugiharwati makes explicit Amelia's implication that ketuk tilu refers not to the name of a musical instrument, but rather to an entire performance context (Sugiharwati 1980:90).

HISTORY Scholars typically assign three main periods of development to the history of ketuk tilu (e.g., Azis and Barmaya 1983–84:7–8; Somawijaya 1990:15–19): (1) prehistory, (2) a period of popularity beginning in the nineteenth century, and (3) a revival in the 1970s (i.e., jaipongan). This approach follows Soedarsono's influential three-stage model (primitive, feudal, and modern) of dance history (see Soedarsono 1974). Many published accounts of ketuk tilu history are based on interviews with Yoyo

4.1 *Goong* and three *ketuk* from a *ketuk tilu* ensemble (photo: Henry Spiller, 1999).

Yohana and the older members of the LS Kandaga Kancana ketuk tilu troupe based in Ujungberung (east of Bandung). Their lore suggests that ketuk tilu was already well known in 1883, because some people dancing at a ketuk tilu event were killed by a coconut tree that fell during the infamous eruption of the volcano Krakatau (Somawijaya 1990:15; Suhaeti 1986:9). Yohana can name two leaders (*centeng*, ronggeng "keepers")— Abah Ariyani and Abah Sarnapi—of Ujungberung ketuk tilu troupes in the mid-nineteenth century as well (Sugiharwati 1980:12; Yohana 1979:35).

Certainly many of the nineteenth-century descriptions presented earlier could be construed to be ketuk tilu performances, although none of them use that term specifically. There is a published reference to *ketoek tiloe* as a dance genre involving ronggeng in 1926 (Saleh 1926). It is within some people's living memories that ketuk tilu–like events were popular throughout the first part of the twentieth century but lost favor after Indonesian independence (Sugiharwati 1980:2). Darul Islam, a political and military movement founded in the late 1940s in West Java that advocated the establishment of an Islamic state in Indonesia, was particularly influential in areas south of Bandung such as Garut, Tasikmalaya, and Ciamis. In the late 1940s and early 1950s, some local governments in the areas south of Bandung, which were under the influence

CHAPTER FOUR

of Darul Islam–imposed Islamic law at the time (Bush 2008:185), interdicted ketuk tilu in public places in response to the events' association with sexual impropriety (Amelia 1996:60; Somawijaya 1990:15). Abun Somawijaya hypothesizes that at least some of the multitude of names were a result of these prohibitions—in some communities, he suggests, fans simply avoided the bans by calling their activities something else (1990:16–17).[7]

As for dance movements, Somawijaya quotes Yoyo Yohana (from Ujungberung), who characterizes men's movement in ketuk tilu as *tarian khusus perorangan* (personal, individualized movements), while the ronggeng's movements follow her male partner's and *melayani* (serve) the man's movements (Somawijaya 1990:56). When dancing, it is the men's foot movements that are supposed to coordinate with the kendang patterns, while the movements of their hands and the rest of their bodies remain unspecified (Sugiharwati 1980:38). Dancing is spontaneous and not in a fixed order (berpola; Fajaria 1996:17). Men are supposed to dance freely, spontaneously, basing their motions on the musical rhythm as well as on the wishes of their own hearts (Sumiati 1996a:31).

Sundanese commentators stress that although the events follow a protocol, they are subject to the whims and desires of the men who attend them. Somawijaya and Sugiharwati both relate a story of naughtiness on the part of the dancers, subverting the protocols: "After reaching a climax with an agile movement the dancer pretends to kick the pole of the oncor (oil lamp) and knocks it over so that the arena becomes dark, whereupon all the male dancers use the opportunity" (Sugiharwati 1980:37).[8] Somawijaya's version is only slightly more specific about this "opportunity"—it is "to do something to his partner" (Somawijaya 1990:57).[9] Presumably "opportunity" is understood to imply physical contact with the ronggeng, the nature of which is limited only by the reader's (and the male dancer's) imagination. These descriptions are reminiscent of Sarluy's early twentieth-century characterization of "seizing opportunities" for contact with the ronggeng at dance events.

KETUK TILU EVENTS A number of Sundanese authors have described the protocols of ketuk tilu events.[10] For the most part, their descriptions are generalized, idealized reconstructions of how events in the past were conducted rather than detailed descriptions of specific traditions. The events were divided into two segments: (1) an introductory, performed segment with a predetermined order of songs, dances, and prayers, and (2) a participatory segment driven by the desires of the male participants. This division is consistent with Goldsworthy's (1979) and Foley's (1989) generalized models of Southeast Asian ronggeng events. An event begins at approximately 10 P.M. and is held outdoors, illuminated by a standing oil lamp called an oncor. The opening ceremony begins with an instrumental overture (tatalu). Next the ronggeng perform dances called jajangkungan (walking on stilts) and wawayangan (acting like a wayang puppet). The ronggeng sit while the troupe leader prays, to the accompaniment of an invocation song ("Kidung"), for a successful evening. The boundary between the two segments of the performance is marked by a special liminal song, "Erang," which belongs in some ways to both sections. It is the last of the predetermined pieces, but also the first piece that invites participation. In contrast to the subsequent free-dance songs, however, men can dance to "Erang" without paying for the privilege. During the second segment, audience members request and pay for songs, which one of the ronggeng sings while the others dance with the men.

Quite a few of the songs associated with ketuk tilu are relatively simple, characterized by short phrases and a four-square formal structure, enabling great freedom for improvisation by the dancer. The singer, too, has considerable freedom in selecting stock verses for these tunes. The man who pays to start the dance gets to choose the piece, and he usually selects a genre and a song that enhances the kind of dancing he wants to do—sophisticated, brutish, humorous, acrobatic, artistic, and so forth.

Ketuk tilu's musical conventions enable this dancing freedom. As described in chapter 2, after the special nyered section, the lagu (main song) begins; each song has a particular, recognizable tune set in one of three pentatonic Sundanese modes (salendro, sorog, or pelog), undergirded by a rhythmic framework that is articulated by strokes on the goong. The main song can be repeated any number of times. Also as discussed in chapter 2, the drumming for the main song has two sections. In the first section, the drumming for each goong phrase alternates static and dynamic drum rhythms, climaxing in a cadential pattern. The second section is mincid.

For the first section, dancers are in principle free to do whatever they like, as long as it fits the drumming. Fitting the drumming means moving during the flurry of drumstrokes that characterize the dynamic portion and striking a pose when the flurry ends. During this section, dancers typically concentrate on moving their upper bodies and arms, with occasional steps. Male dancers often strike poses while balancing on one foot. If there are steps, they are typically large and may include jumps. The male dancers usually move away from their ronggeng partners during the goong phrases, only to approach the ronggeng again as the goong

CHAPTER FOUR

phrase comes to an end. Most typically, the cadence involves stepping up to the ronggeng and pretending to kiss or touch her on the accented beat just before the goong stroke; the stroke itself is met with stillness and is a moment of great aesthetic satisfaction for the performers and viewers alike.

At some point, after a few repetitions of the lagu's cycle, there is a signal to change to the mincid section. The term suggests walking, and dancers focus on their foot movements in this section—stylized stepping, often with complicated patterns involving foot taps without weight shifts. Dancers often maintain a single hand and arm position over the course of several steps. In these sections, if the drums play no cadential figure leading up to a goong stroke, the dancers continue their stepping right through the stroke, as if it were not there. There are different drum patterns for different types of movements; dancers and drummers are involved in a constant give-and-take with regard to what types of movements and patterns should be played. During mincid, for example, a dancer might begin with small steps, which the drummer accompanies with relatively quiet, high-pitched sounds. If the dancers shift to large, jumping steps, the drummer might respond with increased volume and pepper his patterns with low-pitched strokes. Alternatively, the drummer could initiate the pattern variation, to which a dancer would almost certainly respond with larger movements. If there are multiple dancers, one might initiate the change, to which the drummer would respond, compelling the other dancers to follow suit as well. Aside from the ronggeng-only set dances, a ronggeng's dance movements are keyed to those of their male dance partners (but without the dramatic dynamic contrasts).

Following each dance of the men with the ronggeng, there is a second, men-only dance called *oray-orayan* ("moving like a snake"), in which the paying male dancer leads the other men around the performance space in a line. The men-only oray-orayan dance is meant to restore fellowship among the men and prevent arguments or fights among the men over ronggeng. In the past, it is said, such conflicts were sometimes fatal (Herdiani 1996:45).

The protocols of ketuk tilu enable men to experience a sense of freedom in the songs and movements they choose. The first section of the event is formal and presentational, characterized by specific rituals, songs, and group dances performed by the ronggeng. The transition to the second section is effected by the liminal song, "Erang," which has elements of the formality of the first section, but men from the audience are allowed to join in the dancing. The sequence of events in the second section is determined not by custom or protocol, however, but by the collective will of the men involved. They determine the overall progress of the event as well as the small details—who dances, what pieces are performed, and what specific movements and gestures are involved. Men pay for the privilege of leading the dance, and leading a dance means choosing the song (and thus determining the overall character of the dance) and providing a model for the drummer. Ketuk tilu drum patterns, the details of which are well-known to all the participants, provide general guidelines for the kinds of dance movements to be performed, but each man who participates can adjust his movements to suit his own character, mood, and goals. The "loose coupling" of drum patterns to dance movements enables men who are dancing together to perform highly individualized gestures.

Tayuban

Although differences of scale and behavior are apparent between upper- and lower-class dance events in the nineteenth-century descriptions, it is not until the late nineteenth century that a name—*nayuban* or tayuban[11]—and a distinct protocol for elite dance events clearly emerge. From at least the fifteenth century until the nineteenth century, Sundanese society was more deeply stratified by class differences than it is today. The aristocratic class (*kaum menak*) led a lifestyle significantly different from that of Sundanese commoners. The historian Nina Herlina Lubis argues that performing arts were an important symbol of status and differentiation for the Sundanese aristocracy; cultivating and patronizing performing arts contributed to the impression of grandeur, wealth, and power that they hoped to convey (Lubis 1998:243).

In the nineteenth century, under increased Dutch colonial control, the upper class took great pains to differentiate their artistic productions from those of commoners. Aristocrats held their events in large covered porch areas rather than outdoors and danced to the accompaniment of a full gamelan salendro ensemble rather than the minimal three-man ketuk tilu ensemble. It appears, however, that the same ronggeng performed at events for both aristocrats and commoners.

Besides the differences in venue and accompaniment, the protocols of tayuban events also differed from their lower-class counterparts. At a tayuban event, each lead dancer was nominated through a process of presenting him with a tray holding a ceremonial dagger (*keris*) and a

CHAPTER FOUR

dance scarf. The chosen dancer was expected to put the keris into his belt, where it functioned as an attachment point for the dance scarf. The nominator would be either the host of the event or a ronggeng. The lead dancer was expected to choose an accompanying piece appropriate for his dancing.

Aristocrats took their dancing, and the status and power it signified, very seriously. The most powerful hereditary officials often had a *kostim* (dance character and song) that they preferred to dance in tayuban. According to Lubis, the consequence of using somebody else's kostim without permission was said to be *kesurupan*—possession by spirits (1998:245).

Other men were allowed to dance along (*mairan*), provided they sought, and were granted, permission from the lead dancer to do so. Nevertheless, the events focused on solo dancing and the display of individual dancing skill—at least until the consumption of alcohol loosened the men's inhibitions. The kinds of freedom afforded by the event's protocols—freedom to manage the course of the event, the particular character of the songs, and the individual movements—were for the most part identical to those of commoners' events.

This kind of environment inevitably led dancers to strive toward increasingly complex choreography. Changing values and changing contexts led to the development of dance pieces based on men's improvisational dance that were essentially presentational. As will be described in chapter 5, the development of tari kursus—a genre of men's dance that was presentational in focus and more fixed in content than tayuban dancing—was a logical consequence of increasing emphasis on individual dance skill and complexity.

A change in the root word used to describe such dance events also reflects a changing emphasis from process to content. Nasalizing the consonant at the beginning of a word that begins with a "t" (such as "tayub") to an "n" sound is how Sundanese speakers ordinarily transform a word into a verb. In the case of "tayub," however, it appears that Sundanese speakers fabricated a new root word—tayub—out of an existing word—*nayub*. Nayub itself is probably derived from yet another root—*sayub*—that relates to fermented or alcoholic drinks. [12] These linguistic sleights of hand contribute to the shift from process-oriented participatory dance performed at events lubricated with alcohol to a more presentational, product-oriented approach. [13] Ironically, increasing complexity compromised one of the most fundamental characteristics of men's improvisational dance—the feeling of freedom.

Freedom in Dancing

The perception that men's dancing is bebas (free) is one of the principal characteristics of the erotic triangle of Sundanese dance. The discussion in chapter 2 of the ambiguity of drumming's leading and following provides part of an explanation for how men can dance freely while conforming to some very specific constraints. The preceding summaries of ketuk tilu and tayuban protocols reveal a give-and-take for the men and identify places where they could assert control over the course of events. The assessment in chapter 3 of the ronggeng image demonstrates how the conventional reaction to a ronggeng gives permission to men to resist their sense of malu. In doing so, they have a chance to augment their masculine power by performing, onstage, as the sort of man they would like to be, or would like at least to be perceived to be, by others.

Performing Gender and Ideology

Participants in dance events do not think about performing gender identities when they participate in dance activities. They are acutely aware of desires that color the activities they choose and the movements they make. But for the most part they are simply dancing—moving their bodies in ways that seem free, in a context that seems self-evident, and engaging with aesthetic values that seem natural.

Judith Butler's notion of gender performativity provides a way to consider how dance events do the work of creating gender ideology without the participants' explicit collusion. In her book *Gender Trouble* (1990), Butler addresses issues of desire and the enculturation of gender identities. Like Rubin, Freud, and Lacan, she argues that exogamy, kinship systems, and the "natural" laws that support them—incest taboos, compulsory heterosexuality, and the division of humanity into two discrete gender categories—are social constructions. In her view, the psychological transformations emblematized by the Oedipus myth create and enforce "discrete and internally coherent gender identities within a heterosexual frame" (Butler 1990:x). She characterizes these gender identities as performative in that they actually constitute the things they purport to describe. This reversal of cause and effect is accomplished by repeating acts that "congeal over time to produce the appearance of substance."[14] Through constant repetition and reinforcement, people come to believe that their acts are motivated by a stable, natural inner core, when in fact it is the arbitrary acts themselves that create the illusion of such a core

CHAPTER FOUR

(Butler 1990:151). In other words, many things about human behavior that we take for granted—such as sexual desire, rigid gender dimorphism, and even the notion of culture itself—are more arbitrary and less natural than they seem. Although these arbitrary ideologies are rife with contradictions and inconsistencies, somehow people come to believe that the contradictions and inconsistencies are inevitable. These astonishing feats of group self-delusion—smoothing over inconsistencies and reconciling contradictions to make the contingent seem natural—are accomplished by reversing causes and effects.

Triangles, Myths, and Ideology

As discussed in chapter 3, Lévi-Strauss posits that myth is one mechanism for reversing cause and effect. For him, myth is a kind of language, so his point of departure in discussing myth is Ferdinand de Saussure's distinction between *langue* (the structure of language) and *parole* (the deployment of that structure in usage). He suggests that in myth the difference between these two terms is one of time referents: *langue* is ahistorical and synchronic, while *parole* is contingent and diachronic. Myth, he argues, employs a third time referent, which is simultaneously historical and ahistorical.

Myth implements this dual structure by stringing together many different episodes that express the same conflicts and contradictions. Taken individually, the episodes present irresolvable binary contradictions. When put in a sequence, however, a story emerges that appears to resolve the paradoxes. The *langue* of the myth does not change—it is the same relationship of irresolvable contradictions. The contradictions are mitigated by interposing a third term between them to help to resolve them. Each time the impact of a stark contradiction is lessened by insinuating a moderating third term, the sense grows that the contradiction is a fact of nature rather than a humanly imposed artifact.

According to Roland Barthes, too, the ideological function of myth is to transform history into nature (Barthes 1972:142). Barthes relies on the semiological concept of the sign—where meaning lies—as a third term that is produced by the relationship between the signified (the abstract concept that is expressed) and the signifier (the image that expresses it) (Barthes 1972:109–59). He theorizes myth as a higher-order semiological system in which what were signs in the lower-order system become mere signifiers (Barthes 1972:114).

Barthes explains that although in the lower-order system a sign is a self-sufficient entity that comes with a history, a past, and a record of how it came to be the way it is, in the higher-order system of myth a sign loses its sense of contingency and comes to be taken as natural, inviolable truth (Barthes 1972:117–18). It comes to be the image that expresses some higher-order mythic concept. Myth involves converting what was the mitigating third term in the lower-order system into a natural first term in the higher-order system. Myth creates a discontinuity between the lower-order sign, replete with its own history, and its new ahistorical appearance as a signifier for some arbitrary new concept. We perceive the lower-order sign as the cause, foundation, and justification for the new concept rather than as merely the image that stands for it. The history and fullness are drained out of the lower-order sign's meaning and absorbed into the myth's concept. As a result, the myth's concept, which is contingent and intentional, is made to seem eternal and natural by virtue of this appropriated content (Barthes 1972:129).

The nature of the synchronic—the eternal, the Imaginary—is based on absolute, irreconcilable opposites, while the nature of the diachronic—the Symbolic—is based on triangular forms that enable substitutions and mitigations and allow for change. Triangularity is implicated in the foundation of symbolic systems (e.g., the three-part model of the sign), in the formation of the subject (as modeled by Freud and Lacan using Oedipus as a metaphor), and in the external enforcement of societal norms (through mechanisms of myth and ideology). It seems that the form of the triangle can be thought of, in some sense at least, as modeling the slippage between synchronic and diachronic and the reversals of cause and effect that enable the Symbolic, and the heterosexual matrix, to exist.

Dance Performances as Myth

The purpose of myths and ideologies is to make arbitrary cultural constructs seem natural, obscuring their inherent contradictions. Desire comes to be understood as a natural drive rather than as a response to arbitrary prohibitions surrounding kinship, sexuality, and procreation. Masculine and feminine qualities are seen to emanate from natural core gender identities rather than as differentiating behaviors that are performed to support socially imposed prohibitions. Contradictions come to be understood as unavoidable consequences of nature rather than as artifacts of arbitrary ideological stands. As we have seen, the effecting mechanisms involve reversing causes and effects. Myths achieve their ideological goals of making arbitrary values appear natural through the mitigation of the contradictions these values engender by triangulation—interposing third terms between them.

CHAPTER FOUR

Both Lévi-Strauss and Barthes imply that the work of cause-and-effect reversal is accomplished in myth through the deliberate blurring and confusion of temporality. Lévi-Strauss specifically mentions myth's simultaneous presentation of what he describes as reversible and nonreversible time. Barthes cites a rapid alternation between historical and ahistorical views of a sign. Eve Kosofsky Sedgwick summarizes Karl Marx's comparable explanation of the mechanism of ideology in her development of erotic triangles: "The function of ideology is to conceal contradictions in the status quo, by, for instance, recasting them into a diachronic narrative of origins" (Sedgwick 1985:14). Lacan describes the very basis of symbolic process as involving some crossover between synchronic and diachronic registers (cf. Grosz 1990:62).

One of Sedgwick's insights is that ideological statements are always narrative, even when they are explicitly declarative. Such statements draw on history but mask the values that are a function of diachronic history as synchronic axioms. Her example is the phrase "a man's home is his castle," which relies on evoking images of mastery out of a long-lost European past, along with the historically contingent (and ill-fitting) values they suggest, as if they were historical facts, to lend a patina of mastery to a much different economic situation. She concludes: "For the reweaving of ideology to be truly invisible, the narrative is necessarily chiasmic in structure; that is, that the subject of the beginning of the narrative is different from the subject at the end, and that the two subjects cross each other in a rhetorical figure that conceals their discontinuity" (Sedgwick 1985:15). In other words, the consumers of ideology do not notice the crossing of subjects, or that the truth value of the ideological statement relies on a non sequitur.[15] Sedgwick's statement echoes Lévi-Strauss's diachronic/synchronic reading of myths, Barthes's notion of empty signs, and Butler's performative twists. Sedgwick specifically posits that the construction of sexuality relies on the "mutual redefinition and occlusion of synchronic and diachronic formulations."

The erotic triangle of Sundanese dance is a structure that represents the *langue* of Sundanese dance. In addition, each of its three sides functions independently as a kind of myth or empty sign. Each side models a set of contradictions that characterize binary contrasts of Sundanese gender ideologies. The musical dimension of the events, especially the drumming, makes manifest the contradiction that men should follow (be subject to higher authority) yet lead (be independent and self-determining). A ronggeng, who references the benevolent and fertile rice goddess as well as a view of women as sexually and economically greedy, epitomizes contradictions inherent in notions of Sundanese femininity. Male dancers enact the contradiction that men should simultaneously be modest and assertive through their actions, and through the very act of dancing itself. The notions of drumming as both leading and following, of ronggeng as both goddesses and whores, and of men as both malu and bangga are myths in this sense—contradictory, contingent, impossible conditions made to seem not only real, but even inevitable and natural. Like myth and ideology, dance events simultaneously enact diachronic and synchronic elements, and they involve comparable performative twists.

Performances of all kinds provide some kind of diachronic/synchronic simultaneity. Clifford Geertz, among others, suggests that nonnarrative performances—"any . . . collectively sustained symbolic structure" (Geertz 1973a:448)—can be interpreted as texts. He compares the enactment and reenactment of Balinese cockfights, for example, to reading and rereading *Macbeth*. For Geertz, a sustained symbolic structure such as a cockfight represents something synchronic, a "paradigmatic human event" (Geertz 1973a:450), as well as something diachronic, "a story [people] tell themselves about themselves" (Geertz 1973a:448).

The reversal of cause and effect is acted out in dance events through the friction between the various contradictions embodied by each of the three elements. Participants iterate and reiterate slippages between them until they seem natural and inevitable. The perception of naturalness is aided, too, by the feeling of freedom of action that defines the events. Understanding the notion of "freedom" that characterizes Sundanese men's dancing, the way in which this sense of freedom relates to the malu/bangga contradiction, and the way it is paradoxically enabled by regulatory conventions manifested in ronggeng and drumming, is key to the erotic triangle of Sundanese dance.

Freedom

As discussed in chapter 1, the term freedom generally suggests a state in which one feels unrestricted by rules or constraints imposed by others, but as the philosopher Stephen L. Gardner argues, the objects, experiences, and feelings that individuals "freely" desire are, in fact, suggested to them—even imposed upon them—by others. To create an aura of autonomy and power, individuals find ways to obscure the reality that their "free" actions are imitating the actions of others, and that the power

CHAPTER FOUR

they are pursuing is the same power that others covet as well (Gardner 1998:92).

Several people, when I informed them of my interest in men's dancing, warned me that I would probably laugh when I watched some men dance because their movements are not necessarily graceful or beautiful. And indeed, at times, I did laugh. One guest at a wedding, for example, moved much like the movie version of Frankenstein's monster, never bending his elbows or knees, and keeping his gaze blindly straight ahead. For improvised dance, the goal is to appear unconstrained by conventions or restrictions.

My attempts to elicit specific information about dance styles or gestures from Sundanese men usually were answered with statements such as "bebas" (free), "masing-masing" (to each his own) or "apa saja" (whatever). What exactly do Sundanese men mean when they say their dance is free? How does one learn to dance freely? John Chernoff suggests that "to understand and translate the meaning of words like 'freedom,' it is necessary . . . to look at what someone who talks of freedom does" (Chernoff 1979:21).

Nobody actually studies the kind of dancing that men perform at these events; to do so would defeat the ideal of spontaneity. When I asked one young dance fan if he studied dancing, he answered, "No, I'm Sundanese; for me, jaipongan is already traditional" (personal communication, June 20, 1999). His implication was that, as a Sundanese man, traditional dancing was part of his genetic heritage and it was in his nature to dance. Another dance fan pointed out that even his three-year-old son could already dance—it simply is not difficult to learn the drum patterns (personal communication, June 6, 1999).

Ketuk tilu expert Salam Mulyadi told me he learned to dance "all over the place." It was easier to learn when he was young, he said, because there were ketuk tilu performances to watch all around (personal communication, April 18, 1999). On another occasion, I asked whether he had ever studied dancing, and he replied that he studied elmu, by which he meant that he studied esoteric techniques for gaining spiritual strength and physical invincibility (cf. Barker 1999:36–37). Elmu can be acquired through diligent study and can indirectly make a dancer look good because it provides a base of genuine power. But dance movements themselves are not something to study. He said that most people learn to dance by watching other dancers and acquiring a passive understanding of the music and drumming (personal communication, June 17, 1999).

When I expressed interest in learning to dance, many other people told me the same thing: the best way to learn to dance is simply to watch.

One young man at the Bandung Zoo told me that he could already do jaipongan and penca silat, but he was still studying ketuk tilu "from the front" and was not quite ready to try it out yet (personal communication, March 21, 1999). Shortly after this conversation, one of the Zoo ronggeng goaded him into dancing to a ketuk tilu song with her; the assembled crowd appreciated his efforts, applauding after each of his goong cadence movements.

Even when pressed for details about how they dance, most Sundanese men answer vaguely. One man told me he dances "from my heart." To learn to dance, one must come to know the songs, their character, and where the goong strokes fall, he explained (personal communication, June 19, 1999). Another fan explained that he simply follows the "path of the drum patterns." The patterns are often in a fixed order, he said, but you can predict what is coming by the first few notes of a pattern, so you need not know the order perfectly. He also said he follows the "path of the song." There is considerable variety and freedom to do whatever sorts of movements he wants, as long as they fit the drumming and the song (personal communication, June 6, 1999). The Cirebonese dalang topeng and master tayub dancer Sujana Arja clarified the relationship of song and drums. The drumming is the "mouth," he said, while the song is the "thoughts." The song provides a general idea of what to do, but it is the drum that provides specific instructions (personal communication, July 11, 1999).

The typical answer to the question "Why do you like to dance?" was something along the lines of "You should just try it." Because this was the only clue I was given, I followed up on it on quite a few occasions. My experiences and impressions cannot, of course, be thought of as representative of a typical Sundanese man's feelings, but I believe they do, as my interlocutors predicted, provide some insight. Mostly I felt foolish because there were obviously a lot of people watching me, and I was anything but confident about my own dancing skills. At times, however, my experience transcended this self-consciousness. When my focus shifted from the external—how I looked from the outside—to the internal—how my body felt from the inside—my experience changed considerably. I quote from my field notes from April 10, 1999:

I was aware of each drum pattern as it came, and tried to do something that made sense. I tried to be aware of where the gongs were. . . . I was also aware of where he [my dance "partner"] was in my space, and whether our arms were parallel or mirror (I didn't really try to make it one way or another, but I was aware of it). . . . I was aware that people were watching me, but I found that I was actually enjoying myself despite

CHAPTER FOUR

the attention. I felt like my movements made sense in relation to the drumming, and I didn't get obsessed with whether they looked bad or not. It seemed very clear, too, when it was time to end. I can't really say which one of us initiated the *sembah* to end—it was almost as if we did it simultaneously.

The most successful male dancers at Sundanese dance events convince themselves and their observers that they are dancing spontaneously. They focus on their internal sensations of what feels right. They are constrained to move in lockstep with the drumming, however. The trick is to make the drumming seem like a response to the movements rather than vice versa. If he succeeds in doing so, a man commandeers the drumming's regulative power as if it were his own.

Sundanese men's discourse about their free dancing supports an interpretation of freedom as a mask for conformity. The perception of freedom mitigates the humiliation that an individual might feel upon realizing that he must imitate his peers—and his betters—to achieve status and power within a group. As Gardner expresses this contradiction, "One must at all costs pretend that one desires what one wants either because of its inherent worth or because one has invested it with one's own value, as an 'expression' of one's 'self'" (Gardner 1998:7).

Free Dancing in the 1990s

Clearly, a sense of freedom is a key characteristic of Sundanese tayuban and ketuk tilu. Neither tayuban nor ketuk tilu is encountered much in contemporary West Java, however, although tayuban events were common in aristocratic circles before Indonesian independence. In the earlier part of the twentieth century, upward mobility within the Dutch-Sundanese power structure was enhanced by cultivating dancing skills. After independence, the correlation of tayuban and upward mobility contributed to its redeployment by an emerging middle class as an entertainment at celebrations of life-cycle events. At the same time, however, its feudal overtones clashed with the dominant ideology of modern democracy. In the 1970s, an alternative—jaipongan—appeared on the scene, and tayuban became increasingly rare. At present, in most of West Java, tayuban occur only as folkloric presentations, such as those sponsored monthly until the late 1990s by the Geusan Ulun Museum in Sumedang, or the occasional tayuban sponsored by STSI Bandung (such as the one held in December 1998). The situation is different in northern West Java, around Cirebon, where tayuban are still sometimes part of family celebrations. The topeng performances for which the villages around Cirebon are justly famous often incorporate tayuban performances, and some versatile female topeng dance masters double as ronggeng.

Some Sundanese scholars now differentiate two kinds of contemporary ketuk tilu: Priangan style and *kaleran* (northern) style (e.g., Marliana 1996; Turyati 1996). The Priangan style is maintained only by a couple of essentially folkloric groups (the Ujungberung group and the Zoo group) in and around Bandung. A distinctly southern style—ronggeng gunung—apparently also has declined rapidly in popularity.[16] The kaleran style, centered in the lowland cities of Subang and Karawang, however, is a living, vibrant, and changing phenomenon.

Bajidoran

It is precisely this viability that sometimes precludes the categorization of modern versions of kaleran-style performances under the rubric of ketuk tilu—a rubric that has acquired some implications of archaism and is somewhat artificial to begin with. It is true that in many surface details some modern versions do not much resemble the austere, reconstructed versions of ketuk tilu as performed in and around Bandung. From a broader perspective, however, modern men's dancing in Karawang and Subang has much in common with traditional ketuk tilu and tayuban.

In the earlier part of the twentieth century, ketuk tilu troupes followed dalang around to compete for their audiences. Some people speculate that the assimilation of the ronggeng into wayang performance practice as the pasinden (seated, nondancing female singer) was a concession on the part of wayang golek performers in order to outdo their competition. More recently, as ketuk tilu events became difficult to find, fans started going to wayang golek performances and asking the pasinden to dance for them. The pasinden became the focus of the performance, often at the expense of the wayang's ostensible main focus—that is, the narrative. The dalang Tjejtep Supriadi from Karawang describes how some dalang encouraged this practice because it contributed to their own popularity (Suganda 1996), but other dalang sought to impose standards on wayang performance that would preclude dancing by female performers (cf. Weintraub 1997:176–82). So some female performers began performing in a new kind of group, which presented music drawn from wayang and ketuk tilu repertoires for listening and dancing. These performances were called kliningan and/or bajidoran (Dahlan 1996:2, 34–35).[17]

CHAPTER FOUR

Bajidoran groups in Subang typically include ten to fifteen female singer-dancers called sinden, accompanied by a large gamelan salendro, including several kendang players, performing on a high stage (approximately five feet above the ground).[18] Bajidor are male fans of these groups, who often show up at any performance that features their favorite sinden. The performance sponsors do not necessarily know the individual bajidor personally, but they welcome their attendance and even provide them with alcoholic drinks (which the regular guests do not receive) to encourage them to dance. The men dance below the stage, with minimal physical contact with the sinden.

One form of physical interaction that does take place is called egot. A bajidor stands in front of the stage, sometimes on a wooden box placed there for this purpose, and his chosen sinden kneels in front of him. They join hands and swing them back and forth in time to the music. Opportunities to actually grope the sinden are minimized by the height of the stage, but the sinden's bent-over position does provide the bajidor with a particularly close view of her cleavage. The bajidor are expected to tip the women generously and often. After a few minutes, the sinden breaks contact, and will not reengage until the bajidor tips her.[19] A bajidor can also pay the sinden to turn around and dance with her buttocks in his face.

In the 1960s bajidoran/kliningan music in Subang was a hybrid of ketuk tilu drumming, kliningan singing, and gamelan salendro. One particularly famous drummer, Suwanda, caught the attention of Gugum Gumbira Tirasonjaya, who employed Suwanda and many of the style characteristics of bajidoran/kliningan in the 1970s in his seminal jaipongan recordings. Nowadays, most bajidoran groups supplement their "traditional" repertoires with dangdut songs (Dahlan 1996:80; Junengsih 1997:vi), which are often requested by the audiences.

BAJIDORAN'S GROOVES   For the most part, in bajidoran (like ketuk tilu and jaipongan), the dancing and drumming alternate between two main grooves. The first groove, which Tosin Mochtar called bubukaan (personal communication, June 8, 1999), usually includes several iterations of the drumming that Dahlan calls pola ibing and that I introduced as the "standard phrase" in chapter 2. This phrase divides a goong phrase into several segments, with a complete stop of activity (and silence from the drums) at the end of each segment. This first groove may also include other phrases that are similar to the standard phrase in that they include complete stops of movement and silence from the drums. The second

Table 4.1. Effort-shape adjectives

Effort-Action	Space	Force	Time
Dab	direct	light	quick
Punch	direct	strong	quick
Glide	direct	light	sustained
Press	direct	strong	sustained
Flick	indirect	light	quick
Slash	indirect	strong	quick
Float	indirect	light	sustained
Writhe	indirect	strong	sustained

groove is called mincid, and the drummer provides a short, repeating ostinato while the dancers walk around or in place, without the activity stops that characterize the first groove.

Male dancers have considerable freedom in choosing movements to fit the drum patterns (described in chapter 2). In describing the dancing that is freely applied to these drum rhythms, I am adopting terminology for movement analysis developed by Rudolph Laban under the rubric "effort-shape," as explicated by Irmgard Bartenieff and Martha Ann Davis (1972) and Cecily Dell (1977). Effort-shape is useful in this endeavor because it provides vocabulary that can characterize the overall "feel" of a single dance movement, of an individual's movement style, and even (in general terms) of a dance genre, without getting bogged down in the details of body mechanics. Effort-shape analysis looks at several main parameters: gesture-posture, effort flow, and shape flow.[20]

In addition, effort-shape identifies a number of effort and shape qualities. Effort qualities characterize how a body moves with regard to the elements of space (indirectly or directly), force (lightly or strongly), and time (sustained [slowly] or quickly). Laban assigns evocative names to the eight possible combinations of space-force-time qualities, which are summarized in table 4.1.

Shape qualities characterize how the body's shape changes in three dimensions: horizontal (widening or narrowing), vertical (rising or sinking), and sagittal (moving forward [advancing] or withdrawing [retreating]). Cecily Dell provides some useful adjectives for combination shape changes in multiple dimensions, including scattering, unfolding, and

CHAPTER FOUR

opening (for widening, rising, and/or moving forward), and gathering, folding, and closing (for narrowing, sinking, and/or withdrawing). Shape changes might involve only the body or torso, or they may involve limbs as well. Dell also distinguishes opposite ways in which limbs might contribute to shape changes: arclike or spokelike (Dell 1977:45–58).

DANCING TO THE STANDARD PATTERN   I have identified some general tendencies in the choices that most men make for the standard pattern, which includes six different flurries of activity: bukaan, jalak pengkor, capang (two flurries), cindek, and ngala genah (see again fig. 2.12). Men tend to adopt a stance in preparation for the first flurry (bukaan). This stance, called *adeg-adeg* (support post) or *kuda-kuda* (sawhorse or roof-beams), consists of placing the left foot back and the right foot forward (both turned out about 45 degrees from center), with the left knee bent and supporting most of the body's weight. The dancer's trunk leans back a bit, his gaze is downcast, and his arms are relaxed. When the bukaan drum flurry begins, the dancer gestures with his head, arms, and torso, leaving his feet on the ground. He may change directions, but the effort flow is primarily free, and the effort shape is essentially expanding. Most of the gestures could be characterized as floating (indirect/light/sustained), with an emphasis on sustained time quality.

At the end of the flurry, when the drummer performs the characteristic rising drum motive, there is an abrupt change to a bound effort flow, usually accompanied by some sort of a dabbing or punching gesture, following which the dancer stops moving so that his final position becomes a pose. Dancers typically do not move during the inactive portions. Many dancers do not even hold a pose for these periods; instead, they stop dancing and just stand there (i.e., the flow and quality of their effort and shape become "neutral") until the next flurry of activity begins.

Jalak pengkor and capang involve similar movements (although jalak pengkor typically involves stepping as well). The rising drum motive at the end of each flurry inspires an abrupt change to a bound effort flow, a dab or punch, and a pose. The dramatic stop at the end of the ngala genah cadential pattern inspires a similar, but usually more dramatic, change to a bound effort flow accompanied by a punching or dabbing gesture. In contrast to the previous abrupt changes, the shape changes of ngala genah movements are also characterized by a pronounced sinking quality, giving it more of a feeling of finality. Even bajidor who barely dance at all during the other flurries, preferring to watch the sinden dance, move a little bit during ngala genah (Ade Komaran, personal communication, March 4, 1999).

DANCING TO MINCID   For the second groove, mincid, most men match their foot movements to the drumming, stepping in some patterned way (e.g., step left/close/step right/close). They might travel only slightly (e.g., back and forth in a "slot") or else move around the dance arena. The stepping rapidly alternates free and bound flows, giving it an overall continuous feel. Dancers usually supplement their foot movements with floating (i.e., indirect, sustained, and light) head, arm, and torso gestures. Drum cadential figures (and dance movements) that lead to goong strokes in mincid are similar to ngala genah or nibakeun in the standard pattern.

Within these overall guidelines, individuals develop their own unique dancing personalities to express their own masculine identities—or perhaps the identities they would like to project. The descriptions below illustrate three quite different dancing personalities I analyzed from images of a bajidor event I attended and videotaped on June 25, 1999. My descriptions focus on three of the fifteen or so men who were dancing below the stage. I identify them according to the clothes they wore: "Red" (shirt), "White" (pants), and "Two-Tone" (shirt). In the following paragraphs, I provide a running commentary on their movements during approximately two minutes of dancing that included the drum patterns I have described previously as mincid and the standard pattern.

SOME EXAMPLES   When the two-minute clip begins, a musical piece is already in progress, the drummers are providing a driving mincid groove, and several men are dancing. Red, a tall, solidly built thirtyish man wearing jeans, a red T-shirt, and a baseball cap is standing in a rather neutral position, just off camera, but he warms to the idea of dancing by clapping his hands to the beat with an indirect effort. As he begins to step to the music's driving pulse, he changes his effort to be stronger and more direct. Although his arms move in an arclike path while clapping, once he begins to dance in earnest, the directionality of his arm and leg movements becomes more spokelike, with a bound effort flow. His steps are small, with a bound, quick effort; he briskly traverses a rather lengthy path across the camera's entire field of vision. Overall, he holds his limbs close to his body, his shape tends toward folding and closing, and he advances in space. He articulates each musical pulse with his feet, with his arms, and with a slight rising and shrinking of his entire body. Unlike most of the other men, Red stops dancing when the mincid groove ends

CHAPTER FOUR

and the standard pattern begins. Instead, he reverts to a neutral-weight, nondancing body attitude and walks deliberately toward the edge of the stage, where he engages one of the sinden in egot.

White, a very thin twentyish man wearing crisp white Levis and a long-sleeved button-down shirt, is dancing with a male partner as the clip begins. He and his partner face one another but do not maintain eye contact. In contrast to Red, who locomotes across the dance floor, White stays in one place, his feet planted firmly on the ground. He rarely steps at all, articulating the beat instead by bending his knees, rising and falling with light to medium weight. The effort he displays while dancing is mostly indirect, light, free, and sustained. His arms move in arclike fashion, rarely in sync with the music's pulse, in expansive, growing, unfolding, scattering gestures on several planes.

Two-Tone is a shortish man in his twenties; he wears a shirt that has a solid white upper panel and a sheer, diaphanous lower panel. Like Red, he enters the dance space by walking normally, but once in place, he quickly assumes his dance character. Like White, he doesn't locomote very much. He observes the mincid beat with subtle bounces at the knee, and directs most of his energy into the horizontal plane, twisting his entire body from one side to the other in time with music's pulse. He alternates closing and opening gestures, often bending and unfolding his entire torso at the waist. Overall, his use of weight is rather neutral—neither free nor bound—and his movements are more sustained than quick.

The standard pattern begins leading up to a goong stroke, with the drum pattern called ngala genah. Only Two-Tone is visible on the tape for this segment of the dance. When the mincid groove stops, he reverts to a neutral standing position, with his arms hanging at his sides. He steps from side to side, without any deliberate arm gestures, for the steps leading up to the final drum flourish. He plants his feet in a basic adeg-adeg stance with a quick, strong, direct effort and gracefully unfolds his arms, extending them out to his sides at shoulder level. He chooses a quick ribcage shift and a snap of his neck to observe the punch/dab drumstroke that comes just before the goong stroke. By the time the goong stroke occurs, he already has assumed a neutral standing position and dropped his arms to his sides.

Red and White do not return to the camera's view until the standard pattern's second of the flurries of activity, that is, the jalak pengkor section. In keeping with the movement's name, which means "lame bird," all three dancers observe the drumstrokes with steps, amplified with unfolding arm gestures. Red's steps are spokelike, like pistons moving in a cylinder, with a pronounced bend of the knee, but he uses these small steps to move forward in his space. White's steps, in contrast, are arclike, with a more gentle knee bend, and he steps in place. Two-Tone's steps are quite small, but he observes the drumstrokes with hip flexes. All three men reinforce the drum accents with quick, strong, bound upward arm gestures; once again, Red's gestures are spokelike and move in only one plane, while the others use arclike motion in a more three-dimensional space. Only Two-Tone and Red are visible for the final "dang-dut" drumstrokes; Red's movement—an upward arm gesture—is rather sustained and free, and immediately following the end of the pattern he stops dancing and walks toward the stage. Two-Tone, in contrast, unfolds his arms out to his sides and observes the "dang-dut" with a quick, bound jerk of his rib cage.

For the final flurry of the standard pattern, ngalah genah, both White and Two-Tone perform steps leading up to the goong stroke. As before, Two-Tone observes the final accented stroke of the pattern by assuming a kuda-kuda stance using a quick, strong, direct effort, unfolding his arms, and observing the punch stroke with a quick rib-cage shift and a snap of his neck. In contrast, White seems to fold his body; he assumes a stance with his feet close together and his arms at waist level, extended only slightly as he snaps his neck for the last stroke. His snap, however, comes in anticipation of the actual drumstroke; by the time the drumstroke sounds, he already has dropped his dance posture and assumed a neutral standing position.

Clearly, each man is aware of and observes closely the movement conventions associated with each drum pattern. However, the details of each man's execution are quite different, in terms of effort and shape, the amount of space he occupies and traverses, his interaction with other dancers, the degree to which he anticipates or delays synchronizing his movements with the drumstrokes, and the degree of enthusiasm or apathy he displays. Each man performs his own interpretation of Sundanese masculinities in the way he claims space on the dance floor, interacts with and influences his fellow dancers, and negotiates conformance with or independence of the regulating drumming.

NGALA GENAH: THE SENSATION OF ENJOYMENT   The attraction of dancing might be summed up in the phrase ngala genah (or ala genah). In Sundanese, ala or ngala means "to pick (as fruit)" or "to look for"; genah means "delicious" or "pleasing." Ala genah refers to the final gesture of the "standard" jaipongan phrase, specifically to the abrupt stop, accentuated by a loud drumstroke, that comes just one beat before the stroke of the goong. Almost all the men I talked to were unable to express in words

CHAPTER FOUR

what was pleasing about the gesture, but there is no doubt they found it pleasurable—they inevitably broke into a introverted, blissful smile at the moment they stopped talking and demonstrated the movement. Mas Nanu Muda told me that the pleasing part of ngala genah is getting back in sync with others at that particular point in a dance. He said that it is nice to dance according to one's own wishes during the lively drumming that leads up to the goong stroke, but that coming back together at the point where the drumming stops before the goong stroke is especially satisfying. Nanu, like the others, ultimately resorted to demonstrating the gesture, and he affected the typical blissful smile at the moment he stopped moving (personal communication, July 27, 1999).

The dancers consider themselves free to dance in whatever ways they want, but the most pleasurable part of dancing is the moment when they stop dancing freely and pause for a moment, in unison, and shift their focus from the internal to the external. These pauses in the first groove, of which ngala genah is perhaps the most dramatic example, suggest to me a sort of "checking in" with the rest of the dancers—interrupting the introspective, personal sojourn that is free improvised dance to make sure that everybody else is still in the same groove. The dancers' cherished freedom is, in effect, limited quite frequently by these checks—much as their personal freedom to act as they please is held in check by their sense of malu. The second groove, mincid, is blissfully free of these reality checks, and the dancers are given the opportunity to really let loose.

Dangdut

On its surface, the pan-Indonesian popular music and dance genre known as dangdut may seem a significant departure from more traditional Sundanese music, in terms of tonal material (dangdut songs are usually modal or diatonic), ensemble (dangdut is not associated with gamelan), dance groove (the dangdut dance rhythm is continuous, not segmented and varied), and language (most dangdut songs are in Indonesian). In the following section I will compare the dance grooves for jaipongan and dangdut and argue that there is considerably more continuity between them than is immediately apparent. Despite differences in their sonic signatures, dangdut and more traditional musical genres occupy the same musical milieu in West Java and influence one another.

Dangdut music is usually performed using an ensemble that features Western instruments such as guitars and keyboards as well as a transverse flute (*suling* or *bangsing*). The characteristic dance groove is usually played

DANCE EVENTS AND FREEDOM

"dang - dut"

4.2 Basic *kendang* phrase for *dangdut* (from Ade Komaran, personal communication, June 9, 1999).

on a set of two drums called gendang (Weintraub 2006). It is characterized by two accented drum strokes, the first of which is low-pitched and the second of which rises in pitch. On gendang, this rising pitch is effected by striking the drumhead and applying pressure with the heel of the hand to tighten the head and raise the pitch. The emblematic groove can also be played on other drums, including the standard set of Sundanese kendang. Figure 4.2 is a possible kendang rendition of the basic dangdut phrase as taught to me by Ade Komaran.

The key strokes in this pattern are the two low-pitched quarter notes. A kendang player executes the second of these quarter-note strokes (notated on the bottom line of the staff) with his foot on the drumhead. After striking the drum he increases his foot pressure on the head so that the pitch of the sound rises. This creates the eponymous "dang-dut" sounds. Other strokes may be added for variety, but this essential groove is maintained, and the pattern is repeated over and over again, forming a cycle—a continuously repeating rhythm. Weintraub identifies other dangdut rhythms as well, but they all have this cyclic quality.

In everyday language, modern Sundanese typically distinguish between two styles of dancing with different words: joged and *ngibing*. Joged usually implies dancing to modern, popular music with a continuous groove, while ngibing suggests dancing to Sundanese music in which the drum flurries start and stop. The late Sundanese musician Entis Sutisna believed that the underlying approaches to rhythm that motivate jaipongan/bajidoran and dangdut were quite different. What he called *wanda klasik* (classic style) is characterized by the dramatic shifts and variations in effort and shape flow, qualities described earlier for bajidoran drumming. To demonstrate, he assumed a dance position with one arm forward and one arm back, and then slowly twisted his head, neck, and torso, accelerating the speed of the twist until he came to an abrupt stop. The effort involved might be described as a glide of the whole torso accelerating into a press that is abruptly terminated with a punched stop.

CHAPTER FOUR

The *wanda anyar* (new style), in contrast, is continuous. He demonstrated it with back-and-forth movements of his upper torso, his upper arms held at his sides and his forearms bent forward (as if holding a steering wheel), moving in and out, that is, alternating flicking motions of the torso. In his opinion, it is the sudden changes in effort flow of the wanda klasik that distinguishes the wanda klasik from the continuous wanda anyar (personal communication, May 8, 1999).

The examples of the jaipongan/bajidoran standard phrase (see again fig. 2.12) and the dangdut groove (see fig. 4.2) support Entis's contention that the two rhythmic approaches are inherently different. But traditional Sundanese dances, such as ketuk tilu, tayub, jaipongan, and bajidoran, include two main sections or "grooves," and only one of these two grooves is what Entis would call *dinamika*. The other groove, mincid, is cyclical and continuous like the dangdut groove. In contrast to Entis's assertion, Ade Komaran told me that the primary difference between jaipongan/bajidoran and dangdut is the accompaniment—dangdut is diatonic and features the "dang-dut" drum rhythm, while jaipongan/bajidoran uses Sundanese scales and drum patterns. Dancers often use the same dance movements when dancing to dangdut music and jaipongan/bajidoran, he added. The cyclical, continuous nature of the drumming did not seem to him to be as significant a distinction as it did to Entis (personal communications, March 22, 1999, and May 19, 1999). Furthermore, dangdut arrangements typically feature alternate drum patterns that are keyed to specific parts of a song (Andrew Weintraub, personal communication, April 2009).

The dangdut groove (see fig. 4.2) shares some features with drumming for Sundanese dancing with dinamika. For example, dangdut's eponymous rising pitch gesture echoes the rising pitch motive at the end of each of the flurries of activity in the jaipongan standard phrase (see again fig. 2.12) that, as I have suggested, interrupts the introspective, personal sojourn that is free dance to make sure that everybody else is still in the same groove. And dangdut drumming variations often lend the groove a 3–3–2 accentuation pattern (reinforced by the parts played on the kempul and goong, if present) that encapsulates the kind of cadential anticipation described in chapter 2. In a sense, it is as if the two different grooves that characterize traditional Sundanese dance accompaniment (i.e., the standard phrase and mincid) have been conflated into one short, condensed drum pattern (dangdut). Even if, as Philip Yampolsky describes it, "the aim of [male dangdut fans'] dancing is apparently to be transported to a state where they are unaware of their surroundings, free of self-consciousness and inhibition" (Yampolsky 1994:38), a constant reminder of malu is built in to the dangdut groove in the form of the rising drum sound—a sonic emblem of movement stops.

Many of the dangdut songs that are popular in these contexts include significant Sundanese elements, including instruments (goong, kempul, *kecrek* [a stack of metal plates hit with a mallet], and kendang) and jaipongan-like drum "hooks" and cadential patterns as well, to which dancers always set corresponding dance moves. Furthermore, the dangdut groove is not the only case in which a continuous approach to rhythm has replaced more dynamic approaches. The family of the Bejo Group from Subang told me that one of the characteristics of Subang-style bajidoran is that although it still uses gamelan accompaniment and Sundanese songs (as opposed to dangdut's Western instruments), what goes on combines a new, continuous rhythmic groove with bajidoran drumming. The new element is called triping, a term derived from the English slang term "tripping." A 1996 *Kompas Online* article discusses triping as a by-product of ecstasy use and suggests that it is inextricably tied to the rhythm of house music. Ironically, the source interviewed for the article cited jaipongan specifically as a musical groove that was fundamentally incompatible with tripping (*Dampak ecstasy pada tubuh* 1996). This assertion notwithstanding, however, in effect tepak triping is gamelan with a house beat. When dancing to triping, dancers do not move very much. They nod their heads and sway subtly to the rhythm, with an effort-action that is best described as floating, and they do not move their arms very much. The stopped or rising drum sound that I associate with malu is completely absent from the drumming, and the dancers' internal focus is almost unbroken—until the musicians provide a dramatic return to the jaipongan groove just before the goong stroke, and the ineluctable dinamika pattern that signals a sudden change in effort returns. The drum's momentary silence, after a long period of consistent playing, seems deafening as the dancers enjoy the goong stroke together. Although triping provides a more complete negation of constraints—a more perfect freedom for the dancers—the music always returns to something more conventional, such as the jaipongan standard pattern or mincid.

In the late 1990s a number of groups released cassettes with special triping songs. Members of the Bejo Group identify the main difference between Subang-style bajidoran and dangdut as the former's gamelan instruments and nondiatonic tonality, and they imply that people far away from urban centers, such as the people who live around Subang, refer a more "traditional" sound with regard to instrumentation, melodic

CHAPTER FOUR

materials, and language (personal communication, June 25, 1999). With regard to rhythmic groove, however, and the enactment of freedom and malu, their audiences seem to be seeking similar experiences.

Dancing and *malu*

The men—bajidor—who make dancing this way the primary focus of their lives follow their favorite groups around and throw all their money at the sinden (cf. Suganda 1998). Most men, however, indulge in this behavior only occasionally, and some experience it only vicariously by watching others. Yet men often feel compelled to dance despite their sense of modesty, in part because to perform onstage (kaul) will honor their hosts and guests of honor. There is usually some sort of coercion (often mild) involved in getting ordinary men to dance. At weddings, men take the stage to dance as kaul, which in Sundanese literally means repayment of a debt or fulfillment of a vow. According to Sean Williams, kaul "means [to] join in for the fun of it and to lend their support to the event" (Williams 1998a:77). She continues her gloss of kaul in an endnote:

Kaul has multiple layers of meaning; in the context of wayang, it also means fulfilling a vow to one's teacher. Indeed, it is sometimes the teacher (of vocal music, or of dance) who commands his or her students to take the stage. The self-conscious behavior of participants may be a direct reflection of the embarrassment associated with going onstage prior to being fully prepared to perform on one's own. (WILLIAMS 1998A:83)

In other words, kaul is closely connected to embarrassment, humility, and submission to the wishes of another—to malu. Performing some public act, such as dancing onstage, as kaul in honor of the bridal couple is a common activity among wedding guests. On many other occasions I observed friends goading and teasing each other into dancing. Geertz's remark with regard to the Balinese—"to be teased is to be accepted" (Geertz 1973a:416)—is apropos of Sundanese practice as well. It adds one more complication to the network of malu, bangga, and kaul. Kaul is another manifestation of masculine contradictions in that it involves seeking humility by acting bravely—defying convention for the sake of conformity.

I frequently felt foolish when participating at Sundanese dance events. My feelings of foolishness are probably akin to the Sundanese experience of malu—occupying space inappropriately, acting outside one's level of competence, attracting undue attention—and I infer that the experience

138

DANCE EVENTS AND FREEDOM

is not pleasant for Sundanese men, either. When communing with my fellow dancers, however—when all of us were somehow motivated by the rhythms played on the drums to manifest in individualized movement what those patterns suggested to each of us, coming together at times—I felt as if foolishness did not apply to me. Perhaps this, then, is the attraction of men's improvisational dancing: it provides a framework in which to experience malu-inducing activities without malu.

What emerges onstage, then, might be construed as a performance of a man's internal dialogue about malu. At a wedding on March 22, 1999, I watched as a young man was dragged onto the stage, apparently against his will. Once there, he sometimes danced very enthusiastically, rolling his pelvis in a sexually suggestive manner in close proximity to the mother of the groom, who was also onstage. He would alternate the sexy moves with equally convincing spells of boyish embarrassment, laughing as if to deny his association with his previous actions. He did this cycle a few times before returning to the audience, where his friends teased him and he laughed embarrassedly about his behavior onstage. While dancing, however, he successfully embodied a key contradiction of Sundanese masculinity.

The general outline of choreography for the standard jaipongan drum pattern enables a similar trade-off. Dancing to the flurries of drumming involves free-flowing, floating movements; these are contradicted by the sudden effort flow and quality changes that characterize the ends of the flurries. As I pointed out earlier, some dancers do not even maintain their poses throughout the quiet moments between flurries; instead, they drop out of dance position, neutralizing shape and effort flow until the next flurry of drumming begins. While they are moving, they revel in the sense of freedom that dancing provides; their sense of malu, however, stops them in their tracks at regular intervals. It is as if they are simultaneously free and constrained—quite literally performing the contradictions of masculinity.

The freedom afforded dancers gives them a limitless arsenal of external expressions for their internal dialogue. Even something as simple as their use of gesture versus posture—whether they concentrate their movements on particular body parts or allow the movement to spread through their bodies, whether they locomote or stay in place—may provide clues about their internal state. With regard to dancing in general, Bartenieff and Davis remark that "the continuum of gesture-posture reflects greater or lesser degrees of physical and presumably psychological involvement" (Bartenieff and Davis 1972:7). How a dancer combines gestural and postural movement in dancing may provide a visual index of his own

CHAPTER FOUR

focus between malu and boldness. In all cases, it enacts the mythic diachronic resolution of the contradictions of Sundanese masculinity.

The details vary according to social class: what kinds of movements
are manly, what sorts of protocols enhance status, and what type of constraints the dancers face. In men's improvisational dance this variability
in actual movement, irrespective of class and genre, is regarded as an aesthetic value. One of the good things about ketuk tilu, Salam Mulyadi told
me, was that each male dancer does something different and might even
do something unpredictable, so there is a lot of variety. In contrast, he
found choreographed jaipongan dances boring because everybody does
the same thing (personal communication, June 17, 1999).

Salam took this point even further to say that freedom and unpredict-
ability not only make men's improvisational dance interesting to do, they
make it interesting to watch as well. One young Sundanese college student
told me, for example, that he enjoys watching other men dance onstage,
although he himself has never done so. The thrill, he said, comes from
enjoying their bravado. When they dance well, he feels as if he himself is
on top of things. He admitted that the music compels him to dance, but
he is not "brave" enough to do anything but joged "in place" (i.e., sway
and move his body, but not his hands and feet, to the beat, without getting onstage; personal communication, December 15, 1998). At present,
most Sundanese regard men who are seriously devoted to dancing at
such events with an ambiguous mixture of contempt and admiration.
The young man mentioned above also told me that even though he
enjoys watching, he does not necessarily respect and admire the men
who dance onstage, whom he regards as old-fashioned and backward
(personal communication, December 15, 1998). Ade Komaran told me
that he sees a lot of invited guests at the events for which he plays who
are inspired by the music to move but are much too shy to dance onstage.
He can tell because they joged surreptitiously in place, by moving their
legs or arms according to the drum patterns (personal communication,
April 7, 1999).

Being Seen

Even for the audience, then, the focus is internal rather than external. I
believe that viewers imagine what the various dancers' movements feel
like rather than judge their visual impact. Watching men's improvisational dance is, at least in part, a vicarious activity. I am proposing that
observers do not evaluate what they see so much as they assess whether
(and how) the dancer's way of moving might augment their own style of

moving and, more fundamentally, their understanding of self-identity by expanding the realm of possible ways of being. Dancer Sujana Arja condenses the difference between merely watching and holistically experiencing with two assonant Indonesian words: *tontonan* (spectacle) and *tuntunan* (guidance). Tontonan, he explains, is a kind of detached watching, while tuntunan means watching with engagement, learning about life and values from the dancing. Modern stage dances are tontonan, he continued, while ritual and social dances are tuntunan (personal communication, July 11, 1999).

David Hanan's article about the film *Nyi Ronggeng* makes an important point regarding the notion of "the male gaze" as originated by the film critic Laura Mulvey (and subsequently expanded by others). Mulvey asserts that mainstream films provide a male point of view and set up shots so that female characters are the object of "the male gaze" (Hanan 1992:168). Hanan suggests that in Sundanese men's dance events, the male dancer becomes part of the "spectacle"—the male dancer, too, is an object of "the male gaze," both for the audiences at dance events and (more important for Hanan's purposes) for film audiences as well. But perhaps "gaze" is the wrong word—the "viewers" are not "looking at" so much as "feeling with" the men they watch.

Thus, it is not only the male dancers who participate actively in dance events, but the rest of the audience as well. Watching from the sidelines, men compare their own strategies for negotiating these contradictions with those of the men onstage. Women are reminded of the seamier side of men's nature and may even experience a double bind of their own as they are simultaneously aroused, revolted, and made jealous. Children, who watch the activities with rapt attention, form conceptions about masculinity that last a lifetime as the contradictions of Sundanese masculinity are inscribed on yet another generation. Citing and enacting masculine behaviors in an environment where they are sanctioned gives men the opportunity to try on such behaviors and make them natural. Of course, not all men and women are completely convinced that these enacted behaviors are the only available or desirable ones, but by performing and witnessing them, everybody comes to understand the behaviors as "natural," and the dominant paradigm of masculinity is reinforced.

Ronggeng and drumming create a context in which participants—active and vicarious—can do the cultural work of dance events. The context of conventional dance events constructs a position for ronggeng and drummers as professionals, in contrast to the male dancers' status as amateurs. As a result, ronggeng and drummers (and other musicians) distance their true selves from the events to enable the dancers (and the rest of the

CHAPTER FOUR

audience, vicariously) to assume a subject position. As professionals who make a choice to surrender their subjectivity temporarily and partially, they of course remain full-fledged agents. In the sense that they, too, are performing gender identities, drummers and ronggeng retain a certain subjectivity even as they *appear* to forfeit a subject position. In all these ways, the erotic triangle of Sundanese dance makes contingent, arbitrary gender ideologies seem incontrovertible, unassailable, and natural.

Returning to the central idea of this book—that three elements, namely ronggeng, drumming, and participants who dance freely, constitute a durable yet flexible erotic triangle—it is clearer how the migration and reinscription of the triangle onto different genres (ketuk tilu, tayuban, wayang, bajidoran, jaipongan, dangdut) work. All these different dance forms and events provide a means of integrating one's body physically into the maze of contradictions that makes up Sundanese gender identities. Dancing encompasses the contradictory forces of bangga/berani and malu; for the men, the desire to transcend the strictures of malu is redirected as interest in the ronggeng. The drumming provides an excuse and a vocabulary for engaging publicly in an inner dialogue about malu. Those watching the goings-on participate vicariously, imagining their own bodies moving, validating or rejecting what they see, hear, and feel to erase or redraw the lines of contradiction that lie at the bottom of gender identities. All three elements—free dancing, drumming, and ronggeng—play important roles in identifying and working through the issues. In the course of these events, all participants dance the norms of Sundanese gender identities into existence.

FIVE

The Erotic Triangle of Sundanese Dance

Despite its persistence, the erotic triangle of Sundanese dance is not a fixed structure. Rather, it provides a flexible framework not only for affirming ideologies of gender and power through interactive dancing, but for contesting them as well. This chapter begins by looking at the development of a pivotal Sundanese dance genre—tari kursus—through the lens of the erotic triangle to demonstrate how this flexibility operates. A geometric approach clarifies how tari kursus could be seen as maintaining traditional values about men's dancing—exhibiting signs of a participatory nature—while simultaneously being an icon of Sundanese presentational dance. Such an analysis also helps us to understand the always changing, often uneasy relationship between Sundanese classical dance and the enduring Sundanese regard for men's improvised dancing. It culminates in a theoretical exposition of how erotic triangles operate in Sundanese dance.

Tayuban to *Tari kursus*

Tari kursus occupies a pivotal position among modern presentational Sundanese dance genres. Although it clearly grew out of tayuban (aristocratic men's participatory dance), it also provides the basis for modern Sundanese tari klasik (classical dancing). As the use of the borrowed word

CHAPTER FIVE

"classical" suggests, the goal of tari klasik's creators was to ennoble Sundanese culture by establishing a classical tradition on a par with those of European culture.

Chapter 4's historical accounts of tayuban painted a picture of dance events that constituted a complete erotic triangle. Men were free to dance according to their own desires, always aware that the other participants formed judgments about their character and power from their idiosyncratic dancing styles. Over the course of the twentieth century, for a variety of reasons, the dancing at such events was systematized and codified. A new term—ibing tayub—was applied to the genre that began as freestyle dancing, with few constraints, and morphed into a named dance genre with normative conventions and rules.

This shift in emphasis from free dancing to a more strictly defined notion of a dance genre is rooted in changes in the role and position of the Sundanese aristocracy around the turn of the twentieth century. Sundanese aristocratic families trace their position from before Dutch administration. Since the fall of the Sundanese Pajajaran kingdom in the sixteenth century, the Priangan (highland West Java) has been part of non-Sundanese political units. The outside rulers of Priangan, such as the Mataram empire, delegated governing authority to the existing Sundanese aristocracy. The Dutch followed suit and insinuated their political agendas into the existing Sundanese feudal system under the *Preangerstelsel* (Priangan System). Thus, the Dutch perpetuated the great prestige and administrative ability of the local Sundanese aristocratic authorities (called regents by the Dutch and bupati by the local residents) to live in grand style (Sutherland 1973:126). Sundanese regents in the nineteenth and twentieth centuries acted as middlemen between the local realm and the larger realm of the colonial regime. According to Sartono Kartodirdjo, aristocrats embodied their roles as mediators by cultivating courtly manners and practices (1982:188).

In 1871 the regents were relieved of much of their governing responsibilities (Sujana 1993:49), which were shifted to the local Dutch officials. As a result of this diminution of real power, the regents pursued various cultural legitimizing activities even more ardently. Men's dance was one of these status builders, and the differentiation of aristocratic male improvisational dancing from that of commoners, along with its renaming as "nayuban," is likely an artifact of this demotion.

The dual roles of traditional aristocrat and modern bureaucrat became increasingly incompatible as the twentieth century proceeded, so the Dutch implemented various changes in the system to recruit talented nonaristocrats into the bureaucracy (Sutherland 1973:76). One Dutch reform was an increasing emphasis on merit-based promotion. According to Kartodirdjo, membership in the aristocracy became something neither completely hereditary nor completely merit based (1982: 188).

The historian Heather Sutherland describes how someone of common birth could break into and advance among the ranks of the aristocracy by becoming an apprentice in an aristocratic household. Advancement ensued as the candidate curried favor and earned the master's esteem. The bestowing of esteem and status did not necessarily depend on skill or efficiency, but rather on the quality of personal relationships and an understanding of one's place and purpose (Sutherland 1973:32).

When blood alone no longer determines place in society, other factors become more important. Aristocrats (as well as those with aristocratic aspirations) developed elaborate *hormat* or *tatakrama* (etiquette) skills. The publication of a number of Sundanese etiquette books in the early twentieth century attests both to the importance of etiquette among the aristocratic class and to the chance for upward mobility by those who master etiquette's intricacies. Lubis cites a book first published in 1908 entitled *Tatakrama Oerang Soenda* (Sundanese People's Etiquette), by D. K. Ardiwinata, which states that etiquette has three aspects: language, dress, and behavior (Lubis 1998:173).

To address the first aspect, aristocrats cultivated different levels of vocabularies of the Sundanese language. A speaker's choice of language level situated him or her in relationship to an interlocutor. People of lower rank were obliged to use deferential language when speaking to their superiors, creating a palpable distance between them. Proper usage of Sundanese provided a means literally of speaking one's status. Details of dress, too, provided opportunities to situate one's self within aristocratic society.

The final dimension of etiquette was careful attention to one's behavior, or, more specifically, one's bodily deportment. Lubis describes the etiquette of West Javanese aristocrats and identifies as its function the creation of distance between those affecting aristocratic mannerisms and those of lower status. For Sundanese aristocrats, etiquette meant a set of "conventional manners as reflected in postures, movements, and actions" that the elite could use to distance themselves from people of lower status (Lubis 1998:172–73).[1] Status was created and affirmed by particular ways of holding and moving one's body that were clearly distinguishable from the deportment of commoners. Becoming an aristocrat involved learning to *move* like an aristocrat.

For example, *sembah* (a gesture in which the palms of the hands are brought together with fingers pointing up) was used in all sorts of

CHAPTER FIVE

situations, such as greeting somebody or receiving an object. Etiquette required that polite social interactions be punctuated with the gesture, and its proper use was compared to "commas and semicolons in a literary work or gong strokes in gamelan music" (Lubis 1998:174).[2] Dance gestures performed at nayuban doubtless developed into an extension of this bodily etiquette. Sembah and other etiquette gestures have been incorporated into tayub dancing.[3]

Being good at dancing became a requirement of aristocracy. According to Lubis, R. Tumenggung Kusumadilaga once suggested that all aristocrats be skilled in dance (Lubis 1998:246). Irawati Durban Ardjo writes that learning to dance well was "a 'must' for somebody of humble birth to move into a higher social circle, especially from the *santana* [subaristocratic] class to the upper class" (Durban Ardjo 1998:167).[4] Dance was part of the curriculum at Dutch-sponsored schools for native civil servants, such as the Kweekschool voor Inlandsche Onderwijzers (teachers' school) and the Opleiding School voor Inlandsche Ambtenaren (OSVIA, the tertiary-level civil service school) in Bandung (Atmadibrata, Dunumiharja, and Sunarya 2006:100; Sujana 1993:99), where ambitious candidates from all over West Java came to study (Caturwati 2000:20). Among the dance teachers at the Bandung OSVIA in 1926 was R. Tjetje Somantri, who later became one of West Java's most influential choreographers (Caturwati 2000:47–48).

Upward mobility also required, at some level, the imprimatur of the Dutch overlords. Just as they had adopted Javanese customs earlier, including the term tayuban itself, the Sundanese upper classes increasingly adopted European customs. During the period around 1900, drinking whiskey and soda and playing card games were strategies for currying favor with European overlords (Sutherland 1979:43). Upper-class European morals frowned on overt dalliances with women of ill repute. In addition, as Benedict Anderson points out, the worldview of many Indonesian Muslims changed in the late nineteenth century as a result of increased contact with the Near East, and they advocated a more orthodox form of Islam that was more consistent with the practices of the Middle East (Anderson 1972:59). According to Leisbeth Hesselink, Sarekat Islam and other Indonesian societies united as early as 1913 to combat the evils of prostitution (Hesselink 1992:211).

A desire to conform to the Dutch colonialists' standards, combined with similar pressures from increasingly orthodox Muslims, led some aristocrats to "clean up" their tayuban events. Most histories credit the Sumedang aristocrat R. Gandakusumah with modifying tayuban eti-

THE EROTIC TRIANGLE OF SUNDANESE DANCE

quette in several significant ways, including forbidding the ronggeng to stand and dance, redefining them as singers only (e.g., Soepandi and Atmadibrata 1976:84).[5]

Faced with the prospect of being judged on dancing skills and deprived of erotic spectacle from the ronggeng, participating men turned to enhancing their own spectacle. One particularly rich resource in the cultivation of increasingly complex dancing was topeng from Cirebon. This village theater genre featured a solo dancer portraying a variety of characters in an all-day performance. Sundanese dance enthusiasts were intrigued by Cirebonese dance, possibly because of its sophisticated movement repertoire, characterization, and formal structure, so they observed and studied elements of topeng with visiting dancers.

Enoch Atmadibrata, among others, writes that competitions for male dancers, called *konkurs*,[6] became popular in the early part of the twentieth century (Atmadibrata 1998:3). Competitions provided a context in which standards of dancing excellence were developed, extended, and codified. Dancers' improvised movements were judged on *"Bisa, Wanda, Wirahma, Sari, and Alus*, which mean skill, presentation, rhythm, understanding, and harmony" (Atmadibrata 1997b:80).

Individuals who excelled at improvisational dancing were asked to teach others their skills, resulting, in the early part of the twentieth century, in the founding of organizations devoted to dancing, such as Sekar Pusaka in Sumedang; the dance group Wirahmasari, founded by R. Sambas Wirakusumah (son of the *wedana* [district chief] of Tanjungsari in the Sumedang regency and the *lurah* [local official] of Rancaekek in the Bandung regency); and the dance group Gerak Maya, founded by R. Bidin Suryagunawan, son of the bupati [regent] of Sukabumi (Lubis 1998:245–46). Members of these clubs competed in the konkurs.

In 1930 the Dutch-language periodical *Djawa* published an article entitled "De Soendaneesche dans" (Sundanese Dance), written by two Sundanese authors, M. Soeriadiradja and I. Adiwidjaja, that purports to describe the basics of dance as taught in the Wirahmasari club under the leadership of R. Sambas Wirakusumah. The authors characterize the interest in dance as a revival of a practice that was very popular at some time in the past. The article also characterizes the current dance as not "the pure nayub dance from before" because it includes dance movements from other types of Sundanese dance (Soeriadiradja and Adiwidjaja 1930:115). The authors use an apparently new term—*ibing najoeb*—to designate this dance, which is rooted in, but extricated from, the tayuban context. This new ibing najoeb (or *tari tayub* in Indonesian) was a prescribed set of

CHAPTER FIVE

movements, to be performed in a particular order, which overlays an ordered set of rules onto a practice that previously had been characterized as "free." Participants and spectators shift focus from the event to the dance itself. In other words, they formed a presentational dance *genre* out of a flexible, unnamed practice.

In the 1950s the term tari kursus became a synonym for tari tayub. A 1953 article by R. Tjetje Somantri describes how dance moves learned from dance masters visiting from Cirebon were incorporated into a new genre named with the Dutch term *cursus* (course of study), which he marks with scare quotes:

> My own friends studied dance with Wentar and Kontjer [topeng dancers from Cirebon] . . . there are nine basic movements they studied with these two teachers . . . These nine movements were used in *tayuban* for obligatory dancing. This dance spread in West Java. After it spread this dance became ibing "Cursus." (SOMANTRI 1953B:30)[7]

R. Sambas Wirakusumah's book, published the same year, uses a Sundanized version of the term—spelled with a "k" and the Sundanese language's emblematic "eu" vowel—in its title: *Hartos Widji-widji Ibing Keurseus* (1953).

These didactic dances eventually became regarded as presentational dances in their own right. The genre of systematized dances based on the improvised dancing performed at aristocratic tayuban came to be known as tari kursus; the term tari tayub continued to be used, but now to refer to the hitherto unnamed "precursor" to tari kursus—that customary, conventional, but nameless improvised dancing formerly performed at tayuban.

TARI KURSUS AS AN EROTIC TRIANGLE Thus, *tari kursus* became decoupled from the context of men's dance events and in the process lost some of its integrity as an erotic triangle. Its most significant departure from the erotic triangle is the absence of female dancers. At the same time, however, tari kursus remained congruent with traditional ideas about men's improvisational dance, even in the absence of ronggeng, by foregrounding a close coordination between movement and drumming and emphasizing individuality and freedom (Sujana 1996:75).

Presentational tari kursus gained popularity for several reasons. The name, with its Dutch provenance and vaguely scientific ring, gave the emerging dance genre an aura of upward mobility and modernity. The genre also fit well into the political framework of emerging Indonesian nationalism. Throughout the twentieth century, Indonesian nationalists

THE EROTIC TRIANGLE OF SUNDANESE DANCE

called for the crystallization of an Indonesian culture, but determining exactly what constitutes Indonesian culture generated (and continues to generate) much debate. One persuasive model, which emerged in the Undang-undang Dasar (Constitution) of 1945, envisioned Indonesian culture as the sum of the *puncak-puncak kebudayaan* (peaks of culture) in various regional traditions (Yampolsky 1995:704). This approach was a topic of discourse at the time tari kursus began to develop (see, for example, the introduction to Soeriadiradja and Adiwidjaja 1949:3). The sanitized appearance, free of the immoral connotations of ronggeng dancing, made it suitable for the stages of nationalism. At the same time, its references to the erotic triangle enabled it to impart a truly Sundanese flavor.

In chapter 2 I outlined some of the musical conventions—including relatively simple, nonspecific drum patterns strung together in loose formal structures—that enabled dancers to exercise their freedom in ketuk tilu and tayuban, and I examined some of the complicated interactions that arose when drummers and dancers performed with one another, especially an ambiguity with regard to who actually led and who followed. A successfully masculine dancer at a tayuban was able to lead the drummer and influence the movements of others sharing his dance space without appearing to monopolize the proceedings, thus exerting subtle, yet effective power over the other men.

Many Sundanese presentational dances that were developed in the twentieth century include movements with a related, but different, approach to dance-drum relationships. These dances feature significant importations from Cirebonese dance, especially Cirebonese topeng. There are two kinds of movement sequences in topeng: (1) movement clusters (sometimes called *jogedan*), which are complex sequences of gestures that alternate right and left orientations when repeated, and (2) transitions (called *alihan*), which are not repeated (Suanda 1988:11). The movement clusters are similar to mincid patterns in that they repeat several times before moving on to something else, but they tend to be longer and more complex and to have a much more specific, one-to-one relationship between movement and drum pattern. Each movement cluster is named and has a specific drum pattern associated with it.

In the ketuk tilu/penca silat model of dance-drum relationships, interaction between drummer and dance is important primarily for cueing the section changes. The drummer gives a special signal to the dancers when he is about to begin the mincid sections of the dance; alternatively, a dancer might give the drummer a hand signal that it is time to change (Tosin Mochtar, personal communication, January 28, 1999).

149

CHAPTER FIVE

Otherwise, there is no precise one-to-one mapping of movement units to drum patterns, and a single drum pattern may be appropriate for quite a few different movements. Drummers are expected to make sure that their drumming enhances the movements of the dancers, but they are not required to provide a specific, unique pattern for each discrete movement. In other words, drummers and dancers are loosely coupled, with the drummer carrying some (but not all) of the authority to regulate the flow of the dance. Drumming and dancing for tari klasik, in contrast, might be characterized as tightly coupled. There is considerably more specificity with regard to the pairing of dance movements with drum patterns, and there are more junctures in the dance where choices need to be made. A choice on the part of either the dancer or the drummer can have significant ramifications, sending the performance into a new direction. A dancer's choice to continue to repeat a movement cluster, for example, might require that a transition to another section be postponed until the next appropriate point in the musical cycle. A drummer's choice to initiate a transition might force the dancer to begin the transition earlier than he otherwise might have done. The development of presentational Sundanese dance in the twentieth century involves an increasing complexity of dance-drum relationships and shifts of final authority among dancer, drummer, and choreographer.

At the heart of kursus dances is a set sequence of movement clusters that does not vary from performance to performance. All four tari kursus character types are said to use the same basic sequence of movement clusters. In fact, the movements themselves change according to character type, but comparable units for each character are presented in the same sequence. Kursus dances open and close with movements showing respect for the observers. The dancer begins in a seated position and emphasizes hand, arm, and head gestures. After the dancer stands, each movement unit features a more complex combination of walking movements; foot, hand, arm, and head gestures; and directional orientation than does the preceding movement unit. This progressive, incremental, and systematic approach, which explores the different movement resources of Sundanese dance, reflects kursus's pedagogical origins. It is this sequence of clusters and overall form that provides a starting point for most tari klasik choreographies.

Despite this rigid ordering of movement clusters, there remains room for personal expression in kursus (Soepandi and Atmadibrata 1976:87). The character types are consistent with the characterization of wayang or topeng dances but are abstract and generalized. The character types are identified not with names but with verb forms of descriptive words.

THE EROTIC TRIANGLE OF SUNDANESE DANCE

Instead of assuming the personality of a fictional character, the dancer finds the character type within himself. Personal variations include the specific piece chosen for accompaniment and adjustments in many of the movements to suit an individual's body type and personality (Atmadibrata n.d.:120). "Lenyepan" (also called "Leyepan") is the slowest and most refined kursus character type. The name comes from the root word *lenyep*, which means "wise."[8] "Nyatria" is also refined, but faster and more impetuous than "Lenyepan"; the name comes from the word *satria* (knight). "Monggawa" is a strong, quick-moving character type; the name comes from the root ponggawa (warrior in the service of a superior). The final character, "Ngalana" (from *kalana*, a wanderer), is the strongest and most self-assured and represents "an almost perfect man" (Natapradja 1975:105).

TARI KURSUS FORM   Each of kursus's named movement clusters may be repeated a variable number of times before moving on to the next unit. The smallest rhythmic unit of any choreographic interest is a four-beat phrase. Table 5.1 provides a summary of the core movements; in the table, each unit's length is specified according to the number of four-beat units it occupies.

Usually there is transitional material that separates the main movement clusters from one another. In addition, additional material may be infixed between repetitions of a movement cluster, especially when there is a goong stroke in the accompanying music. The dances begin with a section called *lalamba*, which begins with the seated dancer performing a sembah to the audience, and end with another movement, *mamandapan*, intended to show respect to viewers.

In addition to knowledge of each of the movement clusters and the transitions between them, competence in tari kursus involves fitting the clusters tastefully into the formal framework provided by the accompanying musical piece—a kind of musical-choreographic puzzle with many possible solutions, some of which are more elegant than others. The pieces that accompany kursus dances are played on gamelan salendro or *gamelan pelog*, which are similar in instrumentation and tuning to the modern gamelan ensembles of central Javanese courts. Instruments include two *saron* (six- or seven-key metallophones), a *panerus* (a lower-pitch six- or seven-key metallophone), a *bonang* (a two-row horizontal gong chime with ten or twelve small pots), a goong (a large hanging gong) and *kempul* (a smaller hanging gong) suspended from a single frame, a *kenong* (a gong chime with five or six large pots suspended horizontally), and a *gambang* (a nineteen- or twenty-key xylophone). Some ensembles

CHAPTER FIVE

Table 5.1 Summary of *tari kursus* core movements

Movement cluster name	Four-beat units
Jangkung ilo	4
Gedut/gedig	1
Mincid	1
Keupat	2
Tindak tilu	4
Engkeg gigir	1

include additional instruments, such as *rincik* (a higher-pitch version of bonang) and *peking* or *titil* (a higher-pitch version of saron). Rounding out the ensemble are rebab, pasinden, and, of course, kendang.

Many gamelan pieces are defined by a simple sequence of pitches distributed evenly across one or several gong phrases. Instrumentalists construct the parts to play on the gamelan's idiophones by filling in this slow-moving framework with instrument- and pitch-specific motives that end with the goal pitch. A rerenggongan piece generally has eight or sixteen goal pitches per gong phrase. The motives for each instrument have contrasting densities and idiosyncratic ways of moving from one pitch to another. The resulting texture is often described as stratified polyphony. The rebab player and pasinden float melodies that have more variety in terms of rhythm and register, but these still end with the goal pitches, on top of the idiophone parts. They have considerable freedom to vary their rhythmic approaches and add melodic ornaments. The result is a free-moving melodic line that sounds as if it is floating over the rhythmically regular gamelan accompaniment. The drummer follows the dance choreography, providing the appropriate drum pattern for the dancer's movement clusters and transitions. Dancers (and drummers) often strive to push and pull the metrical pulse of the accompaniment slightly, creating moments of rhythmic dissonance as the dance proceeds (for more details about Sundanese gamelan salendro, see Spiller 2004).

"Lenyepan," for example, is most often danced to pieces that have sixteen 4-beat units (i.e., sixty-four beats total) in each phrase. The end of each phrase is marked by a stroke of the large goong. Some call the form of such pieces *rerenggongan*. Popular "Lenyepan" accompaniments include "Banjar Sinom," "Renggong Gede," "Udan Mas," and "Sulanjana."

After examining more than twenty recorded renditions of "Lenyepan" by a number of different dancers, I have concluded that dancers scrupulously observe the order of core movements. It has also become clear to me that no two accomplished dancers follow the strictures in precisely the same way. Figure 5.1 presents a schematic overview of the core sections of three different "Lenyepan" choreographies. Each line of boxes represents a sixty-four-beat goong phrase, and each box represents a four-beat rhythmic unit. Each box is labeled to indicate the dance/drum unit it contains; in the case of movement clusters that are two or four 4-beat units long, the labels have subscripts to indicate which part of the tepak was associated with that rhythmic unit. Some transitions are designed to ease gracefully into the middle of a cluster, and at times transitions ease out of a cluster in the middle as well. Therefore, not all iterations of a multi-four-beat unit movement cluster are complete. Special cadential material that is infixed leading up to a goong stroke is indicated with the label *maen goong* (playing the goong). Table 5.2 summarizes the distribution of iterations of the various tepak for the three renditions.

The outlines demonstrate a few general features of "Lenyepan" choreographies. For example, *jangkung ilu* typically is iterated one full time before a goong stroke and at least two more times after the goong stroke. By limiting himself to two iterations after the goong stroke, a dancer leaves enough time to effect the transition to *gedig*, iterate it several times, and still include a dramatic infixed movement (maen goong) to enhance the goong stroke. Version b, in which the dancer performs four full iterations of jangkung ilu, would be considered a bit awkward because gedig, which is performed only once before the goong stroke, is not firmly established before the goong cadence; it also seems awkward because of the missed opportunity to infix maen goong. The dancer in Version a, in contrast, takes every opportunity to infix maen goong; he includes it after all three of the movement clusters for which it is an option.

There is a great deal of variation about the treatment of keupat as well. Keupat is a very slow walking movement, and dancers must be careful about how much territory they traverse in order to position themselves favorably for the next tepak (*tindak tilu*). Abay Subardja told me he once stretched the keupat section of a dance out for two complete gong phrases because he was so taken by the pasinden's beautiful singing during the relatively peaceful and static rhythm of this movement cluster (personal communication, November 23, 1998). If the dance includes many iterations of keupat, it is tasteful to break things up at times with infixed material, such as a slow pivot to change direction.

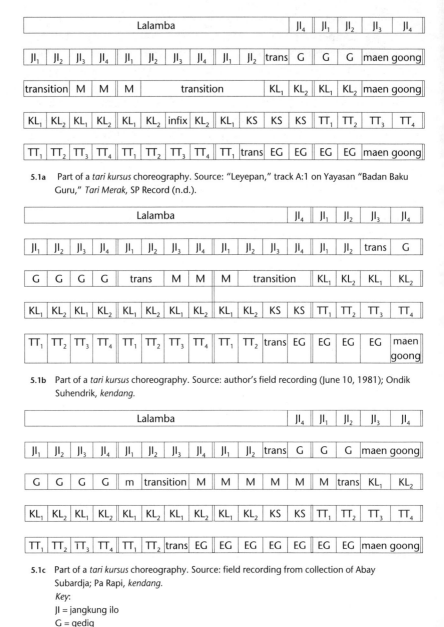

5.1a Part of a *tari kursus* choreography. Source: "Leyepan," track A:1 on Yayasan "Badan Baku Guru," *Tari Merak*, SP Record (n.d.).

5.1b Part of a *tari kursus* choreography. Source: author's field recording (June 10, 1981); Ondik Suhendrik, *kendang*.

5.1c Part of a *tari kursus* choreography. Source: field recording from collection of Abay Subardja; Pa Rapi, *kendang*.

Key:
JI = jangkung ilo
G = gedig
M = mincid
KL = keupat lenyepan
KS = keupat satria
TT = tindak tilu
EG = engkeg gigir

Table 5.2 Comparison of three "Lenyepan" choreographies

Jangkung ilo	Full iterations	3	4	3
	Partial iterations	2	2	2
Gedig	Iterations	3	5	7
	Maen goong	Yes	No	Yes
Mincid		3	3	7
Keupat lenyepan	Full iterations	6	7	6
	Partial iterations	1	0	0
	Maen goong	Yes	No	No
	Keupat satria	3	2	2
Tindak tilu	Full iterations	3	3	2
	Partial iterations	1	1	1
Engkeg gigir	Iterations	4	8	11
	Maen goong	Yes	Yes	Yes

LEADING AND FOLLOWING IN *TARI KURSUS* In the kursus model of dance accompaniment, the drummer is something like to a Foley artist, who creates sound effects for film by emphasizing and drawing attention to particularly dramatic movements. If the drummer's patterns do not match the movements the dancer is performing, observers know that something is amiss. If the dancer chooses to change direction during keupat, for example, the drummer is obliged to anticipate this move and change his drum pattern accordingly. It is also possible for a drummer to elect unilaterally to play the "pivoting" pattern, in which case the dancer is compelled to pivot whether he wants to or not. It is not always clear who is controlling the performance, and there is conflicting rhetoric about who actually leads.

According to some, it is the dancer who controls all aspects of the performance. The drummer is supposed to anticipate the dancer's next moves and not only perform the drum patterns that match the movements, but also execute them in a way that enhances the dancer's personal subtleties and dynamics. To look his best, a dancer might prefer one drummer, who knows his style and predilections, over another. However, these preferred drummers also know how to drum so that the dancer is always reminded of upcoming musical cadences. Drummers are capable of leading dancers through a performance and minimizing any shortcomings in musical knowledge the dancer might have. As a result, some claim that it is the drummer, not the dancer, who leads.

CHAPTER FIVE

Clearly, the framework for tari kursus dances still leaves both performers freedom to execute very personal versions of dances. The goal of studying and practicing kursus dancing was initially to develop the skills required to dance a complex, nuanced piece extemporaneously. Over the course of time, however, some choreographies became ossified: not only was order of the movements fixed, but the number of repetitions and the infixed materials were fixed as well. Some students, especially those who were not particularly gifted, learned only the fixed dance pieces they were taught, without learning the grammar of extemporaneous choreography. Such dancers rely on the drummer to remember their choreography and to cue the various changes as they occur.

Pandi Upandi, in his report on the role of the kendang in Sundanese dance, allows for both possibilities. He first states that "for each basic movement there is always a command given by the drum pattern. Thus the kendang acts as a command-giver for dance movements," implying that it is the drummer who is in control. He then adds: "It does not always happen this way. It happens this way if the dancer is not yet skillful. With a skillful dancer it is the other way around, and it is the dance movements that give commands to the drum patterns" (Upandi 1977:33).[9] By intimating that a "skillful" dancer is the exception rather than the rule, Upandi avoids addressing directly the question of who leads. Some "skillful" dancers assert their control by dancing ahead of the drums. This results in a somewhat jarring asynchrony between sight and sound, but it prevents a drummer from making decisions about the progress of the dance and leaves the spectators with no doubt about who is controlling the performance.

The questions of who leads and who follows, as well as what is improvised and what is fixed, are quite ambiguous. In 1998 I attended a performance billed as a tayuban at STSI Bandung, which included dancing performed by a who's who of tari kursus dancing. I spoke to several of the performers in the days that followed about their performances and the performances of others. When I showed a videotape of an elderly dance master named Aim Salim to the drummer who had accompanied him, Tosin Mochtar, Tosin remarked with some admiration that Aim had done quite a bit of spontaneous dancing in the second part of the dance, which Tosin found challenging to follow (personal communication, January 4, 1999). When I showed the same video to Abay Subardja (a dancer with impeccable tari kursus credentials), he characterized Aim's dance as standard kursus choreography, even the section that Tosin asserted was spontaneous. Abay's intentions for his own performance at the tayuban were to improvise something on the spot, in the way he imagined the aristocrats of the nineteenth century had done. He had even brought his own drummer, with whom he had been rehearsing, to the tayuban to accompany him. The results were not very satisfying, for Abay or the audience. Abay speculated that the gamelan musicians found his dancing too far from the norm to be accompanied easily (personal communication, December 16, 1998). Tosin commented that Abay's dancing could not possibly have been spontaneous or improvised because it was obvious he had been rehearsing with the drummer.

A DEFORMED TRIANGLE Although it is clear that the form, style, and gestures of tari kursus are firmly rooted in men's improvisational dance, differences in context and meaning are profound. In contrast to the vicarious identification with the embodied feelings of the dancers that characterized audience response to men's improvised dancing at dance events, kursus audiences respond primarily to the visual spectacle the dancers create. These changes in meaning are reflected, too, in kursus dancers' garb. The special jacket (*takwa*), length of batik cloth wrapped around the waist (*sinjang*), and head covering (*bendo*) that comprise the tari kursus "costume" used to be simply the formal dress worn regularly by Sundanese aristocrats. Formerly quotidian practices—dancing freely and wearing clothes—have become steeped in new significance.

The development of tari kursus as a Sundanese presentational dance that could contribute to a pan-Indonesian culture involves accomplishing two contradictory aims: deforming tari kursus's triangularity in order to "upgrade" it without completely destroying the elements that are essential to its Sundaneseness. Nowadays these two faces of tari kursus are sometimes called by two different names—tari kursus and tari tayub—and it is not always clear whether tari tayub still exists or has been made obsolete by tari kursus. Tari tayub is improvised and social ("free"), while tari kursus is precomposed and presentational ("fixed").

The term tari tayub came into use to describe a revival of aristocratic improvisational male dancing in the twentieth century. It is as if the term tari tayub were coined to put a name to what had been, in its time, a generic kind of "dancing," with no need of a name; in revival, however, it came to be remembered as a "pure," distinctive, named dance genre. In other words, the degree of self-consciousness with which dance is performed and its conventions articulated make a significant difference in how people talk about it. As tari tayub, the customary way of improvising dance acquires a form and becomes an "invented tradition" (in the

CHAPTER FIVE

Hobsbawmian sense)[10]—that is, an attempt to manufacture continuity with a fictitious past to legitimize modern innovations—in this case, to provide a pedigree for modern, presentational dance.

Slippery discourse allows Sundanese dancers, choreographers, and audiences to believe that tayub/kursus is both free and fixed. They can begin to tell a story by emphasizing the orderliness of tari kursus and its strict rules and scientific pedagogical method. Then, after a breath, they can continue what is ostensibly the same story, but now with talk of tari tayub, freedom, spontaneity, and individuality. By talking around the seemingly contradictory qualities of standardization and spontaneity, of fixed and free, these qualities can be made to coexist (albeit uneasily at times) in modern Sundanese dance.

By complicating the conventional ambiguity of who leads and who follows, kursus performers draw attention to two triangle sides (drumming and free dancing) so that an erotic triangle is perceivable even in the absence of the third side (female dancers). By implying the triangle without explicitly providing all three sides, tari kursus can seem seemly and seamy at the same time. Outsider audiences can watch it as purely presentational dance, while insiders, armed with the appropriate understanding of dance-event geometry, can imagine their own vicarious involvement in the performance.

Ironically, tari kursus's success, in terms of the way in which its basic choreographic structures provided a base upon which other kinds of tari klasik could be built, may be a reason for its waning influence in contemporary Sundanese dance. Even though the fixed choreographies of modern classical dance still reference tayuban dancing, the references are increasingly obscure. One consequence of the growing distance between tari klasik and its participational antecedents, and the concomitant lessening of a feeling of authentic Sundaneseness that congruent dance forms enjoy, is an interest in finding ways to restore that traditional flavor to tari klasik, particularly by attempting to update tayuban in various ways. One approach is to host a tayuban revival. For many years, the Prabu Geusan Ulun Museum in Sumedang sponsored such an event monthly. The museum's own gamelan club provided the music, and interested dancers from the surrounding community attended. Alcohol was strictly forbidden at these events, but other protocols of tayuban were preserved. Those in charge of the event nominated dancers one by one by presenting them with a keris and dance scarf, and the dancer chose a piece. At these events, the ronggeng all but disappeared—replaced by pasinden or "fake" ronggeng, who do not sing and are clearly playing a role. The protocols became the main point of the event, a theatrical frame for presentational dance. Many of the dancers, however, performed a set tari klasik dance that they had studied; some dancers even chose to perform penca silat or jaipongan.[11]

Another approach is staged tayuban. I was intrigued when I saw the designation "Tari Tayuban" on a printed program for a performance I attended at the Centre Culturel Français (CCF) in Bandung on April 8, 1999.[12] The blurb in the printed program read: "In the past tayuban was the social dance of the aristocratic class held in the open porch of the regent's palace. This dance was usually danced while drunk, to eliminate the feeling of malu while dancing with ronggeng."[13] My expectation, therefore, was that we would see a demonstration of the "invented genre" that has come to be called tari tayub. Instead, the troupe presented a brief "dramatization" of a tayuban event.

The performance opened with a gamelan onstage playing "Jipang Kraton," a conventional opening piece for a tayuban (Sedyawati, Parani, and Proyek Pengkajian dan Pembinaan Nilai-Nilai Budaya (Indonesia) 1995:602). A pasinden, dressed in clothes appropriate for a modern pasinden, was sitting next to a second female performer, who was wearing a much more elaborate costume, with flowers and metal ornaments in her hair. She was clearly meant to be the ronggeng. Also onstage were two men dressed in traditional clothing, one at stage right, sitting in a chair and already wearing a dance scarf, and another at stage left, sitting on the floor. The men's costumes were relatively unadorned and not exceptionally stagey, but the dancers did sport painted-on facial hair.

A third male dancer entered, dancing vigorously and carrying a *baki* (tray) with a dance scarf and keris on it to the accompaniment of the piece "Gendu." Each of the men on the sides of the stage made it clear through his mimed movements that he would like the tray to be given to him. The dancer with the tray approached each in turn and pretended he was going to offer the tray, but he jerked it away at the last moment. Finally he danced off the stage and down into the audience, walked to the rear of the hall, and presented the tray to a fourth male dancer, who was back there waiting. These two returned to the stage, where the fourth man donned the keris (inserting it into his belt) and dance scarf (draping it over the keris). One of the men who had been passed over asked in a loud stage whisper, "What piece will he choose?" The chosen dancer emphatically requested "Waled, dua wilet," indicating the piece "Waled" to be played in the metric/rhythmic treatment *dua wilet*. The other dancers murmured among themselves and acted as if they were impressed by his choice.

CHAPTER FIVE

The chosen man's dancing was spectacular. He performed tricky kicks and throws with his scarf, always on the goong stroke. After a bit of dancing, he squatted in front of the ronggeng and invited her to dance. She got up and began very simple movements, stepping and moving her hands in a movement called *lontang*. At some goong strokes, the chosen dancer approached her, but she snapped her dance scarf at him to drive him away. For other goong cadences, she allowed him to get near her, and they moved their faces close together, their motions culminating in a sudden jerk on the accented beat just before the goong stroke.

Each of the remaining male dancers, in turn, asked for permission to take over by pointing his thumbs up. Each male dancer did his own version of the same sorts of movements, each with slightly different styles and tricks. The finale involved all four male dancers joining together and dancing in unison around the ronggeng, who added some very slow and prominent goyang to the spectacle. This section involved considerable *bloking*—predetermined formations and coordinated changes in direction. When the gamelan piece ended, the male dancers loitered at the side of the stage while the ronggeng carried her little tray around to extract a bit of money from each of the four men, one by one. Finally she left the stage. To conclude, the men performed a *sembah* to the audience and filed out of the hall.

Although it was a presentational, staged performance, "Tari Tayuban" showed evidence of an effort to represent a complete erotic triangle. The piece clearly is an attempt to do more than simply present tari tayub extricated from any context: it distilled and dramatized the entire tayuban protocol into a ten-minute piece. Despite its having been staged, the choreographer used several strategies to recover some the flavor of a genuine dance event. Right at the outset, the ordinary boundary between the stage and the audience was broken when the tray-carrying dancer dramatically breached it by descending from the stage and retrieving another dancer from the back of the hall. Passing through the audience, in effect, nominated all those viewing as participants—maybe even as dancers. To distance their dancing from tari kursus, the men's choreography scrupulously avoided most of the emblematic gestures of tari kursus, as well as its characteristic movement order. The melodramatic tone the first chosen dancer affected when requesting his music drew attention to the use of the metric/rhythmic treatment dua wilet, which is not characteristic of tari kursus but was associated with tayuban dancing. To minimize the negative connotations of ronggeng, the roles of singer and dancer were bifurcated, and there was a clear contrast in terms of costume and behavior between the female dancer (who did not sing) and the pasinden (who did not dance). Seating them together at the beginning of the piece, however, allowed viewers to conflate the two individuals and their roles into a single persona. This theatricalized tayuban appeared to reinstate many of the elements—the ronggeng, the freedom to choose movements and songs, and the competition and camaraderie among the male guests—that were eliminated from tari kursus in its journey from dance events to the stage. In many cases, however, these elements were simulated.

Although there was an illusion of freedom on the part of the male performers, the dance obviously was not improvised or free—a fact driven home by the finale, in which the men danced in unison. The audience was reminded that despite the thrilling and acrobatic solo dancing they had seen the individual men perform moments before, the dancers were professionals, not amateurs, and were subject to the choreographer's will. If there was any doubt that this piece was a presentational one meant to be viewed, the last section erased it. Ironically, the element of freedom is precisely what is exaggerated in tari kursus dances.

Although tari kursus explicitly eliminates ronggeng, this staged tari tayuban restored them. The erotic quality of the interaction between the male dancers and the ronggeng, however, is feigned. Their relationship was between two professional actors playing roles. Once again, the cherished freedom—in this case, to behave badly in the presence of a ronggeng—was exposed as illusion. The male dancers' simulated desire for the ronggeng makes uncomfortably visible the imitative nature of sexual desire.

Tari kursus marks an important point of transition between wholly participatory and wholly presentational dances in West Java. Its origins lie in attempts to *teach* improvisation skills in the early twentieth century—skills that individual men developed on their own without instruction until the advent of tari kursus. As the century progressed, tari kursus dances became more and more fixed, leaving less and less room for personal expression; yet the genre continued to rely on a perceived connection with men's improvisational dance for its impact. In triangular terms, as long as tari kursus dances were perceived as congruent with tayuban dancing, observers were able to make the connection regardless of how free the performers actually were, and the fixed tari kursus dances still could impart a sense of authentic Sundaneseness.

The net result of these changes, which I have represented as subtle deformations of otherwise congruent dance triangles, was a gradual disassociation of tari klasik with men's improvisational dance and with the sense of authentic Sundaneseness it references, and a concomitant

CHAPTER FIVE

reassociation of dancing with femininity rather than masculinity in tari kursus. Dance pieces such as the choreographed "Tari Tayuban" represent attempts to restore, or at least make reference to, the traditional values of Sundanese masculinity to classical dance by reinscribing the elements of the erotic triangle back onto it.

With regard to the evocations of the erotic triangle of Sundanese dance and its desirable Sundaneseness even as it accommodates changing values about power and gender identities and relationships, different strategies achieve different results. It is probably safe to say that some are more successful than others, but it is difficult to determine exactly what constitutes success. Jaipongan and tari kursus both have thrived in their own ways in modern West Java, but they have succeeded in accomplishing different goals. Jaipongan slips facilely between participatory and presentational contexts, allowing its fans to entertain old-fashioned Sundanese attitudes about gender identities and masculine power even as they are changing in modern Indonesia. Tari kursus's firm ensconcement as the foundation of presentational stage dance, in contrast, has diminished its ability to explore the values that Sundanese traditionally associate with men's social dancing.

Erotic Triangles

One thing is certain: any claims for tari kursus's authentic Sundaneseness inhere in its derivation from an erotic triangle of Sundanese dance. Tari kursus's aesthetic clout derives from its appropriation of the protocols that encode masculine power and status in dance. The example of tari kursus demonstrates just how powerful the erotic triangle can be for understanding how Sundanese gender ideology underlies broader issues of power. The following discussion explores how erotic triangles facilitate ideologies of gender and power, and how they might shed light on dance and gender in contemporary West Java.

Erotic triangles represent a structuralist approach to thinking about gender ideologies. Structuralist models are theoretical approaches that look for fundamental, fixed patterns of thought and behavior that manifest in the details of beliefs and values. One of the strengths of structuralist thinking is its ability to build representations of the complexity of human experience from starkly basic binary oppositions. The triangle is an arch-structuralist form in that it relies on the introduction of a third term to provide the crucial means for mitigating the differences between any two irreconcilable opposites, and for incrementally weaving individual binary contrasts into a multidimensional web of meaning.

In her influential book *Between Men*, Eve Kosofsky Sedgwick uses erotic triangles to interpret how the European literary canon writes gender and sexuality, and specifically the bonds between men, to consolidate patriarchal power. She justifies her use of the triangle as a graphic schema in her readings with the observation that triangles are a commonsense and time-tested schema for erotic relations (Sedgwick 1985:21). Sedgwick begins by introducing the notion of male homosocial desire, by which she means a variety of social relationships (possibly including, but not limited to, erotic relationships) between men (following Lévi-Strauss 1967:44) who are jockeying for power within a patriarchal system. At their roots, social institutions and conventions involve exchanges of women to establish bonds between men and ultimately are in service of this homosocial desire. As Sedgwick puts it, "This bonding, if successfully achieved, is not detrimental to 'masculinity' but definitive of it" (Sedgwick 1985:50).

Sedgwick bases her notion of erotic triangles on René Girard's model of power as structured by a relation of rivalry between the two active members of a love triangle. Girard's basic premise is that human desires are not innate, but mimetic—individuals mimic the desires they see in "mediators" (role models whom they wish to be like, and whose power they wish to share in or appropriate). Thus, relationships involving desire are basically triangular; one element is the subject, another is the object of desire, and the third is this "mediator"—the role model for the desire.

In Girard's formulation of triangular desire, a role model puts the desires into the subject's head. According to Sedgwick and to Girard as well, in an erotic triangle, the subject should model his desire after the mediator/role model/rival's desire. In Girard's interpretation of *Don Quixote*, for example, Sancho Panza's desire for political power and a beautiful wife "do not come spontaneously to a man like Sancho. It is Don Quixote who has put them in his head" (*Deceit*, p. 3, quoted in Golsan 1993:3). In an application of Girard's model to Sundanese dance events, ronggeng play the "object of desire," the thing upon which the subject's desire to be like the role model is cathected as well as the thing that both the subject and the mediator/role model/rival desire. For Sundanese audiences, drumming plants desires for ronggeng, expressed as movements, in men's heads.

The drummer is the epitome of Javanese power in that he appears to be merely responding to the dancers' movements, yet he is in fact

CHAPTER FIVE

motivating their movements. Even when he is ostensibly following a dancer, he has the power (exercised or not) to influence and change the course of everybody's movement. Yet, his drumming has no corporeal presence—the drummer's power is disembodied and emerges as sound. Thus the drummer represents a true mediator in the Girardian sense—the drumming represents the power that Sundanese men want to gain.

In the triangular relationship, causes and effects are reversed: the ostensible cause of desire is the object and the ostensive effect is rivalry, but the actual cause is rivalry and the effect is desire for the object. The triangular relationship represents a negotiation of power between the subject and the mediator. The negotiation is masked, however, as desire for a third term—the object. The subject denies the importance of the mediator and believes that desire for the object arises autonomously, from within (Golsan 1993:1–8).[14] In Sedgwick's erotic triangles, the subject and mediator typically are male, while the object is female. In effect, erotic desire on the part of a masculine subject for a feminine object is an artifact of negotiating homosocial relationships. Desire for the female object masks the true purpose of the relationships; the "object" of desire is a necessary decoy in the negotiations of status and power between men.

So the male dancers set out to imitate the drumming. Devoid of any means of producing sounds, their only means of expressing the power the drum sounds produce is to dance. Because the ideal is to wield power without moving, however, their project is fraught with a contradiction from the start. The only path to domination for the men lies in wresting control from the drummer. The negotiation between the men and the drummer, then, takes the form of trading off leading and following. "Free" dancing on the part of the men has the hidden agenda of leading the drumming—forcing it to follow—without overtly seizing control. "Fixed" choreographies—pola—have the hidden agenda of leading the dancers, forcing them to follow, while providing them the illusion of freedom (in that they may choose whatever dance movements they want, as long as they fit the drumming). The aesthetic values of free dancing and fixed dancing, and the ambiguities between them as dancers and drummer spar over control, are based in this negotiation for power.

Ronggeng, too, manifest free and fixed elements in their performance. As we have seen, an important aesthetic value for ronggeng performance is the simultaneous presentation of dancing and singing. When she dances, a ronggeng follows her male partners (in some people's view, she "serves" him with her dancing) and, by extension, the drumming. When she sings, however, she resists the constrictions not only of the drum patterns, but even of the regular pulse and meter of the accompanying

THE EROTIC TRIANGLE OF SUNDANESE DANCE

music. She chooses texts that relate to the unique circumstances of the moment and provide free commentary on the proceedings. Her singing remains unmetered, spilling provocatively over the edges of the rhythmic structures set out by drumming.

Erotic triangles depend, then, upon the idea that societies are patriarchal and engage in the "traffic of women."[15] The implication is that the whole system of culture—the fundamental economy of power—is predicated on the identification of a subgroup of people (women) as the objects of desire for another, more powerful group (men). The model neglects, obviously, the agency of the women who appear to be mere "objects of desire" and their considerable power to influence the processes and outcomes of the erotic triangles of which they are an integral part. Nevertheless, erotic triangles provide a powerful tool for understanding at least the male-to-male relationships and the role of their desires in establishing and manipulating power. In sum, erotic triangles model desire and gender division in the service of power and status.

Aesthetics and Erotic Triangles

One way to characterize the process of naturalization that I have outlined in previous sections is to say that participants in dance events perform gender and desire into existence. This kind of gender performativity, as theorized by Judith Butler, is not the same as "performance" as it is usually understood. In her view, the heterosexual matrix constantly reproduces itself because the individual acts that constitute it are "ritualized production, a ritual reiterated under and through constraint, under and through the force of prohibition and taboo, with the threat of ostracism and even death controlling and compelling the shape of the production but not, I will insist, determining it fully in advance" (Butler 1993:95).

In Butler's usage, performativity suggests absorption; the effect of iteration is to erase conscious intent from the repeated acts. In contrast, in the theatrical sense, performativity suggests acute self-consciousness and intentionality (Parker and Sedgwick 1995). If we consider performance as a means for redirecting intent rather than erasing it, however, these two meanings of performativity converge. In other words, dance events enact triangular transactions in service of "performing" (in the Butlerian sense) gender identities. The participants, however, direct their conscious intentions toward "performing" (in the theatrical sense) according to certain aesthetic values. The performance of gender is recast as aesthetic engagement with the symbolic materials of the dance events. Like myth, aesthetic engagement involves, using Barthes's terms, a dissociation of

165

CHAPTER FIVE

form and content; the kinds of transactions—the protocols, gestures, and interactions—that remain when form and content are dissociated become the materials to which aesthetic values are assigned.

Pierre Bourdieu's thoughts about ideology (which he brands "symbolic violence") further clarify the aesthetics of Sundanese dance performances. Bourdieu begins with the idea that symbolic systems are based on distinctions, such as those "between high (sublime, elevated, pure) and low (vulgar, low, modest), spiritual and material, fine (refined, elegant) and coarse (heavy, fat, crude, brutal), light (subtle, lively, sharp, adroit) and heavy (slow, thick, blunt, laborious, clumsy), free and forced, broad and narrow" (Bourdieu 1984:468).

By assigning greater value to one term of each pair, all of these pairs ultimately reduce to an opposition of dominant versus dominated. Although this formulation is radically reductionist, it provides for Bourdieu a starting point for arguing that all cultural interactions are sites in which individuals position themselves in relation to other participants. Although Bourdieu characterizes each individual's understanding of the values and the ways to manipulate them to his or her own best advantage as "strategies" (Bourdieu calls this understanding and deployment habitus), he also understands distinctions to be made at a subconscious level; valuation of one term over the other is experienced consciously as a judgment of "taste," effectively dissociating value judgments from their underlying political meanings and transforming content into form. Freud expresses similar ideas about the relationship between aesthetic values and constructions of reality when he writes, "One thing only do I know for certain and that is that man's judgements of value follow directly his wishes for happiness—that, accordingly, they are an attempt to support his illusions with arguments" (Freud 1961:92).

In the sense that it implies that an aesthetic engagement involves a dissociation of form and content, Bourdieu's approach is not too different from more established philosophies of aesthetics, which hold that an aesthetic engagement with an object involves an immediate enjoyment of an object "for itself," for its interaction with the senses, separated for the moment from any practical meaning. Aesthetic engagement also involves some kind of contemplation and critical judgment, imbuing the object with some level of significance and value separate from its original meaning. When making an aesthetic judgment, the beholder evaluates the form of what is perceived, often neglecting its literal content. Signification and valuation follow but are not necessarily identical to the form's "original" content. Aesthetic valuation, like myth signifiers, privileges form over meaning—it is perceived as form for form's sake. Bourdieu

THE EROTIC TRIANGLE OF SUNDANESE DANCE

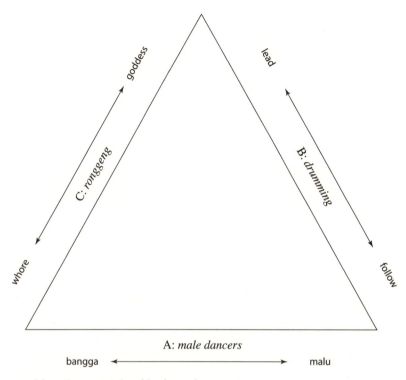

A: *male dancers*

bangga ⟵⟶ malu

5.2   Schematic representation of Sundanese dance events.

would characterize this change in meaning as "misrecognition"—an unconscious denial of a practice's political or economic implications (Swartz 1997:43). At some level, however, the original signification must remain; the form is emptied of, but still refers to, its original signification, "misrecognized" as an aesthetic value.

Each of the three elements of the Sundanese dance triangle—drumming, ronggeng, and free dancing—indexes a rich historicity that encompasses the qualities and characteristics each element has come to signify as well as the irreconcilable contradiction it seeks to resolve. Participants in the events, however, forget the contradictions and concentrate on performing aesthetic forms. The three constituent elements of dance events, as well as the entire event itself, serve as "meanings" and as "forms" (in the Barthesian mythological sense). The diagram in figure 5.2 lays out the three components schematically. At the core is the triangle, formed by three sides: ronggeng, drummer, and male dancers. Parallel to each side is an indication of the binary opposition that each side addresses.

CHAPTER FIVE

The protocols of dance events provide the means for each of these participants simultaneously to explore the extremes of a binary contrast. The other elements provide mediation for each side's contradictions—excuses or motivations to justify acting in contradictory ways. Participants perform these ideologies in the Austinian/Butlerian sense—the actions they perform constitute the things they purport to be, but the participants' intentions are to behave the way their "natures" predispose them to act. As outlined previously, the ronggeng is, all at once, a representation of the rice goddess, a vision of ideal femininity (visual appeal and the promise of sexual availability), and a caricature of all that is undesirable in women (unbridled passion and greed). Dancing with her male partners while singing is a means quite literally to perform these contradictions—to be all of them at once. The discussion of drumming suggested that there is an inherent ambiguity with regard to how much drummers lead and how much they follow the dancing in dance events, modeling an approach to authority in which control is asserted by masking conformity to hegemonic values as freedom. And finally, the male dancers, by simultaneously seeming to submit to and to lead the drumming, as well as by engaging with the ronggeng's sacred and profane sides, dance the line between the contradictory qualities of malu and boldness/bangga (shame and pride/bravado) that are expected of them.

Dance-Event Geometry

In Euclidian geometry, the intersection of two sides creates an angle, and the angles formed by the three sides of a triangle have a variety of interesting and useful properties. This triangular model for dance events suggests ways to analyze the aesthetic values of men's improvisational dance. For example, each of the triangle's three angles can be characterized by considering what the two sides forming the angle have in common. In this I consider first Charles Seeger's model for communication. In his classic essay "Speech, Music, and Speech about Music" (1977:16–30), Seeger presents a three-part model for the raw materials of human communication (i.e., the senses)—tactile (subsuming taste, smell, and touch into a single category), auditory, and visual—and suggests that these three senses are interdependent: "The central, curve-sided triangle formed by the overlapping of the three circles represents the primordial biological function of the brain, upon which the mystical conception of the human 'mind' has ultimately been erected" (Seeger 1977:21). The "curve-sided triangle"

THE EROTIC TRIANGLE OF SUNDANESE DANCE

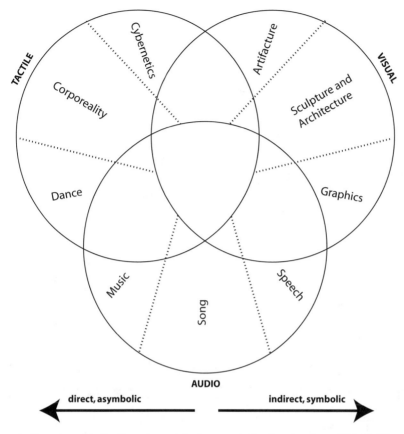

5.3   Seeger's model of tactile, audio, and visual communication (based on Seeger 1977:21–24).

to which Seeger refers can be seen in the center of figure 5.3, which also illustrates his notion of nine "systems of communications" that employ different combinations of sensory media, as well as his generalization that all communication can be characterized as belonging somewhere on a parametric continuum between direct, asymbolic communication and indirect, symbolic communication.

Seeing how speech morphs into song, then into (nonvocal) music, dance, corporeality (sexual intercourse and fisticuffs), and so on, under the rubric of how they involve the three kinds of sensory input and output, provides an illuminating perspective on the similarities among the nine systems of communications that Seeger identifies. All the participants in dance events, of course, are at both the sending and the receiving

169

CHAPTER FIVE

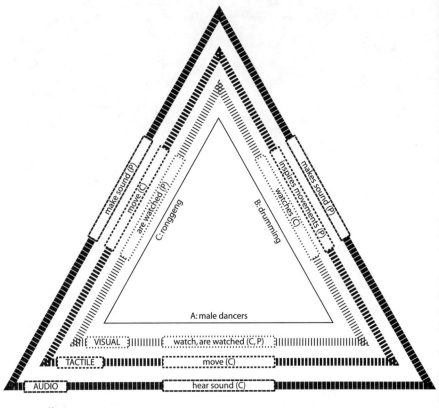

5.4   Tactile, audio, and visual elements in the dance-event triangle.

ends of all three senses. We can begin to analyze the gender implications of dance events and the aesthetic values that mask them by assessing how each side of the dance-event triangle engages with each of the senses.

Figure 5.4 annotates the dance-event triangle with an indication of whether each side is primarily a producer or a consumer of messages in Seeger's tactile, audio, and visual sensory modes. As discussed in chapter 3, ronggeng are producers of visual messages—one of their chief functions is to be watched—while male dancers and drummers consume visual messages (male dancers watch the ronggeng, drummers attend to the dancers). A drummer's chief function is to inspire movement (although it is not always clear whether sounds cause movements or vice versa, as noted in chapter 2). Drumming thus represents cybernetic audio messages. Both ronggeng and male dancers consume these messages, inducing a tactile or, more accurately, a proprioceptive response—dancing. Finally, both ronggeng and drummers make sounds, while male dancers are primarily consumers of sounds. In figure 5.4, each sense occupies a band of different shading around the triangle; each triangle side's primary engagement with that sense and whether the side produces (marked with a "P") or consumes (marked with a "C") that sense are indicated in the appropriate band.

This diagram suggests that each side has a functional profile (with regard to which senses it emphasizes) that complements the other sides and stabilizes the triangular form. Because they are watched by all the others, ronggeng need above all to be seen; in other words, their visual appeal is perhaps their primary function. To integrate fully into the triangle, however, ronggeng also make sound (i.e., they are singers) and make movement (i.e., they are dancers), forming "angles" with the other sides. The aesthetic values of ronggeng performance—singing and dancing at the same time—emerge from this triangular model.

Based on this model, drumming needs, above all, to be effective at inspiring movement. To accomplish this, drummers need to make sound (i.e., play the drums) and to watch (i.e., accompany dancing). Male dancers have as their main purpose the translation of the sights, sounds, and inspirations they perceive into dance movements. Again, these are the aesthetic values for these roles as described in earlier chapters.

Aesthetic "Teams"

Other patterns fall out from this analytical approach as well. For one thing, the three sides group into various two-member "teams" according to how they engage with a particular sense, leaving the third member in each sensory configuration standing alone. Ronggeng and drummers, for example, both make sounds—they are musicians—leaving the male dancers as the lone silent participants. The second "team" comprises ronggeng and male dancers, who both dance, animated by the playing of the drummer, who remains still. Drummers and male dancers form another "team" in that they both watch, leaving ronggeng to be watched. These "teams," portrayed graphically in figure 5.5, are evocative of other cultural values.

PROFESSIONAL VERSUS AMATEUR: SUBJECTIVITY   Chapter 3 established drummers and ronggeng as the professional participants in the erotic triangle of Sundanese dance. They submerge their own subjectivities to produce

CHAPTER FIVE

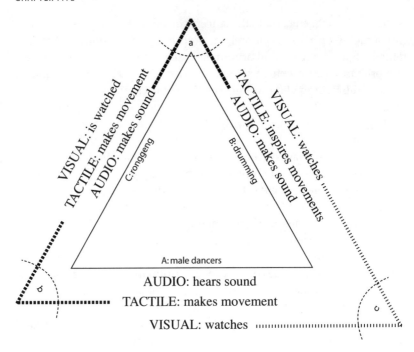

5.5 Dance-event triangle's aesthetic teams.

important components upon which dance-event protocols depend: drumming and the ronggeng image, respectively. Together, these two professional sides of the triangle stand opposed to the amateur male dancers in that they are the "producers" of sensory stimuli (in fig. 5.4, male dancers are "consumers" for all three sensory modes and produce in only one mode). Ronggeng inspire the men with their appearance. Drummers inspire them with their representation of power. Both ronggeng and drummers reinforce their roles as producers by creating a soundscape that marks out a place in which dancers can experience a different reality. In dance-event protocols, participants who might be called "professional," as opposed to the "amateur" male dancers, typically assume these two roles.

Changing this distinction between professional and amateur in dance events—deforming the triangle, in a sense—affects the outcome. As I will describe in chapter 6, putting "professional" male dancers in the roles customarily filled by amateurs leaves audiences who are accustomed to the triangular model unsure of their subject position. The artifice becomes apparent. The resulting confusion, however, is experienced as an aesthetic judgment—the performance may be received as uninteresting and lacking in artistic merit.

STILL VERSUS MOVING: POWER   Ronggeng and dancers join together in movement, while drummers are restricted in their movement; their primary function is to make sound. At some level, then, drummers represent a disembodied impulse, a divine or at least spiritual force that animates human bodies and gives them life, and the drumming they produce operates as a metaphor for power, as discussed in chapter 2. Drumming coaxes dancers to move and reacts to their individual movement styles (recalling, too, Seeger's definition of "cybernetics"; see fig. 5.3). Drummers command by making audible the conventions that guide normative dance behavior. Their conventional drum patterns demand conventional responses, yet dancers perceive their movements to be freely performed.

In the triangular model, drummer and ronggeng share a divine nature. The drummer wields cosmic power, and the ronggeng's associations with the rice goddess establish her divine nature. Ordinary men seek to accumulate this power, made audible in drumming, in their desire for the ronggeng. The defining characteristic of the drumming is its physical stillness—it is pure sound—which, of course, the men cannot imitate because the only medium they have available is movement. Their quest for stillness—for perfect refinement—is doomed from the start; but because of the aesthetic mask of ambiguity between leading and following, dancers can imagine themselves and their movements as the source of the power rather than a mere imitation of it.

In a different interpretation, drumming and ronggeng might be likened to a god and his consort. In tantric thought, gender differences are a manifestation of the god's desire for Sakti. In other words, on a philosophical level, it is the manifestation of creative energy in movement that differentiates the genders on Earth. Although this heavenly genderlessness seems at odds with the Sundanese worldview, it is a part of the cosmology of wayang golek (rod puppet theater) and thus not completely forgotten. The wayang clown figure Semar, a fallen divinity who is thought to be the oldest being in the universe, for example, is half male and half female (Foley 1990b:10). Anderson stresses that the successful reconciliation of opposites is a sign of power and interprets aesthetic objects that simultaneously incorporate maleness and femaleness as representing power (Anderson 1972:14–15).

A bit of wayang narration by the dalang Asep Sunandar Sunarya (as translated by Andrew Weintraub) further illustrates the point: "The situation in Heaven is different from Earth, meaning that on Earth, everything

CHAPTER FIVE

is clearly defined: day-night; dry season–wet season; darkness-lightness; falsehood-truth; female and male" (Sunarya 1998:54). In heaven, then, gender differentiations are unclear. On Earth, existence is clearly split into two different ways of being. These ways of being are gendered: the active energy is feminine, while the passive consciousness is masculine. A combination of the two—a passive, but powerful, consciousness—is at the heart of refined behavior.

The aesthetic ideal of ambiguity between leading and following enables drumming to represent these complex ideas of power and its accumulation. By animating the participants, drumming represents power. The drum sounds' sonic palpability translates abstract power into the realm of the sensual. The ambiguity of leading and following enables participants to imagine that their movements are causing the drumming; thus, participants also can imagine that they are capable of owning the power that drumming represents.

MALE VERSUS FEMALE: GENDER   The preceding discussion presented the drumming as representing power—a genderless force that somehow splits into male and female. It is the third aesthetic team that completes the engendering process. The third team sets drumming and male dancers—the watchers—against ronggeng, who are the watched. This team serves to delineate gender differences between male and female. The bifurcation between male and female is predicated on the notion that drumming is an exclusively male activity, which in West Java is indeed the case.

Characterizing drumming as an exclusively male activity requires some explanation. Historically and ideologically, among Sundanese, playing musical instruments has been primarily a male activity (Williams 1998a:78; Williams 1998b:720; Zanten 1989:47). This is not to say that there are no female instrumentalists in West Java. The most commonly cited exception is Ibu Haji Siti Rokayah, who played kacapi and suling on the radio and for recordings and composed a number of songs of enduring popularity (e.g., "Reumbeuy Bandung" and "Jeruk Manis"). The public was acutely aware that Ibu Haji was a woman but took her work seriously because it met certain standards (Otong Rasta, personal communication, January 22, 1999). Shelly Errington postulates that in general, island Southeast Asians hold that it is the activities that men and women do, rather than the biological differences between them, that determine who becomes prominent and powerful. A woman who has become good at male activities "has not broken the rules but beaten the odds" (Errington 1990:40, 55). The sight of women playing musical instruments, especially degung instruments, has become common

THE EROTIC TRIANGLE OF SUNDANESE DANCE

in recent years. Sean Williams attributes this development to a changing perception with regard to degung music "from the concept of a restricted, difficult, male-only ensemble to a popular, easy, mostly female-oriented one" (Williams 1998b:706). Swindells recounts how *gamelan ibu-ibu* (all-female gamelan) rose to popularity between the 1950s and 1970s in part because of the visual appeal of one of the first such groups, Cahaya Medal (also known as "gamelan mojang" [young women's gamelan]) (Swindells 2004:31–32).

Despite the inroads made by female musicians into the formerly all-male bastions of instrument playing, virtually no Sundanese women play kendang in public. Heins stipulates that even in all-female gamelan, "suling and modern drum style are still not generally performed by women" because it is considered "improper" (Heins 1977:66–67). Of all musical activities, Sundanese appear to consider drumming to be the most exclusively masculine. Otong Rasta insists that there are a number of practical and physiological reasons why women simply cannot play kendang. For one thing, drummers must sit cross-legged on the floor with their feet apart, a position precluded by clothing and etiquette; this point is also mentioned by Heins (1977:67). There are ways to overcome this problem when females play other instruments, but Otong considers it insurmountable in the case of kendang. Furthermore, he says, women do not have the upper-body strength and endurance required for an evening of drumming for dance or wayang (personal communication, January 22, 1999). Tosin Mochtar also told me that drumming is difficult for women (personal communication, March 12, 1999). Rachel Swindells reports that when she sought instruction from Sundanese drummers, she was "repeatedly told that women are not physically strong enough to strike the kendang with sufficient force" (Swindells 2004:33).

One Sundanese observer essentialized the masculinity of drumming in a brilliant pun that comments on an American woman's performance of drumming: "no pak, only bu." The consensus was that her drumming was weak and hard for the dancer to follow, and that it did not provide the excitement and support that drumming is supposed to provide (though these criticisms could just as easily be applied to a male drummer). In the comment, all of the desirable qualities for drumming were essentialized into one onomatopoeic word for a drum sound—the crisp and commanding "pak" sound made by slapping the drum with strength and precise technique, resulting in a sharp attack and quick decay. In Indonesian and Sundanese languages, "Pak" is an honorific for respected men (short for *bapak*), approximately equivalent to the English "mister" or "sir." Instead, the female drummer could only produce a weak,

CHAPTER FIVE

amorphous, low sound—"bu." "Bu" is, of course, the parallel honorific for women (short for *ibu*). The pun relies on the inherent connection between the essence of drum sounds and the gender identities of their producers.

Heins speculates that such physical arguments are dissembling. Women avoid the appearance of having music skill for purely social reasons: "Being publicly proficient in music would cause embarrassment to less skilfull [*sic*] men. Connected with this is a certain reluctance to expose oneself in a traditionally male role; this is considered unwomanly behaviour" (Heins 1977:67). Williams hypothesizes that women's primary role onstage is as a mediator between onstage performers and the audience; she concludes that female performers, when performing as instrumentalists, "appear to abdicate their potential to develop good musicianship in the name of social balance" (Williams 1998a:79). Whether this lack is characterized as a constitutional inability to play drums, a social proscription, or a diplomatic choice, it is clear that drumming and femininity are mutually exclusive, while drumming and masculinity are somehow synonymous. The essential maleness of drumming is part of any aesthetic valuation of drumming, resulting in an unassailable myth that drumming is an exclusively male activity.

The masculinity of drumming is an important component in setting up an aesthetic basis for constructing a bifurcation between male and female in dance events. A female kendang player would wreak serious havoc on the model outlined above. Sundanese women have stepped into quite a few formerly male-dominated roles in the arts over the past decades, successfully challenging the status quo with regard to what men and women can and should do. They have not, however, challenged the fundamental difference between male and female. Female drummers, on the other hand, would challenge this notion. The resistance on the part of Sundanese women to playing kendang, and on the part of Sundanese in general to allow it as a possibility, supports this hypothesis.

Unlike the other two aesthetic teams, which I noted are sometimes broken up in modern music and dance innovations, this fundamental male/female dichotomy is rarely altered. Although the other tenets of gender ideology, masked as aesthetic values, have been challenged, the inherent maleness of drumming has not been breached.

Dance Events as Erotic Triangles

Dance events are erotic triangles that inscribe and reinforce the heterosexual matrix by naturalizing the fundamental division of humans into two genders, one of which controls the bulk of power. By engendering drums as masculine and exoticizing the cathected object of desire (ronggeng) as feminine, male participants dance this gender ideology, along with its contradictions, into perpetuity. By singing and dancing, ronggeng model the negotiations characterized by leading and following, on the one hand, and free and fixed dancing, on the other. The negotiations between the men and the drumming are masked as desire for the ronggeng. Men dance a line between conformity and independence by imitating in movement the sounds of the drums, while imagining that they are moving freely and controlling the drums. Observers witness and affirm the proceedings, internalizing and naturalizing these gender identities for themselves.

I have considered a variety of theoretical approaches to understanding the power of the individual elements ("sides"), teams ("angles"), and the totality of the model ("erotic triangle") of Sundanese dancing and dance events that I have developed in this chapter. Structuralist models clearly have contributed a great deal to my formulations. The apparent universality of comparable myths among many different human populations, including the Sundanese Sangkuriang story, lends additional credibility to structuralist approaches. Yet structuralist models have been subjected to considerable—and hardly unwarranted—criticism in recent decades. Although structures that determine values and behaviors may appear to unify societies' solutions to many different problems, indeed they also tend to reject the agency of individuals, the uniqueness of historical moments, and the trajectories of cultural change. On a more particular level, variations in the details—who does what to whom—of the so-called universal Oedipus myth dilute any claims of universality for Freud's, Lacan's, and Lévi-Strauss's interpretations.

Barthes's *Mythologies* is, at heart, a structuralist account of the mechanisms of myth and ideology. However, Barthes acknowledges that the apparent ahistoricality of structures is the result of an ongoing process of accruing and changing signification. His clear explanation of how myth and ideology accrue meaning over time points toward his later deconstructionist approaches and allows for changes. As discussed in chapter 1, William H. Sewell views structures as comprising generalizable procedures (schemas) and individuals' unique outcomes (resources). Sewell considers the agency of individuals in transposing and applying structures to meet their own needs and to produce new kinds of resources, which in turn can account for modifying the structures that helped to generate them. Structures, then, do not simply determine behavior, but

CHAPTER FIVE

rather "empower and constrain social action and . . . tend to be reproduced by that social action" (1992:19).

In Judith Butler's formulations, the mechanisms that seem to guide the behavior of individuals are not perpetual, preexisting structures, but rather arbitrary acts that are repeated to take on the appearance of a natural, eternal core identity. The rules are not fixed, but continuously and actively constructed through performance and discourse. Bourdieu's concepts of doxa, field, and habitus provide a nuanced poststructuralist approach to theorizing the actors, mechanisms, and conventions of social phenomena such as Sundanese dance and dance events. According to Bourdieu, individuals' actions are informed by deep-seated beliefs—doxa—that individuals regard as self-evident, such as gender identities. Doxa are akin to what structuralists might characterize as structures, what Barthes calls myth and ideology, and what Butler dubs the heterosexual matrix. Doxa influence the conventional rules that govern any social setting in which people interact, which Bourdieu dubs a field. Fields also are shaped by each individual participant's unique habitus—a personal disposition toward a field's rules as well as strategies for coping with them, acquired through a lifetime of experience. Judith Becker extends this notion to articulate a habitus of listening that predisposes individuals to listen and engage with musical stimuli in particular, predictable ways.

Richard Dawkins famously applied the biological notion of a replicating entity (in biology, a DNA molecule or gene) to human culture; he coined the term meme to apply to units of cultural transmission that "propagate themselves . . . by leaping from brain to brain via a process which, in the broad sense, can be called imitation" (Dawkins 2006 [1989]:192). Like genes, which vie with other genes for space in a given chromosome, memes compete for limited resources (space in the brains of their human hosts and representation in media). Like genes, which coadapt with other genes to form stable sets of physical characteristics defined by gene complexes, memes often cluster together to create meme complexes—stable, self-replicating sets of persistent ideas that resist change (Dawkins 2006 [1989]:199).

The erotic triangle of Sundanese dance can be viewed as a structure, a field, a meme cluster—or all of the above. As powerful as they might be, none of these disparate theoretical approaches could ever hope to provide a complete picture of Sundanese dance practice. And if postmodern approaches to culture, texts, and meaning have taught us anything, it is that a complete picture is both undesirable and impossible. Sedgwick emphasizes that the erotic triangle should be construed

> not as an ahistorical, Platonic form, a deadly symmetry from which the historical acci-
> dents of gender, language, class, and power detract, but as a sensitive register precisely
> for delineating relationships of power and meaning, and for making graphically intel-
> ligible the play of desire and identification by which individuals negotiate with their
> societies for empowerment. (SEDGWICK 1985:27)

In other words, the participants in an erotic triangle are not fated mindlessly to enact and reenact the same relationships over and over again. Rather, she argues, interpreting the terms of the relationships between the elements of a specific triangle provides insights into how these persistent myths are created, recreated, and even modified in particular times, places, and contexts. The changing picture of aristocratic Sundanese men's dancing, as illustrated through the examination of tayuban dancing, the invented genre tari tayub, and the presentational genre tari kurus, demonstrates just how the erotic triangle of Sundanese dance provides a flexible schema for exploring gender ideologies under changing circumstances.

My goal in bringing a variety of theories to bear on the erotic triangle of Sundanese dance is to make clear this flexibility. As the specific protocols of dance events change, the contradictions expressed by each side are mitigated and modified. In some cases, an element of the triangle is attenuated, as when female dancers are eliminated from tari kursus, or intensified, as when kursus intensifies the relationship between movement clusters and drum patterns. The power of the triangle lies precisely in how participants and audiences can still perceive the entire complex of myths, ideologies, assumptions, and power relationships that are indexed by even a partial instance of a dance triangle.

Sundanese dance events are replete with symbols and protocols that reference and enact aspects of ideology in rich ways. Many values are represented in ways that are overdetermined—they are redundantly articulated and reinforced in a variety of ways. The erotic triangle of Sundanese dance elucidated in the preceding chapters schematizes some of the ways that meaning and values are produced through dancing and presents the flexibility of dance events as sites for the production of culture. In other words, by citing the dance event, as modeled by the dance-event triangle, in various ways and guises, the event expresses a static meaning: how men as a group, as well as how individual men, with the complicity of women, imagine and create their power and status relationships with other men and, to a limited extent, with women. By changing, minimizing, or elaborating some of the protocols—that is, "deforming" the

CHAPTER FIVE

triangle by changing its sides and angles—nuances of that meaning can be explored and expressed, contested or affirmed, reified or changed. The next chapter will develop further a trigonometry for Sundanese dance events and apply it to several twentieth-century dance expressions in order to explore these continuities and changes.

SIX

Triangulating Sundanese Dance

Sundanese dance derives meaning from the relationships between three readily recognizable elements: ronggeng, drumming that animates male dancers, and a sense of freedom on the part of the dancers. These elements comprise three "sides" of an erotic triangle, each of which explores a cultural contradiction; when taken together, these model the twists and turns of Sundanese gender ideologies. Although I do not mean to suggest that this triangle is a real entity, I have demonstrated that considering Sundanese dance in relation to a variety of three-part theoretical models illuminates its cultural significance.

Congruent Triangles

Marshaling yet another body of tripartite theory to contribute to the analysis, in this chapter I will develop the notion that participants recognize an erotic triangle in Sundanese dance by applying a kind of dance-event trigonometry. In Euclidian plane geometry, two triangles are considered congruent if and only if all six of their elements—their three sides and three angles—are congruent. However, Euclid demonstrated that it is possible to prove that two triangles are congruent given only three congruent elements, provided they are the elements specified in the various triangle congruence theorems. These theorems are often represented with a shorthand notation in which a pair of congruent angles is

CHAPTER SIX

represented by the letter "A" and a pair of congruent sides by the letter "S." The congruence theorems are SSS, SAS, SAA (= AAS), and ASA. Thus, if all three of the corresponding sides of two triangles (SSS) are congruent, it can be proved that the three angles, too, are congruent. Similarly, if two sides and the angle they create between them (SAS) are congruent to the corresponding elements of another triangle, it can be proved that the remaining side and the other two angles also are congruent.

Although the elements I have characterized as the erotic triangle's sides readily emerge from an examination of a variety of Sundanese social dance traditions, establishing "angles" between them requires some more fanciful theorizing. The "aesthetic team" relationships described in chapter 5 (see fig. 5.6) provide one means for imagining the form angles between the dance triangle's sides might take. Each team has a different sensory engagement with the dance event—visual, aural, and tactile—and references a different ideological realm. I characterize each of the three metaphorical angles with an easily discernible stylistic feature that (1) involves the two sides in question (2) in the appropriate sensory mode that (3) somehow indexes the relevant ideological parameter.

Angle c is the angle between sides A and B (male dancers and drumming, respectively) and operates primarily in the visual register. Angle c is opposite side C (ronggeng), whose visual splendor is a significant part of her role. Angle c itself is the close coordination of movements with drumming, especially the perception that male dancers are moving in tandem with the drum patterns in a free, individual manner.[1]

Angle b is the angle between sides A and C (male dancers and ronggeng, respectively) and operates primarily in the tactile register. Angle b is opposite side B (drumming), who produces drumming that demands a tactile, embodied response—namely dancing—in both of the remaining sides. Angle b is the perception that there is physical contact between male and female participants.

Angle a is the angle between sides B and C (drumming and ronggeng, respectively) and operates primarily in the aural register. Angle a is opposite side A, which represents male dancers who respond with desire to two different aural cues—a provocative female voice (from the ronggeng) and animating drumming. These two aural cues have different approaches to rhythm; the free rhythm of female singer's vocal style contrasts sharply with the regular pulse and duple meter of the accompanying music and the drumming. Angle c, then, is the perception of this contrast between a free-moving female voice and the regular pulse of the instrumental accompaniment. Figure 6.1 summarizes the sides and angles of the dance-event triangle's geometry.

TRIANGULATING SUNDANESE DANCE

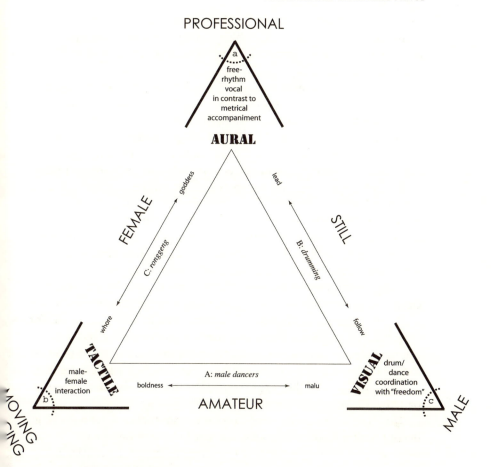

6.1 Dance-event triangle geometry.

The exercise of applying these theorems to cultural activities, of course, must be taken with an enormous grain of salt. I do not imagine that Euclid's demonstrations, as compelling as they are in their two-dimensional plane, can conclusively prove anything about the multidimensional universe of cultures and values. Although it is clear that references to some of the elements of what I have called the dance-event triangle can metonymically suggest a whole complex of values and customs to Sundanese audiences, it is untenable to suggest that a too-literal application of plane geometry to Sundanese dance can survive close scrutiny. Nevertheless, as I hope to demonstrate, this Euclidian approach does provide an enlightening framework for considering the mechanisms through which

CHAPTER SIX

dance expressions give an aesthetic form to cultural ideology and for examining the protocols through which dance events constitute a powerful and meaningful arena for participants to explore, affirm, and challenge normative values.

In the case of a dance expression, by "congruent" I mean that it is recognizable as an instance or a derivative of "traditional" men's dancing and thus triggers a host of associations, preconceptions, and mythologies in the minds of enculturated audiences and participants. A given side or an angle of a dance expression is congruent if it has the qualities I have described for the corresponding element of the dance triangle. It is not congruent if these qualities are absent, or if they are so altered as to be unrecognizable. As a heuristic for this quasi-geometric analysis of Sundanese dance, I propose the following: if three elements are recognizable in a dance event and they conform to the Euclidian theorems outlined above, then the event is likely to be judged within the framework of the ideal type and perceived as consistent with normative values.

Congruence does not necessarily mean that the dancing expresses precisely the same values as old-fashioned dancing, but it does suggest that audiences are likely to regard the dancing as traditional and consonant with traditional values. I contend that the new values given form by the more recent approaches to dancing are more likely to be received as "good" in such situations; new values are implicitly given the sanction of "tradition" if they are associated with traditional approaches to dancing.

This book opened with three dance scenarios that represented a range of contexts for modern Sundanese dances. I chose those scenarios in part because they all present most of the elements of the dance triangle. At this juncture I return to those scenarios, this time to examine them as dance triangles, trying out the trigonometry outlined above.

SCENARIO 1: *KETUK TILU* IN LEMBANG   This performance of ketuk tilu, sponsored yearly by the village of Paneungteung, is among the very few old-fashioned ketuk tilu events still held in the Bandung area for ritual purposes. The hosts hired a professional troupe, Lingkung Seni Manggu Sari, to manage the ketuk tilu parts of the event. This troupe also regularly presents folkloric performances of ketuk tilu at the Bandung Zoo.

The troupe brought along the appropriate musical instruments for ketuk tilu (goong, three ketuk, kendang, and rebab) and several musicians, including two female singers (a mother-daughter team) who know the special repertoire of ketuk tilu songs. They also brought several dancers, both women and men, who perform regularly at the weekly folkloric ketuk tilu performances at the Bandung Zoo. The women dressed in formal dress appropriate for ronggeng, while the men wore the traditional clothes of Sundanese agricultural workers. For this occasion the troupe also subcontracted two additional ronggeng from Subang, who were considerably younger and wore much flashier outfits than the ronggeng from the Zoo.

Although jaipongan and penca silat were performed at times, most of the music was conventional ketuk tilu music, in which the female vocal soloist and rebab player float a melody with elastic rhythm in heterophony over the metrical pulse of the ketuk and drum parts, with periodic punctuation by strokes of the goong. For the most part, the two seated female singers alternated in providing the singing. Although the Zoo ronggeng never sang, both of the Subang ronggeng took the microphone from the seated singers at times to sing while performing simple dance steps.

The troupe's male dancers danced frequently, and so did a few male villagers. Each male dancer partnered with a ronggeng for the first section of each dance piece. For the second section, the ronggeng sat at the side of the stage while the men danced in a line. In contrast to the troupe dancers' laborer's costumes, the village men wore their street clothes. The troupe dancers appeared very confident and self-assured while dancing, while some of the villagers at times looked a little lost. Nevertheless, each villager appeared to be trying to match his dance movements to the drum patterns and to display his own individual style. The troupe dancers unobtrusively directed the men's dancing, gently prodding participants onto the stage and indicating what to do when the ronggeng left the stage.

Figure 6.2 distills these narrative details into a dance triangle graphic. This ketuk tilu performance includes all the elements—sides and angles—that characterize the dance triangle. A few details that are at odds with the dance triangle, however, deserve some discussion.

In figure 6.2, side A (male dancers) is bifurcated into two segments (A_1 and A_2) to suggest the inclusion of male dancers who might be characterized as professional (A_2) as well as the requisite amateur male dancers (A_1). The A_2 men mark their professionalism by wearing a costume of sorts; although the loose pants and shirt and rakishly tied head cloth of an old-fashioned Sundanese farm laborer is hardly flashy, it is rarely worn in everyday modern life, and so it sets its wearers apart. Their role as directors of the event, too, contradicts the usual subjectivity associated with

CHAPTER SIX

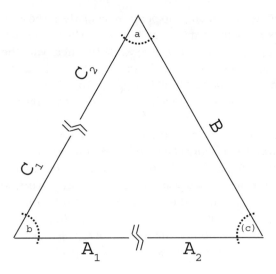

6.2   *Ketuk tilu* in Paneungteung.

Side

Male dancers
A_1 = Amateur male dancers, including host and men from the audience
A_2 = Professional male dancers associated with the lingkung seni

Drumming
B = Conventional ketuk tilu drumming (interplay of leading and following)

Ronggeng
C_1 = Ronggeng associated with lingkung seni who only dance
C = Two "free-lance" ronggeng who dance and sing
C_2 = Pasinden who sit with musicians and only sing

Angle

Voice/accomp contrast
a = Either pasinden (seated singer) or ronggeng (female dancer) sings

Male/female interaction
b = Both professional and amateur men dance on stage with ronggeng

Drum/dance coordination
c = Male dancers follow conventional drum patterns with individual style; ronggeng use simple movements

male dancers in dance events. Although the amateur men are willing dancers and each attempts to improvise according to his own personal style, they appear to be quite self-conscious about dancing "correctly," especially under the watchful gaze of the professional male dancers, and some of them come across as very awkward. This self-consciousness compromises angle c (the parentheses around "c" in the figure denotes this compromise) and suggests that the success of their quest for freedom, too, is compromised.

Side C (ronggeng) is divided as well. C_1 represents the Zoo ronggeng, who dance but do not sing; C_2 represents the seated pasinden, who sing but do not dance. However, these modifications to the ronggeng image are mitigated by the appearance of two younger ronggeng, who do, in fact, both sing and dance.

My impression was that the participants, audience, and passers-by indeed regarded the event as a traditional one—as I would expect given such a complete dance triangle. The event was sparsely attended, however. Many passers-by, who would have been welcome to stop and watch for a while, appeared to regard it as a dull event worthy of little or no attention. The compromised sides and angle provide a possible explanation for these negative assessments; the event's failure to empower the male participants to forget themselves and enable them to dance freely, I suspect, made it lackluster despite the presence of all the dance triangle elements.

SCENARIO 2: *BAJIDOR* IN SUBANG   What a different response came from the crowd at the bajidor event in Cikaum! The summary of that event in figure 6.3 demonstrates that all the triangle elements are present. Eager male fans (the bajidor) dance alone and with each other below the high stage, inspired by the frenetic drumming, the elastic rhythm of the amplified female singers, and the line of erotically dressed female performers. Although their movements are closely coordinated with the drum patterns, each man blissfully surrenders to dance with whatever movements strike his fancy. Bajidor who are willing (or goaded) to pay can come to the edge of the stage and exchange money with one of the female performers in return for the privilege of holding her hand and swaying together (egot).

Subang-style bajidor events also evidence a number of compromises to the dance triangle, however. The placement of the female performers on a high stage limits their intimate contact with the male dancers. But egot enables enough physical proximity to satisfy urges for physical interaction. None of the women sing while they are dancing, but many of the female performers are given a chance to sing at some point during the evening. The bajidor are not necessarily local residents, but the event's hosts invited many of them to come because of their skill and passion for dancing. They cannot be construed as professionals, however, because it is they who pay (and many of them pay quite dearly) for the opportunity to participate. They are amateurs in the original sense of the word, and

CHAPTER SIX

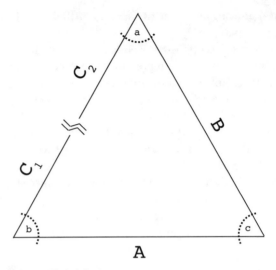

6.3   *Bajidor* in Subang.

Side

Male dancers
A = Male fans (bajidor) dance below the stage—alone, with each other, or with sinden (egot)

Drumming
B = Drummers provide drum patterns easily recognized by all participants

Ronggeng
C = Professional female entertainers (sinden) sing and dance, although not at same time

Angle

Voice/accomp contrast
a = Featured singer's voice floats on top of loud gamelan accompaniment

Male/female interaction
b = Female entertainers dance solos on a high stage; other female entertainers sit at front of stage to hold and swing male participants' hands (egot)

Drum/dance coordination
c = Male participants dance below the stage; they closely follow drum patterns in highly individual ways

everybody who watches them dance experiences a vicarious, rather than aesthetic, thrill.

Although both the Paneungteung and Subang performances arguably outline complete dance triangles and therefore reference traditional values, their outcomes are nevertheless quite different. The Paneungteung event, perhaps, is perceived as too traditional—a rigid portrayal of ossified values in an old-fashioned setting. The Subang event, in contrast, is both traditional and fun, and puts those old-fashioned values in a modern setting that participants—and passers-by—find compelling.

SCENARIO 3: A MAN DANCES AT A WEDDING In this scenario, the troupe that had been hired to perform at the wedding presented a variety of forms of entertainment. The piece at hand was a choreographed jaipongan dance performed by three trained female dancers in brightly colored matching costumes to the accompaniment of gamelan salendro music.

Previous chapters have touched upon aspects of jaipongan's history, style, and rise to popularity; at this point it is helpful to recapitulate jaipongan's transformation from its roots in men's dance (such as the bajidoran discussed above) to a stage dance. The lion's share of the credit for jaipongan's development is usually given to Gugum Gumbira Tirasonjaya, whose influence on Sundanese music and dance over the past thirty years has been undeniably profound—as a choreographer and composer, as an entrepreneur and taste maker (he cofounded the influential Jugala recording company with the singer Euis Komariah), and as a government official.

Tati Saleh, who was one of Gugum's first jaipongan dancers, relates in her biography that Gugum originally conceived jaipongan as a dance for the stage. Gugum found ways to adapt the energy and vitality of participatory dance to a purely visual spectacle. His first choreographies, dubbed *ketuk tilu perkembangan* (developed ketuk tilu), combined movements from tari klasik, ketuk tilu, and penca silat. According to Tati Saleh, Gugum coined the name "jaipongan" from the drum syllables for a common drum pattern for the dance—"plak ting pong, plak ting pong"—and the catchy name stuck (Amilia 2001:96). The dances, along with their choreographer, first gained visibility in the Sundanese arts community when Gugum and Tati performed them for a high-profile cultural mission in Hong Kong for the Third Festival of Asian Arts in 1978 (see Suwandono 1978–79), as well as for local dance festivals.

Many amateur dancers, inspired by their performances, came to Jugala to learn the new dance style, and Jugala's releases of the cassettes *Oray Welang* and *Daun Pulus/Keser Bojong* provided students with a convenient, if inflexible, accompaniment to which to practice. Gugum's choreographies were either couple (male-female) dances or group dances for women. Most of the students who came to study were young women, however, whose goal was to learn the stage versions of the dances for performances in minor venues. The group dances were more popular than the couple dances.

CHAPTER SIX

Gugum often attributes the impetus for his creation of jaipongan to a directive from the former Indonesian president Sukarno in 1961 to eschew Western popular music and look to traditional Indonesian genres instead (e.g., Broughton, Ellingham, Muddyman, and Trillo 1994:428; Yampolsky 1987). Although this is well before the beginnings of jaipongan in the late 1970s, it is still significant in that it inspired Gugum and others to consider local alternatives to imported popular music. Gugum's own account of jaipongan's genesis features a self-conscious analysis of what was missing from Sundanese dance that made imported rock'nroll more attractive, followed by a focused search for means of reinfusing some missing quality back into a socially acceptable, but still exciting, "traditional" dance genre (Myers 1992:45).

Gugum's jaipongan dances were meant to be presentational and were performed at presentational venues. Some of the dances' appeal included the vicarious excitement of watching a skilled male dancer perform in an individualistic style. Even in the absence of a male dancer, however, the groups of well-dressed female dancers were an attraction. The basic stance for female jaipongan dancing involves feet set quite far apart, in contrast to the closed-thigh leg positions of refined female dance characters, and suggests a sexual freedom. Another common position features a deep plié accompanied by a pronounced extrusion of the dancer's hips and buttocks to the right or left, and the buttocks take a prominent role in a number of other gestures as well. Taken as a whole, in West Java jaipongan movements are often considered to be quite provocative.

This exaggeration of the visual temptations of the ronggeng image is reinforced by an exaggeration of the sounds associated with the aural aesthetic team: jaipongan accompaniments feature virtuosic female singing and loud, dynamic drumming adapted from ketuk tilu and bajidoran. Serendipitously for Gugum and Jugala, this particular aesthetic team's focus on the aural dimension made it easy to package and sell on cassettes. Oray Welang featured the singer Iyar Wiarsih, and Daun Pulus/Keser Bojong introduced Idjah Hadidjah, whose sirenlike voice attracted a host of fans. Both releases (and many, many subsequent ones) were enlivened by the dynamic drumming of Suwanda, from Karawang, whose superhuman tempos and crisp sounds, abetted by modern recording technology, seem to leap from the audio speakers.

It took fewer than ten years for jaipongan to become regarded as one of the crown jewels of traditional Sundanese performing arts (Broughton, Ellingham, Muddyman, and Trillo 1994:429). By the late 1980s, presentational jaipongan had become an important part of the curriculum at STSI Bandung, and now virtually all professional dancers include jaipongan in their repertoires. The success of jaipongan has inspired a variety of other choreographed adaptations of improvisational dance forms for presentational contexts.

Figure 6.4a lays out the elements of the dance triangle present in staged female jaipongan performance, such as the one that constitutes Scenario 3. Side A (male dancers) is completely missing, as are the two angles side A forms with the rest of the triangle. Side B (drumming) is quite prominent in the accompaniment, and both components of side C (female dancers and female singer) are present, although provided by different performers. Together, they provide angle a—the fluid female vocal with a metrical gamelan accompaniment. The congruence of sides A and B,

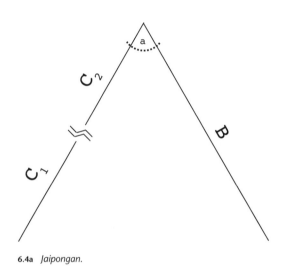

6.4a *Jaipongan.*

Side

Male dancers
A = None

Drumming
B = Drummer provides dynamic jaipongan drumming following a set choreography

Ronggeng
C_1 = Conservatory-trained professional dancers in matching costumes
C_2 = Pasinden sings seated with the gamelan

Angle

Voice/accomp contrast
a = Seated pasinden singing contrasts with gamelan

Male/female interaction
b = Professional women dance in unison for the viewing pleasure of an audience

Drum/dance coordination
c = Female dancers are in sync with drums, but dance in a unison that precludes "free" dancing; no male dancers

CHAPTER SIX

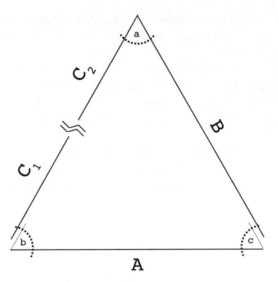

6.4b A man dances at a wedding.

Side

Male dancers
A = Male guest joins female performers in stage space

Drumming
B = (see Figure 6.4a)

Ronggeng
C = (see Figure 6.4a)

Angle

Voice/accomp contrast
a = (see Figure 6.4a)

Male/female interaction
b = Male guest approaches female performers

Drum/dance coordination
c = Male dancer does his own moves that fit with the choreographed drumming

along with angle a, form a triangle congruent with the dance triangle, as "proved" with the SAS (side-angle-side) theorem.

According to Philip Yampolsky, jaipongan "was created expressly to provide an alternative to disreputable dance genres too closely allied with prostitution and vulgar sexuality" (Yampolsky 1995:719). Conspicuously absent are the elements that some modern Sundanese might find objectionable: women who interact too closely with men from the audience (angle a) and the freedom of expression on the part of men (angle b) that is associated with a kind of moral turpitude. A triangular analysis clarifies how observers might overlook such grand exclusions. One of jaipongan's chief assets is that its conventions allow, even encourage, an ambiguity about whether it is presentational or participatory. The drumming is complex and interesting, but the patterns are few in number so that amateur dancers can learn to dance to them quickly. The dance movements can be as simple or as complex as a dancer's abilities allow. Although this triangle is incomplete, it provides enough information for an observer to complete the triangle in his mind, or even in the flesh, as the guest at this particular wedding did. Figure 6.4b demonstrates how the simple act of getting up to dance with the female performers restored the missing side and angles to the triangle.

It is not uncommon in social situations involving all social classes for presentational jaipongan dances to be turned into participatory dance in this way. Indeed, in most contexts, the boundary between presentational and participatory jaipongan is quite fluid. Featured female dancers often find themselves partnered with guests, and guests often pay the musicians to follow them instead of the formal program. It is this dual nature—seeming to be presentational and participatory at the same time—that contributes to the success of jaipongan and (as chronicled in chapter 5) tari kursus.

Puppet Ogres Dance for Fun: Side-Angle-Side

As described in chapter 5, tari kursus's prolonged dissociation from some elements of the erotic triangle has contributed to a lessening of its popularity and compromised its success as a congruent erotic triangle. In contrast, jaipongan occurs in several partial triangular configurations. Andrew Weintraub's transcriptions and translations of a wayang golek (rod puppet theater) performance near Bandung by the famous dalang Asep Sunandar Sunarya (Sunarya 1998) provide an example that complements the wedding scenario. In it, the men's freedom to dance—precisely the element that is eliminated in staged jaipongan—that is brought to the foreground, while the female object of desire, which is emphasized in staged jaipongan, is referenced only obliquely.

As is the case for wayang forms in Bali and other parts of Java, Sundanese puppet theater thrives in modern West Java for a variety of reasons. Wayang shows have something for everybody and every mood—they combine drama, comedy, action, political and social commentary, and philosophy. The most popular dalang (puppet masters) know how to flesh out the basic plots (taken for the most part from the Indian epics *Mahabharata* and *Ramayana*) with jokes, physical comedy, and breathtakingly athletic fight scenes. They find clever and subtle ways to correlate the arcane machinations of the ancient Hindu gods and heroes with the foibles of modern-day public figures and politicians. A skilled dalang can

CHAPTER SIX

hold his audience spellbound with the evocative beauty of his narration or the honest sincerity of his singing; make them roar with laughter at his silly or sophisticated jokes; and moisten their eyes with the pathos of a sad turn of events. The dalang and the large cast of elaborately carved and painted wooden puppets he manipulates are accompanied in the often marathon performances by a gamelan ensemble.[2] In addition to the accompaniment they provide for the puppets' actions, at times the gamelan musicians, especially the pasinden, are featured in renditions of popular songs for the audience's listening pleasure. Finally, even if one is not interested in watching the play or listening to the music, the atmosphere at a wayang is desirably *ramé*—full of sounds, sights, and aromas, and crowded with all sorts of people.

This particular performance relates the story of the mythical hero Gatotkaca. For this excerpt, however, the dalang has just finished a cigarette break, during which the gamelan's two pasinden entertained the audience by singing stock aphorisms called *sisindiran*. The dalang now resumes but postpones the serious business of the main narration to interject a comic scene.

Several ogres (the bad guy's flunkies) are trying to stay awake. The intricately carved puppets themselves are marvels of grotesqueness, with bulging eyes, misshapen teeth, bizarrely shaped heads, and ridiculous clothing. Their voices, too, are caricatures of human voices. At some level, however, these ogres represent ordinary people, and the audience identifies with them. When they speak, they speak in the language of "regular guys."

One of the ogres (let's call him Ogre no. 1) points out that they could all do something upbeat to keep from getting sleepy. He suggests dancing and asks the gamelan musicians to accompany him. They agree. Ogre no. 1 says he wants to do jaipongan. The ogre warns the musicians: "The drumming patterns must be exact" (Sunarya 1998:28–29).

After Ogre no. 1 finishes his dance, Ogre no. 2 jumps on the jaipongan bandwagon, too. His instructions to the gamelan seek to distinguish his style from that of the first ogre: "But for me, with my kind of style, I want a drummer who plays with feeling, one who's really raucous, so that your ears can hear it. What I do is also jaipongan, but I use the entire length of the stage. That's 'cause my dancing is lively, you see, different from others" (Sunarya 1998:28–29). The drumming gets lively, but Ogre no. 2 remains absolutely still. "Boy, jaipongan is tiring, isn't it? I'm gasping and panting already!" he says, eliciting a laugh from the audience.

Ogre no. 3 dances, inspiring Ogre no. 4 to comment, "All you guys are overacting. What's with all these new styles? Either you can dance with

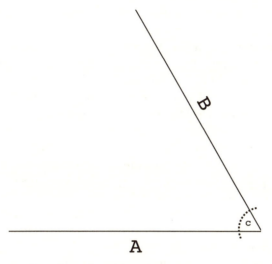

6.5 Puppet ogres dance *jaipongan*.

Side

Male dancers
A = Puppet ogres dance in turn

Drumming
B = Drumming responds to the individual requests of each ogre character

Ronggeng
C = No female dancers

Angle

Voice/accomp contrast
a = Pasinden seated with gamelan, but not singing for this part of the performance

Male/female interaction
b = No female characters involved

Drum/dance coordination
c = Each puppet character cultivates an individual style of movement

the drum or you can't!" After Ogre no. 5 dances, Ogre no. 6 comments: "His body's too loose. Look at the way he squirms; it's like he's just swallowed insecticide. God forbid I should ever get that way. I want to see it done right, according to tradition, so that the people can see a good performance" (Sunarya 1998:28–29).

This wayang scene clearly articulates two sides of the dance triangle: side B, animating drumming, and side A, male characters who cultivate individual, "free" styles of dancing (see fig. 6.5). Using the terminology developed in chapter 5, together they constitute the male aesthetic team. Angle c, formed by these two sides, is expressed in the relationship between the drum patterns and the dance movements. In this case, the

CHAPTER SIX

angle is exactly as described in the ideal triangle: although the drumming regulates each dancer's movements, each ogre cultivates an individual style. Furthermore, the different ogres make it clear in their dialogue that the exact relationship between dancing and drumming—who leads and who follows—is a point of contention.

Together, Ogres no. 1 and no. 2 neatly outline the fundamental contradiction of the free-dancing side of the triangle. Ogre no. 1 emphasizes the synergy between drumming and dancing when he places the drummer in the role of the follower, specifying that "the drumming must be exact." Ogre no. 2 also speaks of this drum-dance connection, but he seems to rely on the drumming for inspiration; he wants the drumming to animate him—lead him—rather than vice versa.

Ogre no. 2 also asserts his freedom to dance the way he wants to dance. He claims that he will use the whole stage and boasts about the uniqueness of his dancing. It is significant that after all his bragging, Ogre no. 2 does not actually move—his idiosyncratic, free style of dancing involves no movement whatsoever! To let the viewers know for sure that Ogre no. 2's performance is finished, the dalang has his stationary puppet complain that dancing is very tiring. For Ogre no. 2, dance's value lies in doing it in whatever manner suits the dancer—in this case, standing absolutely still. The dalang invites his audience to laugh at the ogre's so-called dance, but at the same time, he reminds his viewers that dancing without moving is well within the limits of conventional practice and indeed may be the most powerful, divine way to dance.

Ogre no. 4 criticizes the previous dancers because they follow fads. His ideal for dancing, apparently, is simply moving according to the drumming (whatever that might mean). Ogre no. 6, in contrast, makes specific criticisms of Ogre no. 5's movements; it seems that Ogre no. 6 does not value freedom in dancing but rather adherence to a set of strict standards.

Obviously, missing from the scene is the triangle's third side— ronggeng—along with the angles this third side forms. The ogres never mention that a female object of desire might be a motivation for their activities, either in the tactile dimension (as a dance partner) or in the sonic dimension (as a singer). This sonic dimension of the ronggeng is hinted at, however, by the sound of the pasinden's voice, which is still ringing in the audience's ears from the previous scene. Many scenes in a typical wayang performance involve interaction between the dalang, the dancing puppets, and the pasinden.

The values that the ogres explore are those concerned with male subjectivity, power, and status. Assuming that we can extrapolate to ordinary men from the behavior of these ogres, we see that dancing is and remains a men's activity—something that men do in the company of other men. They explore the limits of their own freedom and the boundaries of conformity. It is clear from their discussions that drumming can be either a force that dictates their actions or a phenomenon that endorses their choices—or both. Whether the drumming signifies cosmic power in a general sense, the weight of real or invented tradition, or peer pressure is left ambiguous in their patter.

Each of these contrasting versions of jaipongan—a staged dance that puts women on display and a site for camaraderie and competition among men—presents a different partial erotic triangle. Participants and audiences are able to triangulate the values and implications of full events from them. There is constant reinforcement of all the various elements of the dance triangle in different jaipongan contexts, even though any particular context is incomplete. This situation contrasts with the case of tari klasik, which are missing the same elements in virtually all the contexts in which it appears; as a result, people who can recognize the congruence of any tari kursus–based dance with its roots in men's improvisational dance are increasingly rare. Even though the fixed choreographies of modern classical dance still reference tayuban dancing, the references are increasingly obscure. In the case of jaipongan, however, a complete erotic triangle remains easy to reconstruct.

Noncongruent Dances

In each of the dance triangles examined so far, different sides, angles, and aesthetic teams were attenuated or exaggerated to dissociate the dance from questionable values. Each succeeds, however, by virtue of the audience's ability to imagine a complete triangle. By submerging the questionable values just enough to remove any objections they might raise, but not enough to eliminate them completely, these dance expressions reinject traditional ideas of masculinity and femininity into modern presentational dancing. Striking the right balance is difficult; remaining faithful to a core of Sundaneseness associated with the protocols of men's improvisational dancing while the particulars of those protocols become increasingly objectionable is a narrow tightrope to walk.

Choreographers face a difficult situation if they want their dances to be both presentational and received as Sundanese. If Sundaneseness is a function of the erotic dance triangle, which relies on freedom and ambiguity, dances that are choreographed cannot possibly reference the

CHAPTER SIX

triangle completely. I already have examined a variety of ways in which choreographers infuse their works with a sense of the participatory in order to cite convincingly the gendered implications of Sundanese dance.

Jaipongan and tari klasik reflect the changing values of Sundanese and Indonesian society. Viewers and participants, for the most part, are aware of meaningful echoes of traditional arts and traditional values in them. I have explored how these new values both connect to the past and break with it by presenting the various dance expressions as congruent, yet incomplete, triangles. Even music and dance forms that on the surface seem far removed from traditional Sundanese culture can be compatible with traditional values if they reference the erotic triangle of Sundanese dance. Dangdut, for example, derives much of its popularity in West Java from the successful integration of the triangle into performances, which is achieved by casting female dangdut singers as ronggeng-like figures who encourage their male fans to mount the stage and dance to the accompaniment of drum rhythms that compel people to move (Spiller 2004:257; 2006).

Not all modern dance expressions, however, are received as congruent with traditional values. Such dances are likely to strike viewers as somehow skewed, or wrong, or "missing something." These aesthetic evaluations can be accounted for metaphorically with a quasi-Euclidean explanation: the dances reference the elements and qualities of triangular dances in noncongruent ways. Geometry texts warn students that there are two three-element formulas that do *not* demonstrate congruence: AAA and SSA. And primers are quick to point out that the equivalent retrograde of SSA—that is, ASS—is an appropriate label for the geometry student who erroneously uses it to demonstrate triangle congruence (Calkins 2005). As the following analyses demonstrate, dance expressions that have an noncongruent relationship to the dance triangle are less likely to be judged "good"; I hasten to stress that such noncongruent dance expressions are not necessarily of low quality—only that they do not reinforce or subtly manipulate normative values about power, subjectivity, and gender the way congruent expressions do. When unsuccessful, noncongruent dances are deemed not good, and the new values they give form to are repudiated. When successful, however, such dance expressions may contribute to changing normative values.

The dances analyzed below do indeed reference triangular elements, but in a manner that audiences often find to be at odds with their expectations. The dissonance may be exactly what the creative forces behind them intended—perhaps as a strategy to capture attention, or to make a particular point about conventional social relationships, or to reflect changes in social values, or even to effect such changes. Whatever the motivations, the result is an artistic experience that contradicts the status quo in some way and thus contributes to the inevitable changes that characterize culture.

Earlier chapters discussed how the aesthetics of dance events grow out of the performance (in Butler's sense) of gender. Because the genesis of Sundanese presentational dances takes place in a multicultural context, however, I suggest that they have a somewhat different function. Rather than performing gender, participants are performing an ethnic Sundanese or a regional West Javanese identity. A significant difference between the two approaches is a shift of focus from an internal, embodied engagement with dance to a visual, disembodied experience. The consequence of this disconnect is twofold: (1) most Sundanese men and women, accustomed to judging dance with the aesthetic values that proceed from the triangular model, have, at best, only a passing interest in presentational dance; and (2) proponents of presentational dance look for ways to incorporate into their choreographed works elements that suggest an internal, embodied focus, thus recapturing the interest of Sundanese consumers. One means of accomplishing this reincorporation is to reference clearly the triangular model in choreographed dances. In the sections below, I will illustrate this disconnect and various approaches toward addressing it with specific examples.

Group Dances—"Tari Baksa"

One of the hallmarks of modern Sundanese choreography is the arrangement of group dances—dances in which three or more dancers, usually in matching costumes, perform in unison (or in simple counterpoint). This practice can be tied historically to *badaya* dancing, in which a group of women danced in unison, as well as to the wawayangan and jajangkungan dances, performed by a group of ronggeng at the beginning of a ketuk tilu event. A dance such as R. Tjetje Somantri's "Tari Puja," in which a group of women enact movements depicting devotional acts (such as praying and lighting incense), harks back to badaya as well as emulating the popular modern Balinese dance of greeting called "Panyembrama," developed specifically to frame Balinese presentational dance performances (Bandem and deBoer 1981:94–95). Other Tjetje creations, such as "Tari Kupu-kupu," in which a group of women depicts butterflies fluttering about, and "Tari Merak," in which the women imitate the movements of peacocks, seem to recall badaya dances as well, despite their mimetic subject matter. Although "Tari Kupu-kupu" and "Tari

CHAPTER SIX

Merak" are performed exclusively by female dancers, both dances allude to mating behaviors, adding yet another layer of gendered significance to the choreographies.

Key to these women's group dances is their bloking (from the English word blocking, a theatrical term), which refers to complex deployments of the dancers in the performing space. As the dance scholar Lilis Sumiati puts it, "Making an interesting choreography cannot be separated from floor patterns/plans" (Sumiati 1996b:15).[3] Each section of a typical group dance features a unique formation, known as a floor plan, in which dancers arrange themselves in aesthetically pleasing patterns on the stage; the transitions between these sections are carefully planned as well. The effect is comparable to the complex maneuvers of a marching band during a halftime show, or choreography for a corps de ballet.

Dances with bloking guarantee that *only* observers can apprehend their full aesthetic effect—the individual dancer's internal engagement with her body movement is put into the service of a composite visual effect that she can only imagine. In addition, bloking and complex floor plans, by their very nature, minimize any sort of improvisation or personal expression on the part of the individual dancers. Such dances are antithetical to what I have demonstrated are archetypal Sundanese aesthetics of men's dance—namely, the internalized experience of free movement and observers' vicarious enjoyment of that freedom.

It is no surprise, therefore, that group dances tend to feature groups of female dancers, both because of the historical precedent of badaya outlined above and because it is not difficult for Sundanese to imagine regulating the behavior of women in this way. Certainly, the all-female jaipongan dances discussed above, in which a group of attractive women are made the object of the audience's gaze, fall into this category. "Tari Merak" and "Tari Kupu-kupu" mask a comparable objectification of women only slightly by casting them as animals.

A choreographed all-male group dance entitled "Tari Baksa" provides a vantage point from which to examine these issues. I saw the dance performed at a benefit concert at Taman Budaya in Bandung in December of 1998. The choreographed dances were billed in the invitation/program as "Tari Klasik & Kreasi" (classical and modern dance) staged by an alliance of several prominent choreographers and dance teachers, including Aim Salim, who choreographed "Tari Baksa," as well as Irawati Durban Ardjo, Indrawati Lukman, and Yetti Mamat.

On the surface, the name "Tari Baksa" is somewhat redundant, because the terms tari and *baksa* both mean "dance." Currently, however, the term baksa is not commonly used in the sense of "dance"; instead, it is recognized as the root of several other terms associated with tayuban—*baksarai* (a type of stepping movement) and *ngabaksaan* (the protocol in which a dancer is offered the tray holding the dagger and scarf). Baksa also is the name of a circumcision custom in parts of southern West Java that involves a group of male dancers carrying the boy to be circumcised to the spot where the operation is to take place (Soepandi and Atmadibrata 1976:74–75). Thus, the title "Tari Baksa" evokes both tayuban and ceremonial group male dance.

"Tari Baksa" featured seven young men dressed in matching costumes based on traditional aristocratic clothing and glitzed up with the addition of gold rickrack. The dancers also wore rather prominent fake moustaches and quite a bit of stage makeup. The dance gestures were derived from the tari kursus dance called "Gawil," which typically is performed as a solo. The basic "Gawil" movements were modified, however, to include complex bloking. For each section of the dance, the dancers arranged themselves into a different floor plan. Some of the dancers performed gestures in mirror image to the other dancers to enhance the observers' impression of symmetry. At times, some of the tari kursus gestures were modified to include interaction with another dancer. For example, one characteristic tari kursus movement, called *sepak soder* (kicking the dance scarf), in which a dancer picks up his dance scarf with the toes of one foot and flings the scarf over his shoulder or head, was modified so that each dancer picked up and kicked another dancer's scarf.

A Sundanese dancer and choreographer later told me that he thought this piece was not particularly successful, primarily because the dancers did not seem to be enjoying themselves—the young men dancing seemed too preoccupied by the demands of the complex bloking to bring any joy to their movements. He added that it is male dancers' own enjoyment of moving that makes such dancing worthwhile to perform and to watch. He also pointed out that twenty years earlier, it would have been impossible even to find seven dancers who could match tari kursus gestures closely enough to perform in unison, because individual dancers always cultivated a personal, idiosyncratic style. Only because the teachers at STSI have standardized tari kursus dances is such choreography possible (personal communication, December 5, 1998). The same commentator found the rendition of "Tari Merak" on the same program, however, to be quite satisfying. This version of "Tari Merak" featured no fewer than fourteen female dancers, in colorful costumes, executing extraordinarily complex floor plans; my commentator noted that these dancers, in contrast to the "Tari Baksa" dancers, appeared to be enjoying themselves. The operative difference between these two pieces is the gender of the

CHAPTER SIX

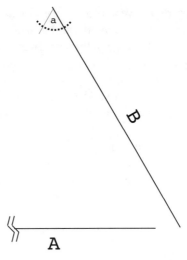

6.6   Tari baksa.

Side

Male dancers
A = Group of trained male dancers in unison

Drumming
B = Animating drumming based on tari kursus

Ronggeng
C = No female dancer

Angle

Voice/accomp contrast
a = Seated pasinden sings with gamelan

Male/female interaction
b = No male-female interaction

Drum/dance coordination
c = Drums and dance are coordinated, but unison dance precludes "free" interaction with drums

dancers. As schematized in figure 6.6, "Tari Baksa" includes two sides (side A, male dancers, and side B, animating drumming). However, the bloking erases any possibility of angle c—freedom.

"Tari Baksa" represents an audacious attempt to challenge the contradictions between freedom and fixity that characterize tari kursus. In effect, the choreographer is forcing the male dancers to conform to an external ideal at the expense of their individual personalities. They must forfeit their cherished sense of freedom. The choreography makes it difficult for viewers to be unaware of the usually subtle gender differences that characterize Sundanese dance. "Tari Baksa" carries to a logical extreme the process of deforming the triangular model of Sundanese dance events exemplified by tari kursus. It makes it clear that the hints of freedom that seem to emerge in choreographed dances are illusions. It objectifies the male dancers, who are accustomed to being watched but not objectified in this manner.

My informed male Sundanese observer found the combination of tari kursus movements with complex bloking to be uncomfortably dissonant and somehow disturbing, perhaps even threatening. A female choreographer, however, expressed her opinion that "Tari Baksa" represents a beautiful extension of Sundanese tradition. In either case, the dance represents a clear break with tradition; its noncongruence with the erotic triangle of Sundanese dance provides a way to examine its disjunctures.

"Tari Cikeruhan"

"Tari Cikeruhan" is a duet performed by one man and one woman, who present a "dramatization" of a triangular dance event. I saw "Tari Cikeruhan" performed several times during my stay in Bandung. It is presented frequently in part because students in several dance degree programs at STSI Bandung are required to study it, and hence quite a few dancers know "Tari Cikeruhan."

"Cikeruhan" is the name of a ketuk tilu piece. According to Tosin Mochtar, male ketuk tilu dancers often choose "Cikeruhan" to accompany dancing that features *kocak* (funny, amusing) movements. He identifies a number of special drum patterns with surprising goong cadences associated with "Cikeruhan" (personal communication, February 11, 1999). The musical accompaniment for the choreographed "Tari Cikeruhan" includes the piece "Cikeruhan," along with several other tunes.

The choreographed dance piece begins with an *arang-arangan* (free rhythm piece, typically played on rebab), to which the female dancer, dressed in the costume of a ronggeng, enters. This type of opening is associated especially with *topeng banjet*, an entertainment genre from the area around Karawang that features ronggeng (cf. Hamid 1976–77; Martasasmita 1978–79; Spiller 1999). The drummer joins in, playing first one accented beat (joined by the gamelan), then another after a bit of time, then more accents, gradually shortening the time interval between accents until they come very quickly. During this time, the dancer slowly moves forward, then backward, while jerking her head back and forth. This opening section ends abruptly, at which point one of the gamelan

CHAPTER SIX

instrumentalists plays the *pangkat* (introductory phrase) for the musical piece "Gonjing Miring."

The female dancer continues her opening solo to the accompaniment of "Gonjing Miring." After another dramatic stop, the gamelan begins playing another piece called "Cangkurileung." After a few repetitions of "Cangkurileung," the male dancer, dressed in a gaudy version of an outfit appropriate for a jawara (tough guy, or a ketuk tilu fan), gets ready. He enters to the strains of the characteristic ketuk tilu drumming and the musical phrase called nyered (see chapter 2). At this point, most of the gamelan musicians drop out, leaving the much smaller ketuk tilu ensemble (three ketuk, kendang, rebab, and goong) to play the ketuk tilu song called "Cikeruhan." The previous pieces have been instrumental; "Cikeruhan," however, features a pasinden and a *wiraswara* (solo male vocalist).

The male dancer's entrance dramatically establishes his character's lecherousness. He rushes in and attempts brazenly to grab the female dancer. She avoids him deftly, and he jumps and spins as if recoiling from a powerful physical blow. The rest of the dance features both dancers, sometimes dancing separately, sometimes interacting. There are frequent sequences of penca silat movements, and the male dancer routinely draws his *golok* (machete) to show off his skills with it for a moment before resheathing it. At frequent intervals throughout this section of the dance, the male dancer approaches the female dancer and attempts to touch her, and she usually sends him flying with a mock blow from her dance scarf or hand. At one point, she actually knocks him to the ground. Often they lock hands and wrestle; the woman invariably "wins" these tussles.

Also at frequent intervals, the male dancer stares intently at the female dancer's swaying buttocks as she executes the movement called goyang. At times, such as after being knocked to the ground, his head is at the same level with her hips, a vantage point the male dancer's character clearly relishes. At some point the musical accompaniment changes to another ketuk tilu piece with more frequent goong strokes (either "Ucing-ucing" or "Kangsreng"). This section ends with another nyered, at which point the male dancer bows and the female dancer takes the opportunity to push him away again. This leads to the female dancer's final goyang. The male dancer crawls on his knees closely behind her, thrusting his head toward her buttocks in a manner that suggests pelvic thrusting, until they both exit the stage.

The dance as it is taught at STSI requires the dancers to personalize and interpret their parts but provides very little room for other kinds of improvisation. The specificity with which the dance is choreographed is evident from STSI student papers on the dance, which include detailed lists of the dance movements and floor-plan diagrams. According to one such paper, the dance is meant to express

two dancers (male and female) in a fresh, coquettish, erotic, happy, warm atmosphere, and also show self-confidence to the male dance fans/participants. The strong feeling for the male dancer is to try to win the sympathy of the ronggeng in order to attract her, by showing off his skill in martial arts along with elements of humor.
(ROSDIANI 1997:5)[4]

The author also describes as very minimal the changes she makes to the choreography to suit her own tastes. She says her revisions are meant only to clarify the structure of the dance movements or make it work better given the exigencies of the performing space. In other words, she does not think it is a good idea to change (or to admit to changing) much about the dance (Rosdiani 1997:48). I reviewed videotapes of three "Tari Cikeruhan" examinations from STSI.[5] The three different sets of dancers turned in extremely similar performances, which also closely matched the choreography documented in Rosdiani's paper (Rosdiani 1997:37–40).

The non-STSI performances I saw, however, included more deviations from the STSI version. In a version I watched at CCF on February 6, 1999 (performed by two STSI graduates, Umi and Akuy), for example, the male dancer, Akuy, twitched his exceptionally large moustache in synchronization with the drumming patterns, garnering big laughs from the audience. Also during this performance, the female dancer, Umi, substituted a brutal kick to Akuy's groin for one of the more typical slaps. The rendition I saw performed by IKIP students (again at CCF) on April 6, 1999, featured a male dancer who acted afraid of the audience, as if he were embarrassed by his dancing. Given his obvious dancing skills, his attempts to outmaneuver and touch the ronggeng were so inept as to be unbelievable.

This mixture of grace and goofiness on the part of the male dancer is consistent with Rosdiani's statement that the male dancer is trying to win the ronggeng's affection by showing off his martial arts skills and by being humorous. He never, however, actually succeeds in winning her favor, or even in groping her. He comes off, in other words, as an incompetent buffoon. The impression is enhanced by elements of the male dancers' costumes. Akuy, for example, wore satin pangsi and a matching shirt, and his hand-tied *ikat kepala* (head cloth) was enormous, as were the golok stuck in his belt and his fake moustache. These costume elements portrayed an image of masculine bravado without substance by enlarging these emblems of masculinity to grotesque proportions. The ronggeng,

CHAPTER SIX

on the other hand, is portrayed as a competent, confident, self-assured figure, who wields her feminine charms with calculated precision.

A couple of blurbs from program notes provide quite different characterizations of the dance. STSI students who performed at CCF on February 6, 1999, wrote, "The folk dance ketuk tilu illustrates the happiness of young people who dance in couples. The name 'Cikeruh' is taken from a village name."[6] The description of the dance evokes a pair of equals in an innocent, bucolic romp in a nostalgic, rural setting—an image that is contradicted by the actual dance piece. The Kadewan group from IKIP Bandung sets a rather different mood for the dance in the program note from their April 8, 1999, performance at CCF: "In this couple dance the female dancer challenges and avoids the male dancer's attempts to touch and get near her."[7] Kadewan's description paints a more realistic picture of what is at stake in the piece—a contest between the man and the woman—but provides no inkling of its final outcome. As it turns out, the woman is successful at fending off the man's advances; he does manage to gawk at her, although only because she allows it. The piece's subtext is that the female character takes charge by using the ronggeng image, and the man's weakness for it, to her own advantage.

Such an outcome is not consistent with the outlines of the erotic triangle of Sundanese dance, although both components of the outcome—the ronggeng's agency and the man's weakness—are not necessarily precluded absolutely by the triangle. But "Cikeruhan" is not about male freedom and power, or about men interacting with other men. The character's desire for the ronggeng is not redirected desire for the power and status of other men. His dancing is meant to impress only the ronggeng, not his compatriots. The drumming no longer signifies power, and the male character is not especially interested in imitating it; in fact, the predictability of the drumming is resignified to enable the ronggeng to parry his thrusts more ably. Although "Tari Cikeruhan" appears to mimic an erotic triangle, it surreptitiously reduces it to an interaction between one man and one woman. Rather than reifying the power of men, the dance represents an empowerment of women to exploit existing structures in order to change Sundanese gender ideologies.

These subversions are reflected in the musical accompaniment as well. The addition of a solo male singer, called a wiraswara or *juru alok*, to gamelan salendro ensembles has become standard practice over the past few decades. However, the presence of a wiraswara in the accompaniment for "Tari Cikeruhan" suggests that this musical change may be part of a profound shift in Sundanese gender ideologies. Just as the choreography adjusts the gender roles of men and women in dance in decidedly nontraditional ways, perhaps the encroachment of men into the once all-female world of solo singing with gamelan salendro points toward a real transformation of gender ideologies.

Conclusions

A sense of freedom for men to dance from the heart and the enjoyment of watching men express their illusory freedom within the powerful constraints of drumming form the essence of Sundanese dance. Contexts that enable this sort of dancing are always participatory, and they always involve a reference to a third party—a ronggeng—who acts as an object of desire to enable the illusion. In a nutshell, the erotic triangle of Sundanese dance is composed of men who are empowered to dance by the presence of inspiring drumming and a female object of desire. The very act of making a spectacle of oneself by succumbing to the allure of a ronggeng and overcoming the strictures of malu to stand out in public is simultaneously and contradictorily reviled and admired. It is precisely this ambiguity—dancing on the line between propriety and lasciviousness—that makes men's dance such a fertile site for exploring gender identities, which are themselves fraught with ambiguity and contradiction.

Developments in Sundanese dance in the twentieth century were generally responses to changing standards about how explicit, how overt, and how pronounced this ambiguity could be made in public. Expanding contexts for presentational dance forms in the twentieth century also gave impetus to developing dances that were interesting enough to be watched, and emphases on regional and national identities encouraged the preservation in presentational dances of some element of the masculine energy that characterized old-fashioned Sundanese dancing. The two most successful presentational forms—tari kursus (and the tari klasik dances which built upon tari kursus), with its roots in aristocratic tayuban events, and jaipongan, with its roots in the ketuk tilu events of the lower classes—succeeded by providing enough references to participatory forms and their discourses of masculinity to invoke that crucial sense of authentic Sundaneseness. They perpetuated the ambiguities of men's dance forms, in part by empowering men from the audience, under certain circumstances, to dance along. If these presentational dance forms strayed too far from this ambiguity, however, as some tari klasik creations did, they ran the chance of being unpalatable—boring—to some audiences.

Sundanese individuals, whether they are avid dancers, avid dance fans, or silent observers of dance activities, do not perceive dance in terms

CHAPTER SIX

of the erotic triangle developed in this book. Yet discussing twentieth-century developments in Sundanese dance in terms of erotic triangles sheds light on the complex yet crucial part artistic activities play in the articulation and contestation of fundamental values. A long Sundanese history of associating the potent triangular formation of ronggeng, drumming, and men's free dancing with values about masculinity, femininity, power, and agency renders any event that involves dance into a site for exploring those values.

In analyzing Sundanese dance, dances, and dancing, I have drawn upon a wide variety of theoretical approaches and models. The rigid structure of the triangle itself conjures the ghost of structuralism, and it appears to act as a persistent, inevitable template that determines in advance a single unchanging set of values and behaviors. It does seem to have, in a sense, a life of its own; as, say, a meme complex that "can be said to propagate itself, spreading from brain to brain" (Dawkins 2006 [1989]:192). As entrenched as it may be, however, it is hardly immune to change, and the actions of individuals and the trajectories of histories affect it mightily. Given its complex ambiguities, it is easy to see how the erotic triangle of Sundanese dance acts as a field (à la Bourdieu), and how the unique habitus that each individual brings to dancing (or watching) creates a rich environment for revision. Whatever it is called—structure, field, meme complex—the erotic triangle of Sundanese dance represents a framework that is durable enough to conserve values, yet flexible enough to enable changes, both large and small, in those values.

At the beginning of the twenty-first century, the two dance domains discussed throughout this book—tari klasik and jaipongan—are prominent in the world of Sundanese traditional dance. The development of tayuban protocols in the early twentieth century eliminated or minimized the ronggeng side of the triangle while greatly expanding the drumming and male improvisation sides in tayuban and konkurs contexts. The trend for tayuban's derivative tari kursus, however, was to eliminate another side of the triangle—the improvisational free side—as well. I have argued that tari kursus's waning popularity can be attributed to the elimination of two triangle sides, thus making any vestiges of the triangle more difficult to recognize and hobbling observers' ability to apply dance-event trigonometry.

The geometric analyses of the various manifestations of these forms tracks how they introduce changing values to their consumers. Tari kursus and jaipongan echo new approaches to Sundanese masculinity without challenging entrenched ideas of masculine behaviors beyond recognition. Other important spheres of Sundanese dance, such as topeng (masked dance) and dangdut, have not been addressed in much detail, but I predict comparable analyses of these forms would present similar results.

Clearly, new social standards can be suggested, introduced, enacted, perhaps even enforced via interventions in the triangle, but if interventions go too far—if the triangle is so deformed that it is impossible to recognize—people may look right past them. Innovations that are congruent, on the other hand, might invite responses that shore up existing values by reintroducing the missing aesthetic elements. Once a certain amount of order is imposed on men's dancing and it strays too far from this fundamental freedom with regard to movement, ordinary Sundanese men lose confidence in it. Constraining their freedom to move disempowers the dancers; they may come to regard the movements as too "difficult" and lose interest in doing them at all.

Some dance expressions, however, are more aggressive about challenging conventional values. "Tari Baksa" and "Tari Cikeruhan," for example, present visions of men's dance that are not congruent, as I have defined it, with the erotic triangle of Sundanese dance and may leave some audiences unsatisfied. At the same time, their citation of the erotic triangle might provide exactly the sort of stimulation that eventually fosters significant changes. There are twenty-first-century individuals who find some of the values to which erotic triangles give form, such as male domination and an unequal hierarchy of power, to be reprehensible. Ironically, many of these same individuals profess to admire and strive to preserve the aesthetic expressions of those very values that emerge from Sundanese dance. How to solve such a dilemma? The erotic triangles that undergird Sundanese dance have been reconciling intractable contradictions for generations, and I have no doubt that Sundanese men and women will dance their way to a compromise of continuity and change.

Notes

CHAPTER ONE

1. *Lingkung seni* (often abbreviated LS) means "arts circle"; in West Java it refers to a performing arts troupe. It is a Sundanese-language rendition of the borrowed Dutch term *kunstkring*, which refers to any arts-related association or club.

2. The Bandung branch of STSI, formerly known as Akademi Seni Karawitan Indonesia (ASKI), currently grants diplomas indicating advanced practical studies as well as academic S-1 degrees (roughly equivalent to an American bachelor's degree).

3. The five penca silat tepak are *paleredan, tepak dua, tepak tilu, padungdung,* and *golempang*. For each of the tepak, one of the drummers plays a tepak-specific ostinato pattern, while the second drummer provides a unique pattern for each of the different movements the dancers perform. Tepak dua and paleredan are characterized by slow tempos and infrequent gong strokes. The rhythmic groove called tepak tilu also includes two sections but is faster, with more frequent gong strokes. Padungdung is the fastest of the tepak, and the dancing tends to be free-form. Dancers also spar, perform incredible feats, and demonstrate their prowess with weapons to the accompaniment of padungdung (cf. Harrell 1977; Maryono 1999).

4. *Priyayi* means "upper-class."

5. First published in Dutch in the journal *Djawa* in 1930 (Soeriadiradja and Adiwidjaja 1930) and subsequently in the Indonesian language in the book *Tari Djawa dan Sunda* (Javanese and Sundanese Dance) in 1949 (Soeriadiradja and Adiwidjaja 1949).

NOTES TO PAGES 26–39

6. Cast in the *pupuh* poetic form known as *sinom* (another Sundanese borrowing from the courts of central Java).
7. The equivalent concepts in Sundanese are *era* and *isin*; in Javanese, *isin*; in Balinese, *lek* (Boellstorff 2004:474).
8. The Sundanese equivalents are *wani* and *wantun*.
9. According to Atik Soepandi, a *bajidor* is a kind of drum, and *bajidoran* is music played by an ensemble including such a drum (Soepandi 1985; Supandi 1970:24). Jaap Kunst and C. J. A. Kunst–van Wely report that a very large one-head drum called badjidor was part of the *monggang* ceremonial gamelan in the Tasikmalaya regent's palace (Kunst and Kunst-Van Wely 1923:32). Bajidor as a term for male dancers has been in use in Subang/ Karawang at least since the 1950s (see Junengsih 1997:15).
10. I have run across a number of variants of this kirata, including *barisan jiwa durhaka* (row of rebels; Suganda 1996) and *bajingan doraka* (sinful bad guys; Ade Komaran, personal communication, June 17, 1999). Mas Nana Munajat Dahlan corroborates this (his brother Nanu's) explication but supplements it with a second, less sociological kirata for bajidoran: *BAnjet, tanJI, dan boboDORan* (*banjet* is a dance/theater form; *tanji* refers to Sundanese music performed on Western brass instruments, and *bobodoran* suggests humorous movement—clowning around). He explains that this acronym shows the similarities of bajidoran to banjet and tanji with regard to the dance, music, and drum patterns, as well as the humor that pervades bajidor events (Dahlan 1996:5).
11. Sundanese scholars often discuss men's dance events as having three elements, which are similar in concept, if not exact details, with the model I set forth here. The scholar and choreographer Mas Nanu Muda, for example, frames his discussion of men's dance events in Subang (a small city north of Bandung) by identifying three elements: *sinden* (in this context, a singer-dancer), *panjak* (musician), and *bajidor* (dancing audience members; Muda 1997). Several Sundanese authors suggest a similar model for understanding ketuk tilu; Amelia says that ketuk tilu is an art form that blends three elements, namely "gerak, lagu dan iringan" (movement, song, and accompaniment; Amelia 1996), while Fajaria suggests that three elements—*instrumen-instrumen* (musical instruments), *nyanyian* (singing), and *tarian* (dance)—complement each other to create a performance (1996:30), and Turyati and Suhaena both identify the elements as tarian, nyanyian, and *tetabuhan* (instrumental music; Turyati 1996:1; Suhaenah 1996:16). Amelia also frames her description of the general characteristics of ketuk tilu–type events along the three axes I propose (although she does not enumerate them specifically). The points of similarity she finds in several different traditions are (1) the role of ronggeng as singer-dancers, (2) the presence of a simple musical accompaniment including drums, and (3) participation by the audience in free dancing based on the rhythm of drumming (Amelia 1996:83–86).

NOTES TO PAGES 39–52

12. This aphorism is sometimes called the *trias politika Sunda*. *Trias politika* refers to the French Enlightenment philosopher Baron de Montesquieu's separation of powers (legislative, judicial, and executive), which, in effect, correlates Sundanese values with modern democratic principles.

13. ASA, angle-side-angle, proposition 26 from Book I of Euclid's *Elements* (Euclid 1998).

CHAPTER TWO

1. "Ia menari-nari dengan mengucapkan bunyi-bunyi kendang atau bertepuk tangan meniru ritmis kendang. Secara tidak sadar ia telah berperan sebagai pengendang."

2. In the past it appears that Sundanese drummers performed with only one drum, the large *indung*, as in the current practice of dance drumming in central Java. Nondance drumming probably involved a second, smaller drum, as it does in the *kendang kalih* practice of central Java (see Spiller 2004:106). Sundanese drummers began to use this smaller drum in dance drumming as well, perhaps to provide timbral variation. Photographs from the 1890s (DeVale 1978:4) and 1930s (Kunst 1973:ill. 161, 164) show this configuration. More recently, a second kulanter was added. Even more recently, some drummers have added more kulanter to enrich their timbre and pitch vocabularies. The impressive visual array of as many as six or seven drums contributed to their prestige as well (cf. Weintraub 2001).

3. Exceptions include the ensemble that accompanies penca silat, which features two kendang players; some modern versions of kliningan and bajidoran, which can include an extra drummer or two; and the spectacular drum extravaganzas called *kendang rampak* (literally, kendang chorus), which feature several kendang players performing in unison, often with clever choreography; these reached the zenith of their popularity in the 1980s and 1990s.

4. The system comprises glyphs composed from symbols available on a standard typewriter. The letter "a" is the basis for right-hand strokes, and the letter "U" is the basis for left-hand strokes (assuming a left-oriented drummer); these letters are modified in various ways to indicate the various right- or left-hand strokes. The glyphs are arranged on a one-line staff; right-hand symbols are above the line, and left-hand symbols below the line (Soepandi and Suaman 1980:50). Rhythm is indicated in the same fashion as in standard Sundanese cipher notation, which is familiar to all academically educated Sundanese musicians.

5. For example, Entjar Tjarmedi and colleagues describe the kendang's function in the degung ensemble as the *yasa* [*sic*] *wirahma* (carrier of rhythm) (Tjarmedi, Suparman, Sutisna, and Resmana 1997:21). The prolific theoretician Atik Soepandi typically used the phrase *pangatur embat/irama*

213

NOTES TO PAGES 52–63

(regulator/governor/controller of tempo/rhythm) (Soepandi 1985:109) and compared the drum's role to that of a conductor in Western music, giving cues for transitions and endings and setting the tempo and dynamics of the piece (Supandi 1970:24).

6. "Fungsi kendang hanya mengatur jalannya gending dan menjaga irama . . . type-type dari suara kendang selalu harus mengisi gerakan-gerakan tari."

7. Benjamin Brinner differentiates cues and signals: a cue is an "act specifically produced for the purpose of initiating an interaction . . . that would not occur otherwise," while a signal is a cue that "reaffirms a planned action rather than conveying new information" (Brinner 1995:183–85). In Sundanese performance practice, whether a drum pattern is a cue or a signal depends on whether the form of the piece is fixed (i.e., the goong strokes are predictable) and, if it is, whether the goong player actually knows when the goong strokes fall or relies on the drummer to tell him.

8. The term *melem* derives from the Sundanese word *pelem* (delicious, enjoyable; Burhan Sukarma, personal communication, December 4, 1999; see also Eringa 1984:568; Panitia Kamus 1969:373).

9. The four drums are (from smallest to largest) *tilingtit* (first dogdog), *panempag* (second dogdog), *jongjrong* (third dogdog), and *bangbrang* (fourth dogdog).

10. *Mincid* apparently is a Sundanese word but is not in common use and does not appear in either of the authoritative Sundanese dictionaries I consulted; but dictionaries define *mincig* as walking in a dancelike manner (Eringa 1984:501; Panitia Kamus 1969:314; Tamsyah, Purmasih, Purmawati, and Supratman 1998:212). Atmadibrata glosses mincid as "stepping" (Atmadibrata 1980:212), and Natapradja translates it as "making steps" (Natapradja 1975:106) and as "stepping—one step or in place" (Natapradja 1975:108). *Keupat* means a swinging, swaying movement where the hands and arms move back and forth while the feet step in opposition to the hands (Eringa 1984:398).

11. As a modern technical term, *sekar tandak* refers to songs in traditional poetic meters that are fitted into regular, quadratic musical structures (Soepandi 1985:105, 186), but this usage is quite specialized. Most native Sundanese speakers I asked did not know the word at all, and many Sundanese dictionaries do not define it. Sources from the nineteenth and early twentieth centuries in European languages tend to use the term tandak to refer to most Indonesian and Malay dance. Jonathan Rigg defined the term in his 1862 Sundanese-English dictionary as "to dance, especially as the natives do by making postures rather than by dancing as Europeans" (Rigg 1862:478). It is a common term in Malay, where it means dancing in general and also refers to a female entertainer (Goldsworthy 1979). Dutch readers were apparently familiar enough with the term to apply Dutch grammatical endings to create such hybrid words as *tandakken*. The late Cirebonese dalang topeng Sujana Arja told me that he had heard the word

NOTES TO PAGES 63–76

tandak used by a Dutch observer once to describe his dancing, so he assumed it was a Dutch word (personal communication, July 11, 1999).

12. Although there are still pieces in the Sundanese repertoire that work this way, they are primarily for use in wayang fight sequences; Foley calls such pieces "free tunes" (Foley 1979:146). Weintraub uses the term *lagu perang* (fight/war song) for these pieces in wayang (Weintraub 1997:147). It is common in central Javanese wayang wong (wayang drama performed by human actor-dancers) to adjust the structure of pieces to conform to the action (cf. Susilo 1984).

13. The tari kursus repertoire includes a couple of unusual musical changes instigated by the choreography. One movement sequence in the refined "Lenyepan" dance called *eungleuk tujuh* calls for an extra goong stroke (*goong maling*, "stolen goong") to be played to mark a dance cadence at a spot where no goong stroke would ordinarily be placed, and some dancers perform the movement *naek monggawa*, which serves as a transition between two character types, in such a way that it requires an extra four-beat phrase, ending with a goong stroke, to be infixed—but these are rather insignificant structural changes and are rarely performed these days. Otong Rasta told me that the flexible piece "Kareangan" was once used in tayuban to accompany carrying the tray (which held the keris and soder) to the next designated dancer (personal communication, March 10, 1999).

14. Abun Somawijaya characterizes this introduction as a distinct piece—*gending Sorong/Nyorong* (1990:52).

15. These structures are often "irregular" in themselves, however; for example, the ketuk tilu song "Geboy" has four goong phrases with 40, 4, 4, and 8 beats, respectively.

16. The Jugala company, for example, has produced few new recordings since 1989 (Euis Komariah, personal communications, August 5, 1999, and April 18, 2007); however, their existing catalog of recordings is widely available, and their studios are in use for other (pop and dangdut) projects.

17. "Dengan sebuah kaset, setiap orang bisa menari ketuktilu/Jaipongan berdasarkan/mengikuti irama kendang dan atau melodi gendingnya."

18. "Penyajian Karawitan terutama tepak-tepak kendang yang dinamis, telah merangsang setiap orang untuk bergerak dan akhirnya menggemarinya."

19. *Kejanggalan* and *tidak berekspresi*.

20. A video of Asep Sunandar Sunarya performing such a routine can be seen on YouTube at http://www.youtube.com/watch?v=vEp-E8m02KE (accessed December 18, 2008). I thank Maria Mendonça for bringing this video to my attention.

CHAPTER THREE

1. For summaries of the Sangkuriang story, see Aman 1976:10–14; Aveling and Sontani 1979:26–27; Knappert 1977:98–100; Roelcke and Crabb

NOTES TO PAGES 76–92

n.d.:20; Rosidi 1984b:16–26; Soebiantoro and Ratnatunga 1978:9–13; Sumardjo 1988:396–97.

2. He does not explicitly use a triangular model, however, in his "provisional" example of how he interprets myth.

3. Lévi-Strauss himself does not employ this argument in his discussion of the Oedipus myth, but John Peradotto points out that it works well with Lévi-Strauss's homology between the assertion and denial of autochthony, on the one hand, and the over- and undervaluation of kinship, on the other (Peradotto 1983:188).

4. My encapsulation of Lacan's ideas owes much to explications by Grosz (1990) and Rimmer (1993).

5. Kleden-Probonegoro provides perhaps the most comprehensive list: "gandrung, ronggeng, taledek, ledek, kledek, tandak, joged, cokek [and] sinden" (Kleden-Probonegoro 1991:41). Sutton provides a few names that Probonegoro missed: *ringgit* and *lengger* (Sutton 1984:120). I have also come across the term *doger* in West Java. In some theatrical traditions, such as *topeng Betawi*, the term *topeng* also implies a ronggeng-like figure.

6. And by C. M. Pleyte in his 1916 article "De Eerste ronggeng."

7. The makeup of the Sundanese ketuk tilu ensemble, which accompanies some of the oldest types of dance events, exhibits the same layers of influence. The bronze goong and three ketuk hark back to a uniquely Southeast Asian approach to music; double-headed conical drums, such as the kendang played for ketuk tilu, have Indic roots; and the rebab is an import from the Arab Middle East. David Goldsworthy and William Malm point out that the Sumatran and Malaysian ronggeng ensembles likewise encompass three historical strata, although the mapping of instrument to stratum is rather different. These ensembles include a gong (Southeast Asian), frame drums (Arab), and violin (European) (Goldsworthy 1979:436; Malm and Sweeney 1974:10).

8. "Ze staan niet bekend als kuische maagden. . . . als er ronggengs bij zijn, dan zijn ze er als de kippen, beter als de hanen bij."

9. Prostitutes are known as "chickens" in Java. See Geertz's classic essay "Deep Play: Notes on the Balinese Cockfight" for more on cocks as "masculine symbols par excellence" (Geertz 1973a:418).

10. "Armen ende beenen van haer treckende, ende tgheheele lichaem draeyende, als de Honden die uyt haren nest comen cruypen."

11. "Gerak pinggul dan mincid."

12. "Ronggeng Ketuk Tilu sekarang ini, tidak lagi menari sambil menyanyi, namun lagu-lagu tersebut dinyanyikan oleh pesinden khusus."

13. Salam Mulyadi reports that some troupes sidestepped this limitation by hanging microphones from the ceiling for roving ronggeng (personal communication, June 17, 1999).

14. "Het mooiste danseresje van het geheele onderdistrict . . . dat bovendien een mooie stem had."

216

NOTES TO PAGES 96–114

15. Originally published as a serial in the Jakarta daily *Kompas* (Foulchera 1987:90). An English version, translated by René T. A. Lysloff, has been published by Lontar Press (Tohari 2003).
16. "Soal bakat bisa dibentuk. Yang penting penampilannya dulu harus aduhai."
17. For example, a fan identified as "Eri from Surabaya" writes on myhero. com that the dangdut star Inul Daratista "has shown power, strength and greatness as a female. From her, we can learn that women are as good as men. . . . Her potential can make our nation, Indonesia, feel proud" (Eri 2004; cf. Weintraub 2008:374).

CHAPTER FOUR

1. "Om beurten worden manlijke toeschouwers genoodigd, door het toewerpen der slendang, om met een van hen te tandakken. De overige vrouwen dansen dan niet doch begeleiden het met hun zang. Wanneer de danser zijn partij heeft gedanst is het usance deze 'n geldstukje in de kring door de danseressen gevormd, toe te werpen."
2. Buitenzorg was the Dutch name for the city currently called Bogor.
3. Probably modern-day Kalipucang on the southern coast of Java.
4. "Ze zijn ambulant en trekken van dessa tot dessa. Ook worden ze gevraagd op inlandsche feesten, soms op feesten van hooge inlandsche ambtenaren te dansen. Of wel op cultuur ondernemingen verschijnen ze b.v. wanneer de suiker maal, koffie- of theepluk is afgeloopen en er voor de koelies een slametan wordt gegeven ter eere van de goede afloop der werksaamheden."
5. "Des avonds was het een vreeslijk geraas van de gammelang en anklong. Alle de hoofden uit het district en die van Garut waren bij een en vele van hun dansten op eene zeer Statige wijze met de rongings. De drie kinderen voor welke dit feest voornamenlijk plaats had zaten fraaij uitgedost terzuide tusschen de Kandoeroean van Selles en de radeen pattie van Trogon van waar ze tondong naar de ronggengs wierden gevoerd."
6. "'Savond's dansten de meeste hoofden met de rongeng's het welke zeer statig geschiedde, de hoofden die en het rond waren gezeten klapten daarbij de maat met hunne handen de radeenpattie zelve gaf hun daartoe het voorbeeld, hij was ook een van de beste dansers, en de anders zoo stille ingetogen inlanders, wierden door hem zoo op gewouden en zoo vrolijk dat het een genoegen was omtezien; de rang van den eene tot den andere wierdt daarbij echter niet uit het oog verloren en alhoewel veele ander hun door het drinken van arak niet meer in hunne normale toestand waren wierd de eerbied voor hunne meerdere toch niet vergeten."
7. His list of euphemisms includes *baksa, belentuk ngapun, jipeng, doger, kursus, melodi senang hati, ngalaga, ngareueus pare, sirimpi, sampiyung, topeng, topeng babakan, ronggeng gunung, dombret, tari dadung*, and *ketuplak*.

217

NOTES TO PAGES 114–118

8. "Setelah mencapai klimaknya dimana terjadi gerakan yang cukup lincah tiang oncor itu pura-pura tersepak dan terguling sehingga arena itu mejadi gelap, disitulah para penari pria mempergunakan kesempatannya."

9. "Untuk melakukan sesuatu terhadap partenernya."

10. Amelia 1996; Atmadibrata 1996:80–81; Atmadibrata 1997c:45–46; Atmadibrata n.d.:96–102; Atmadibrata, Dunumiharja, and Sunarya 2006:59–62; Azis and Barmaya 1983–84; Fajaria 1996:35–39; Herdiani 1996; Johana 1974–75; Sedyawati, Parani, and Proyek Pengkajian dan Pembinaan Nilai-NilaiBudaya (Indonesia) 1995; Soepandi and Atmadibrata 1976:76–81; Somawijaya 1990:27, 35; Sugiharwati 1980:36; Suhaenah 1996; Sukarya 1997; Sumiati 1996b; Tirasondjaja 1979–80; Turyati 1996.

11. Although many descriptions of events that would be described today as tayuban are extant, and a number of them include glosses for other terms now associated with tayuban, such as ronggeng, none of them mention terms related to tayub. Historians of the present era are quick to apply the label tayuban to these events, despite the apparent anachronistic use of the term (e.g., Caturwati 1992:37; Lubis 1998; Sujana 1993). Terms involving the root tayub/nayub to describe a dance event appear to be in common usage by the early twentieth century. The term tayuban is most likely borrowed from the Javanese, but some have suggested a Sundanese origin for the term. Enoch Atmadibrata reports that according to the older generation of Sundanese dancers, the term tayub is closely connected to the Sundanese term *nayubkeun*, a technique for harvesting fish from a pond (Atmadibrata 1998:2). Entis Sutisna independently provides this etymology, glossing *nayubkeun* as "mancing di kolam" (fishing in a pool; personal communication, June 8, 1999).

12. According to Sumarsam, one of the earliest Javanese references to tayuban is in the *Serat Centhini*, an early nineteenth-century Javanese manuscript (personal communication, August 17, 1999). What Sumarsam translates as tayuban (in another manuscript), however, is in the original Javanese *ananayub* (Sumarsam 1995:35, 271 n. 43). Zoetmulder glosses the old Javanese *sayub* as "fermentation" or "a fermented drink"; the verb form *anayub* refers to drinking such a drink (Zoetmulder, Robson, Darusuprapta, and Suprayitno 1995:1063). It appears that the verb for drinking came to be applied to the dance events at which drinking took place—*nayuban*. Poerbatjaraka speculates that Javanese speakers later assumed the word *nayub* came from *tayub* and ascribed to it the meaning "to dance" or "dance events" (Poerbatjaraka 1954:4). Given the base word *nayub*, the noun form *nayuban* most likely referred to an event. In Sundanese, however, a base word can also be transformed into a locative verb by nasalizing the initial sound and adding the suffix *-an*. In other words, upon hearing the word *nayuban*, Sundanese speakers, like Javanese speakers, might reanalyze the word's base as tayub and interpret the word as a verb form of this new root, meaning something like "to do that which is done at tayub."

NOTES TO PAGES 118–129

13. More recent exegeses of the origins of the term tayuban further reflect these changing values. Anis Sujana reports a couple of *kirata* (retroactive etymology by acronym) for the word tayub: (1) *maTAYa* (dance) plus *guYUB* (together) and (2) *menaTA* (put in order) *paguYUBan* (togetherness) (1993:24–25). Narawati reports that in Cirebon, the term tayuban is sometimes said to come from the Arabic *tayyibah*, which means good, to disassociate it from alcohol (2003b:115) and provide an Islamic stamp of approval.

14. Butler's ideas about performativity are based in J. L. Austin's theory of speech acts, which proposes two types of utterances: constative utterances, which can be evaluated as true or false, and performative utterances, which attempt to "do" something (Austin 1975).

15. This is hardly a new insight. Carl Sagan quotes the fourth-century Neoplatonic philosopher Sallustius: "Myths . . . are things which never happened but always are" (Sagan 1977:8).

16. The Indonesian press has run several articles in recent years that interview the sole remaining traditional practitioner of ronggeng gunung, Nyi Raspi (Arcana 2004; Sudrajat 2004; Suganda 2002), who was about fifty years old in 2004. Raspi's young daughter is also a ronggeng, but she is not following in her mother's footsteps to maintain the traditional protocols of ronggeng gunung; rather, she performs in a newer style, *ronggeng tayub dan organ tunggal* (accompanied by solo keyboard), which allows her more flexibility in choosing songs to sing (Arcana 2004).

17. In the past, *kliningan* referred to a small ensemble for accompanying *kawih* singing (see Hermantoro 1991). *Klining, kilining,* or *kilinding* is an obsolete instrument resembling a Central Javanese *gender* (Soepandi 1985: 111). Kawih singing might also be accompanied by a zither-dominated ensemble called *celempungan* (see Koizumi, Tokumaru, and Yamaguchi 1977:32).

18. Junengsih reports 102 such groups in and around Subang (Junengsih 1997:6), while Dahlan reports 105 (Dahlan 1996:39). Her Suganda estimates the number of sinden in Subang and Karawang to be greater than one thousand (Suganda 1998).

19. Usually about 500–1000 rupiah in 1999.

20. Bartenieff and Davis distinguish between a gesture and a posture and characterize effort and shape flows in the following ways: "Gestural movement is movement in a part of the body; postural movement is movement that spreads throughout the body, visibly affecting all parts and usually involving a weight shift"; "The term 'effort flow' describes the continuum between degrees of 'free' or uncontrolled and of 'bound' or controlled movement. Effort flow is the under-current, the continual aliveness and going on of movement"; "Shape flow characterizes the continuous change in the form or spatial relationship of body parts either towards or away from each other" (Bartenieff and Davis 1972:7–8).

219

NOTES TO PAGES 145–159

CHAPTER FIVE

1. "Bentuk sopan santun secara konvensional sebagai pencerminan suatu sikap, tindakan, dan kelakuan."

2. "Koma atau titik dalam suatu karangan atau pukulan gong dalam gamelan."

3. Lubis describes four particular movements associated with etiquette—*sembah*; *sila* or *émok, cingogo,* and *mando* (sitting cross-legged); *dongko, sampoyong, mamandapan, tapak deku, ngorondang, géngsor,* and *mendék* (walking in a respectful manner); and *ngampil* (carrying a symbolic object solemnly)—which have great visibility in modern Sundanese tari klasik (Lubis 1998:173).

4. "Suatu 'keharusan' untuk menaikkan gengsi seseorang dalam pergaulan di kalangan atas, terutama bagi para santana yang ingin menjadi menak."

5. A.k.a. Aom Doyot; *Aom* is a title bestowed on the son of a regent.

6. From the Dutch word *concours* (competition).

7. "Rerentjangan djisim kuring anu sareng dialadjar ngibing di Bapa Wentar sareng Bapa Kontjer . . . Patokan pangadjaran anu katampi ti 2 guru bieu, aja 9 rupi: . . . Tah anu 9 rupi ieu anu sok dianggo ku umum teh, babakuna dina tajuban dina waktos pepestaan anu gaduh karia. Ieu ibingan njebar di Djawa-kulon. Saparantosna mentjar, nja ieu ibingan didjadikeun ibing 'Cursus.'"

8. Strictly speaking, the verb form is *ngalenyepan.*

9. "Setiap gerak pokok . . . selalu deberi aba-aba oleh tepak kendang. Dengan demikian kendang berperanan sebagai pemberi aba-aba pada gerak tari . . . tidak selamanya terjadi. Hal seperti ini hanya terjadi jika penari belum mahir. Sedang penari yang mahir akan sebaliknya, justru gerak tari yang memberi aba-aba pada tepak kendang."

10. Hobsbawm contrasts "invented tradition" with "custom" (repeated practices that allow changes by giving the sanction of precedent; Hobsbawm 1983:2) and "convention or routine" (sets of practices that are repeated for convenience and efficiency; 1983:3). Custom, convention, and routine all have mechanisms for change, while tradition's "object and characteristic" is "invariance."

11. The museum stopped hosting the tayuban events in 1999 owing to a lack of funding and interest.

12. The CCF provides a European-style venue for both European and Indonesian performances, as well as a café, library, and French language classes. This performance featured a dance group called Kadewan using dancers from IKIP Bandung's (Bandung Teacher's University) theater and dance program.

13. "Tayuban pada awalnya, merupakan tari pergaulan di kalangan bangsawan atau ningrat di pendopo di kadipatenan. Tarian ini biasanya ditarikan sambil mabuk, yang tujuannya untuk menghilangkan rasa malu saat menari dengan ronggeng."

NOTES TO PAGES 164–206

14. Girard applies this model in his analysis of European literature in his books *Deceit, Desire, and the Novel* (1961) and *Dostoïevski: Du double à l'unité* (1963).

15. Sedgwick locates her book's focus on male homosocial desire as expressed in male traffic in women as theorized by Girard, Freud, Lévi-Strauss, and Rubin (Sedgwick 1985:16).

CHAPTER SIX

1. Angle c might also be present where female dancers' movements coordinate with drumming, although in the case of female dancers, whose movements are conventionally supposed to serve and follow the movements of men, a perception of freedom of movement is not necessary.

2. All-night wayang are still the norm, although shorter performances are increasingly common.

3. "Untuk membuat sebuah koreografi menarik, tidak akan lepas dari posisi/ pola lantai."

4. "Dua penari putra/putri dalam suasana segar, centil, erotis, kegembiraan, dan kehangatan serta memperlihatkan rasa percaya diri pada para jawara. Perasaan kuat pada penari pria adalah berusaha merebut simpati ronggeng agar terpikat, yaitu dengan cara memperlihatkan keterampilan bela dirinya disertai unsur humor."

5. I thank Ben Arcangel for sharing his tapes of these examinations with me.

6. "Tari rakyat Ketuk Tilu yang menggambarkan keceriaan pergaulan muda-mudi yang menari perpasang-pasangan. Nama Cikeruh diambil dari nama desa." There is indeed a village and a district called Cikeruh near Sumedang. The title of the dance, however, probably refers to the well-known ketuk tilu song that accompanies it, which in turn, probably does come from the name of the village. Azis and Barmaya suggest that a prince from Sumedang originally brought the song and dance out of its birthplace in Cikeruh into the standard Sundanese repertoire (Azis and Barmaya 1983–84:13).

7. "Dalam tari berpasangan ini penari wanita menantang dan menghindar apabila si penari laki-laki mencoba menyentuh dan mendekatinya."

References

Acciaioli, Greg. 1985. Culture as Art: From Practice to Spectacle in Indonesia. *Canberra Anthropology* 8 (1–2):148–72.

Aman, S. D. B. 1976. *Folk Tales from Indonesia*. Jakarta: Djambatan.

Amelia, Lia. 1996. Jenis tari rakyat dalam kategori ketuk tilu: Kajian teknik dan bentuk terhadap pertunjukan ronggeng gunung, bangreng dan doger. Bandung: STSI Bandung.

Amilia, Aam. 2001. *Bintang Panggung: Biografi Tati Saleh*. Bandung: Granesia.

Anderson, Benedict R. 1965. *Mythology and the Tolerance of the Javanese*. Monograph Series, Cornell University, Modern Indonesia Project. Ithaca, NY: Modern Indonesia Project, Southeast Asia Program, Department of Asian Studies, Cornell University.

———. 1972. The Idea of Power in Javanese Culture. In *Culture and Politics in Indonesia*, edited by Claire Holt. Ithaca, NY: Cornell University Press.

Arcana, Putu Fajar. 2004. Raspi, Nyanyian Sepanjang Malam. *Kompas*, October 7.

Arcangel, Benjamin Fernando. 2006. The System of Communication Cycle and Gender Codes in the Presentational Dances of West Java. Master's thesis, University of Hawai'i, Honolulu.

Ashworth, Matthew. 1996. Tembang Sunda: The Evolution of a Form of Sung Poetry as a Product of Social Change. Bachelor of Science honors thesis, City University of London.

Atmadibrata, Enoch. 1977. Kreativitas dalam seni tari Sunda. *Kawit* I–II:7–11.

———. 1980. Indonesia: West Java: Dance. In *New Grove Dictionary of Music and Musicians*, edited by Stanley Sadie, vol. 9. London: Macmillan.

REFERENCE LIST

———. 1996. West Java: Ketuk Tilu and Tayuban. In *Indonesian Heritage: Performing Arts*, edited by Edi Sedyawati. Singapore: Archipelago Press.

———. 1997a. *Ibing Sunda*. Bandung: Granesia.

———. 1997b. Memahami nilai di balik tarian Sunda. *Kawit* 49:76–86.

———. 1997c. Penelitian kesenian Sunda: Menungjang kebijaksanaan pembinaan kesenian daerah di Jawa Barat. *Kawit* 50:36–50.

———. 1998. Dari ibing tayub ke ibing keurseus: Sumber berbagai kemungkinan pengembangan tari. Bandung: STSI.

———. n.d. *Kuliah di ITB, "Lulusnya" jadi Jago Tari Sunda*. Bandung: n.p.

Atmadibrata, Enoch, Nang Hendi K. Dunumiharja, and Yuli Sunarya. 2006. *Khazanah Seni Pertunjukan Jawa Barat*. Bandung: Dinas Kebudayaan dan Pariwisata Jawa Barat.

Austin, J. L. 1975. *How to Do Things with Words*. Edited by J. O. Urmson and M. Sbisa. 2nd ed. Cambridge: Clarendon Press.

Aveling, Harry. 1996. Theatre of the Underclass: Utuy Tatang Sontani. In *Indonesian Heritage: Performing Arts*, edited by Edi Sedyawati. Singapore: Archipelago Press.

Aveling, Harry, and Utuy Tatang Sontani. 1979. *Man and Society in the Works of the Indonesian Playwright Utuy Tatang Sontani*. Southeast Asia Paper no. 13. Honolulu: Southeast Asian Studies Program, University of Hawaii.

Azis, Abdul, and Nandang R. Barmaya. 1983–84. Tari ketuk tilu sebagai materi kuliah tari rakyat. Bandung: Proyek Pengembangan Institut Kesenian Indonesia, Sub Proyek Akademi Seni Tari Indonesia Bandung.

Baier, Randal. 1986. The Angklung Ensemble of West Java. *Balungan* 2 (1–2):8–16.

———. 1988. Is Trance Tuning Theorized? or, One Musician's View of the Ancestors in West Java, Indonesia. Paper read at the 33rd annual meeting of the Society for Ethnomusicology, Tempe, AZ, October 19–23.

Balkin, J. M. 1998. *Cultural Software: A Theory of Ideology*. New Haven, CT: Yale University.

Bandem, I Madé, and Fredrik Eugene deBoer. 1981. *Kaja and Kelod: Balinese Dance in Transition*. Kuala Lumpur: Oxford University Press.

Banner, Hubert. 1927. *Romantic Java as It Was and Is*. Philadelphia: J. B. Lippincott.

Barker, Joshua David. 1999. The Tattoo and the Fingerprint: Crime and Security in an Indonesian City. Ph.D. diss., Cornell University.

Barrow, Sir John, Pieter Jan Truter, and Kenneth E. Hill. 1806. *A Voyage to Cochinchina, in the Years 1792 and 1793*. London: Printed for T. Cadell and W. Davies.

Bartenieff, Irmgard, and Martha Ann Davis. 1972. Effort-Shape Analysis of Movement: The Unity of Expression and Function. In *Research Approaches to Movement and Personality*, edited by I. Bartenieff, Martti Takala, and Philip Eisenberg. New York: Arno Press.

Barthes, Roland. 1972. *Mythologies*. Translated by Annette Lavers. New York: Hill and Wang.

REFERENCE LIST

Bastin, John. 1973. The Java Journal of Dr. Joseph Arnold. *Journal of the Malaysian Branch of the Royal Asiatic Society* 46 (1):1–92.

Becker, Judith. 1968. Percussion Patterns in the Music of Mainland Southeast Asia. *Ethnomusicology* 12 (2).

———. 1988. Earth, Fire, Sakti, and the Javanese Gamelan. *Ethnomusicology* 32 (3):385–91.

———. 2004. *Deep Listeners: Music, Emotion, and Trancing*. Bloomington: Indiana University Press.

Benamou, Marc. 1998. Rasa in Javanese Musical Aesthetics. Ph.D. diss., University of Michigan.

Best of the Best: Maheswara Musik, Vol. 1. 2000. Jakarta: Musica. Dangdut Karaoke VCD.

Bik, J. Th. 1819. Journaal van eene reis door het Buitenzorgsche en de Preanger regentschappen met den Directeur tot de zaken van Landbouwkunsten en Wetenschappen op Java en naburige Eilandenn gehouden. KITLV: Leiden.

Boellstorff, Tom. 2004. The Emergence of Political Homophobia in Indonesia: Masculinity and National Belonging. *Ethnos* 69 (4):465–86.

Bourdieu, Pierre. 1984. *Distinction: A Social Critique of the Judgement of Taste*. Translated by Richard Nice. Cambridge, MA: Harvard University Press.

Brakel-Papenhuyzen, Clara. 1995. Javanese Talèdhèk and Chinese Tayuban. *Bijdragen tot de taal-, land-en volkenkunde* 151 (4):545–69.

Brandts-Buys, J. S. n.d. Krantenartikelen over Javaanse dans. KITLV: Leiden.

Brenner, Suzanne A. 1995. Why Women Rule the Roost: Rethinking Javanese Ideologies of Gender and Self-Control. In *Bewitching Women, Pious Men: Gender and Body Politics in Southeast Asia*, edited by Aihwa Ong and Michael G. Peletz. Berkeley: University of California Press.

Brinner, Benjamin. 1995. *Knowing Music, Making Music: Javanese Gamelan and the Theory of Musical Competence and Interaction*. Chicago: University of Chicago Press.

Broughton, Simon, Mark Ellingham, David Muddyman, and Richard Trillo, eds. 1994. *World Music: The Rough Guide*. Rough Guides Music Reference Series. London: Rough Guides.

Burnham, Clara Louise. 1894. *Sweet Clover: A Romance of the White City*. Boston: Houghton, Mifflin.

Bush, Robin. 2008. Regional Sharia Regulations in Indonesia: Anomaly or Symptom? In *Expressing Islam: Religious Life and Politics in Indonesia*, edited by Greg Fealy and Sally White. Singapore: Institute of Southeast Asian Studies.

Butler, Judith. 1990. *Gender Trouble: Feminism and the Subversion of Identity*. New York: Routledge.

———. 1993. *Bodies that Matter: On the Discursive Limits of Sex*. New York: Routledge.

Calkins, Keith G. 2005. *A Review of Basic Geometry, Revised* [online textbook]. http://www.andrews.edu/~calkins/math/webtexts/geomtit.htm (accessed 22 May 2006).

REFERENCE LIST

Caturwati, Endang. 1992. R. Tjetje Somantri (1892–1963): Tokoh pembaharu tari Sunda. S-2 thesis, Studi Sejarah, Jurusan Humaniora, Universitas Gadjah Mada, Yogyakarta.

———. 2000. *R. Tjetje Somantri (1892–1963): Tokoh Pembaharu Tari Sunda.* Yogyakarta: Tarawang.

Chernoff, John Miller. 1979. *African Rhythm and African Sensibility.* Chicago: University of Chicago Press.

Clark, Marshall. 1994. Men, Masculinities and Symbolic Violence in Recent Indonesian Cinema. *Journal of Southeast Asian Studies* 35 (1):113–31.

Collins, Elizabeth, and Ernaldi Bahar. 2000. To Know Shame: Malu and Its Uses in Malay Society. *Crossroads: An Interdiscipinary Journal of Southeast Asian Studies* 14 (1):35–69.

Colombant, Nicolas. 1997. Classical Music for Youth, and by Youth. *Jakarta Post,* November 23.

Connell, R. W. 1995. *Masculinities.* Berkeley: University of California.

Cook, Simon. 1992. *Guide to Sundanese Music.* Bandung: Simon Cook.

———. 2001. Indonesia: West Java. In *New Grove Dictionary of Music and Musicians,* edited by Stanley Sadie, vol. 12. London: Macmillan.

Cooper, Grosvenor, and Leonard B. Meyer. 1960. *The Rhythmic Structure of Music.* Chicago: University of Chicago Press.

Cooper, Nancy I. 2000. Singing and Silences: Transformations of Power through Javanese Seduction Scenarios. *American Ethnologist* 27 (3):609–44.

———. 2004. Tohari's Trilogy: Passages of Power and Time in Java. *Journal of Southeast Asian Studies* 35 (3):531–56.

Couperus, Louis. 1921. *The Hidden Force.* Translated by Alesander Teixera de Mattos. New York: Dodd, Mead.

Dahlan, Mas Nana Munajat. 1996. Bajidor: Dalam pertunjukan kliningan-bajidoran di Kabupaten Subang. S-1 skripsi, Jurusan Tari, STSI Bandung, Bandung.

Dampak ecstasy pada tubuh. 1996. Kompas Online, July 14. http://www.kompas .co.id/9607/14/iptek/damp.htm (accessed December 6, 2000).

Dawkins, Richard. 2006 [1989]. *The Selfish Gene.* Oxford: Oxford University.

Dell, Cecily. 1977. *A Primer for Movement Description Using Effort-Shape and Supplementary Concepts.* New York: Dance Notation Bureau.

DeVale, Sue Carole. 1977. A Sundanese Gamelan: A Gestalt Approach to Organology. Ph.D. diss., Northwestern University.

———. 1978. The Gamelan. *Field Museum of Natural History Bulletin* (January): 3–12.

Djadja, S., H. 1998. *Pangandaran dan Ronggeng Gunung.* Ciamis: Seksi Kebudayaan Departemen Pendidikan dan Kebudayaan.

Djajadiningrat, Pangeran Aria Achmad. 1936. *Herinneringen van Pangeran Aria Achmad Djajadiningrat.* Amsterdam: G. Kolff.

Durban Arjo, Irawati. 1989. Women's Dance among the Sundanese of West-Java, Indonesia. *Asian Theatre Journal* 6 (2):168–78.

———. 1998. *Perkembangan tari Sunda: Melacak jejak Tb. Oemay Martakusuma dan Rd. Tjetje Somantri*. Bandung: Masyarakat Seni Pertunjukan Indonesia (MSPI).

———. 2007. *Tari Sunda Tahun 1880–1990*. Bandung: Pusbitari Press.

Dyck, J. Z. van. 1922. *Garoet en omstrenken: Zwerftochten door de Preanger*. Batavia: G. Kolff.

Earl, George Windsor. 1837. *The Eastern Seas, or Voyages and Adventures in the Indian Archipelago in 1832–33–34*. London: Wm. H. Allen.

Edmunds, Lowell, and Alan Dundes, eds. 1983. *Oedipus: A Folklore Casebook*. New York: Garland.

Ekadjati, Edi S. 1995. *Kebudayaan Sunda (Suatu Pendekatan Sejarah)*. Jakarta: Pustaka Jaya.

Eri. 2004. *Musician Hero: Inul Daratista*. The My Hero Project. http://myhero .com/myhero/heroprint.asp?hero=Daratista (accessed June 16, 2008).

Eringa, F. S. 1984. *Soendaas-Nederlands woordenboek*. Dordrecht: Foris.

Errington, Shelly. 1990. Recasting Sex, Gender, and Power: A Theoretical and Regional Overview. In *Power and Difference: Gender in Island Southeast Asia*, edited by Jane Monnig Atkinson and Shelly Errington. Stanford, CA: Stanford University Press.

Euclid. 2006. *Elements Book I: The Fundamentals of Geometry*. http://aleph0.clarku .edu/~djoyce/java/elements/Euclid.html (accessed May 11, 2006).

Fajaria, Ria Dewi. 1996. *Ketuk tilu dalam konteks tari pergaulan*. Bandung: STSI Bandung.

Fessler, Daniel M. T. 1999. Toward an Understanding of the Universality of Second Order Emotions. In *Biocultural Approaches to the Emotions*, edited by Alexander Laban Hinton. New York: Cambridge University Press.

Foley, Kathy. 1979. The Sundanese Wayang Golek: the Rod Puppet Theatre of West Java. Ph.D. diss., University of Hawai'i.

———. 1989. Of Gender and Dance in Southeast Asia: From Goddess to Go-Go Girl. In *Proceedings of the 20th Anniversary CORD Conference*. New York: Congress on Research in Dance.

———. 1990a. My Bodies: The Performer in West Java. *TDR* 34 (2):62(19).

———. 1990b. *The World of the Wayang: Puppetry of Indonesia*. Atlanta: Center for Puppetry Arts Museum.

Foulchera, Keith. 1987. Historical Past and Political Present in Recent Indonesian Novels. *Asian Studies Review* 11 (1):87–99.

Freud, Sigmund. 1955. *The Interpretation of Dreams*. [1st] ed. New York: Basic Books.

———. 1961. *Civilization and its Discontents*. Standard ed. New York: W. W. Norton.

Fryer, Ruth M. 1989. Sundanese Theory and Practice in the Performance of Gamelan in Bandung, West Java. Ph.D. thesis, Queen's University of Belfast.

Fryke, Christopher, and Christopher Schweitzer. 1700. *A Relation of Two Several Voyages Made into the East-Indies*. London: D. Brown, S. Crouch, J. Knapton, R. Knaplock, J. Wyate, B. Took, and S. Buckley.

REFERENCE LIST

Fukuoka, Shoto. 2003. Chapter 6: Gamelan Degung: Traditional Music in Contemporary West Java. In *Globalization in Southeast Asia: Local, National and Transnational Perspectives*, edited by Shinji Yamashita, Teruo Sekimoto, and J. S. Eades. New York: Berghahn Books.

Gandamihardja, Suhari. 1978–79. Kesenian ketuktilu. *Kawit* 19:33–37.

Gardner, Stephen L. 1998. *Myths of Freedom: Equality, Modern Thought, and Philosophical Radicalism*. Westport, CT: Greenwood Press.

Geertz, Clifford. 1973a. Deep Play: Notes on the Balinese Cockfight. In *The Interpretation of Cultures*, edited by Clifford Geertz. New York: Basic Books.

———. 1973b. Person, Time, and Conduct in Bali. In *The Interpretation of Cultures*, edited by Clifford Geertz. New York: Basic Books.

Goldsworthy, David. 1979. Melayu Music of North Sumatra: Continuities and Change. Ph.D. thesis, Monash University.

———. 2005. Cyclic Properties of Indonesian Music. *Journal of Musicological Research* 24:309–33.

Golsan, Richard Joseph. 1993. *René Girard and Myth: An Introduction*. New York: Garland.

Grosz, Elizabeth A. 1990. *Jacques Lacan: A Feminist Introduction*. London and New York: Routledge.

Gutman, Matthew C. 1997. Trafficking in Men: The Anthropology of Masculinity. *Annual Review of Anthropology* 26:395–409.

Hamid, D. H. Nurendah. 1976–77. Banjet: teater rakyat Jawa Barat bercakal bakal para pendekar. *Buletin Kebudayaan Jawa Barat* 10:30–31.

Hanan, David. 1992. The Ronggeng Dancer: Another Paradigm for Erotic Spectacle in the Cinema. *East-West Film Journal* 6 (1):156–90.

Hardjana, Suka. 1996. Keroncong and Dangdut. In *Indonesian Heritage: Performing Arts*, edited by Edi Sedyawati. Singapore: Archipelago Press.

Harjantho, Jen. 1970. Sebuah Tjatatan tentang Nji Ronggeng. *Pikiran Rakyat*, November 2, 4.

Harrell, Max Leigh. 1974. The Music of the Gamelan Degung of West Java. Ph.D. diss., UCLA.

———. 1977. *Penca, the Art of Self-Defense, and Topeng Babakan, Masked Dance, from Sunda, West Java*. New York: Performing Arts Program of the Asia Society.

———. 1980. West Java. In *The New Grove Dictionary of Music and Musicians*, edited by Stanley Sadie, vol. 9. London: MacMillan.

Hatch, Martin. 1985. Popular Music in Indonesia. In *Popular Music Perspectives 2: Papers from the Second International Conference on Popular Music Studies, Reggio Emilia, September 19–24, 1983*, edited by David Horn. Göteborg: IASPM.

Hatley, Barbara. 1990. Theatrical Imagery and Gender Ideology in Java. In *Power and Difference: Gender in Island Southeast Asia*, edited by Jane Monnig Atkinson and Shelly Errington. Stanford, CA: Stanford University Press.

Hefner, Robert W. 1987. The Politics of Popular Art: Tayuban Dance and Culture Change in East Java. *Indonesia* 43:75–96.

REFERENCE LIST

Heider, Karl G. 1991. *Landscapes of Emotion: Mapping Three Cultures of Emotion in Indonesia*. Cambridge: Cambridge University Press.

Heins, Ernst L. 1977. Goong Renteng: Aspects of Orchestral Music in a Sundanese Village. Ph.D. diss., University of Amsterdam.

Hellwig, Jean. 1993. Jaipongan: The Making of a New Tradition. In *Performance in Java and Bali: Studies of Narrative, Theatre, Music, and Dance*, edited by Bernard Arps. London: School of Oriental and African Studies, University of London.

Herdiani, Een. 1996. Ketuk tilu dalam konteks upacara. Bandung: STSI Bandung.

Hermantoro, Dwiono. 1991. *Garap lagu kiliningan materi kuliah karawitan Sunda di STSI Surakarta: Laporan penelitian*. Surakarta: Sekolah Tinggi Seni Indonesia.

HERS/NAR. 2002. Jaipong, Goyang Teruuuussss . . . ! *Kompas*, July 11.

Hesselink, Liesbeth. 1992. Prostitution: A Necessary Evil, Particularly in the Colonies: Views on Prostitution in the Netherlands East Indies. In *Indonesian Women in Focus: Past and Present Notions*, edited by Elsbeth Locher-Scholten and Anke Niehof. Leiden: KITLV Press.

Hobsbawm, Eric. 1983. Introduction: Inventing Traditions. In *The Invention of Tradition*, edited by Eric Hobsbawm and Terence Ranger. Cambridge: Cambridge University Press.

Holt, Claire. 1967. *Art in Indonesia: Continuities and Change*. Ithaca, NY: Cornell University Press.

Hood, Mantle C. 1967. The Enduring Tradition: Music and Theatre in Java and Bali. In *Indonesia*, edited by Ruth T. McVey. New Haven, CT: Southeast Asian Studies, Yale University.

Hugh-Jones, Jonathan. 1982. Karawitan Sunda: Tradition Newly Writ; A Survey of Sundanese Music since Independence. *Recorded Sound* 82:19–34.

Ingleson, John. 1986. Prostitution in Colonial Java. In *Nineteenth and Twentieth Century Java: Essays in Honor of Professor J. D. Legge*, edited by David P. Chandler and M. C. Ricklefs. Clayton: Southeast Asian Studies, Monash University.

Iskandar, Rachmat. 2005. Menyoal kultur keberanian orang Sunda. *Pikiran Rakyat*, February 5.

Johana, Jojo. 1974–75. Ketuk tilu di Ujungberung. *Buletin Kebudayaan Jawa Barat* 2:33–37.

Johnson, Carolyn Schiller. 1998. Performing Ethnicity: Performance Events in Chicago 1893–1996. Ph.D. diss., University of Chicago.

Jones, Gavin W., Endang Sulistyaningsih, and Terence H. Hull. 1998. Prostitution in Indonesia. In *The Sex Sector: The Economic and Social Bases of Prostitution in Southeast Asia*, edited by Lin Leam Lim. Geneva: International Labour Office.

Jukes, Joseph Beete. 1847. *Narrative of the Surveying Voyage of H. M. S. Fly*. London: T. & W. Boone.

Junengsih. 1997. Bajidoran Subang: Tinjauan khusus sekarannya. S-1 skripsi, Jurusan Karawitan, STSI Bandung, Bandung.

Jurriëns, Edwin. 2004. *Cultural Travel and Migrancy: The Artistic Representation of Globalization in the Electronic Media of West Java*. Leiden: KITLV Press.

REFERENCE LIST

Kartodirdjo, Sartono. 1982. The Regents in Java as Middlemen: A Symbolic Action Approach. In *Papers of the Dutch-Indonesian Historical Conference held at Lage Vuursche, the Netherlands 23–27 June 1980*, edited by Gerrit Schutte and Heather Sutherland. Leiden: Bureau of Indonesian Studies under the auspices of the Dutch and Indonesian Steering Committees of the Indonesian Studies Programme.

Keeler, Ward. 1975. Musical Encounter in Java and Bali. *Indonesia* 19:85–126.

———. 1983. Shame and Stage Fright in Java. *Ethos* 11 (3):152–65.

———. 1990. Speaking of Gender in Java. In *Power and Difference: Gender in Island Southeast Asia*, edited by Jane Monnig Atkinson and Shelly Errington. Stanford, CA: Stanford University Press.

Kilborne, Benjamin. 2002. *Disappearing Persons: Shame and Appearance*. Albany: State University of New York Press.

Kincheloe, Joe L. 2005. On to the Next Level: Continuing the Conceptualization of the Bricolage. *Qualitative Inquiry* 11 (3):323–50.

Kleden-Probonegoro, Ninuk. 1991. Seks dalam seni pertunjukan tradisional. *Prisma* 20 (7):36–52.

Knappert, Jan. 1977. *Myths and Legends of Indonesia*. Singapore: Heinemann Educational Books (Asia).

Koizumi, Fumio, Yoshihiko Tokumaru, and Osamu Yamaguchi. 1977. *Asian Musics in an Asian Perspective: Report of Asian Traditional Performing Arts 1976*. Tokyo: Heibonsha.

Kornhauser, Bronia. 1978. In Defence of Kroncong. In *Studies in Indonesian Music*, edited by Margaret J. Kartomi. Melbourne: Centre of Southeast Asian Studies, Monash University.

Kost, K. S. n.d. Dari ronggeng sampai jurukawih. *Kawit* 16 (IV–II):11–13.

Kubarsah, Ubun. 1996. *Waditra: Mengenal alat-alat kesenia daerah Jawa Barat*. Bandung: CV Beringin Sakti.

Kunst, Jaap. 1973. *Music in Java*. 3rd enlarged ed. 2 vols. The Hague: Martinus Nijhoff.

Kunst, Jaap, and C. J. A. Kunst–van Wely. 1923. Over toonschalen en instrumenten van West-Java. *Djawa* 3:26–40.

Lamster, J. C. 1929. *The East Indies*. Translated by F. C. Cole. Haarlem: Droste's Cocoa and Chocolate Manufactory.

Lazarus, Richard S. 1991. *Emotion and Adaptation*. New York: Oxford.

Lee, Dorothy Sara, ed. 1984. *The Federal Cylinder Project, Volume 8: Early Anthologies*. Washington: Library of Congress.

Lévi-Strauss, Claude. 1967. *Structural Anthropology*. New York: Anchor Books.

Lubis, Nina H. 1998. *Kehidupan kaum ménak Priangan 1800–1942*. Bandung: Pusat Informasi Kebudayaan Sunda.

Lysloff, René, and Deborah Wong. 1998. Popular Music and Cultural Politics. In *The Garland Encyclopedia of World Music*, vol. 4, *Southeast Asia*, edited by Terry E. Miller and Sean Williams. New York: Garland.

Malm, William P., and Amin Sweeney. 1974. *Studies in Malaysian Oral and Musical Traditions: Music in Kelantan, Malaysia, and Some of Its Cultural Implica-*

tions. Ann Arbor: Center for South and Southeast Asian Studies, University of Michigan.

Manuel, Peter. 1988. *Popular Musics of the Non-Western World*. New York: Oxford University Press.

Manuel, Peter, and Randall Baier. 1986. Jaipongan: Indigenous Popular Music of West Java. *Asian Music* 18 (1):91–110.

Marliana, Lina. 1996. Ketuk tilu gaya Priangan. Bandung: STSI Bandung.

Martasasmita, Ahmad. 1978–79. Naskah dokumentasi topeng banjet Karawang. *Kawit* 19:16–21.

Maryono, O'ong 1999. Pencak Silat in the Indonesian Archipelago. *Rapid Journal* 4 (12):38–39.

Masunah, Juju, Rita Milyartini, Oya Yukara, Uus Karwati, and Deni Hermawan. 2003. *Angklung di Jawa Barat: Sebuah perbandingan: Buku 1*. Bandung: P4ST UPI.

Muda, Mas Nanu. 1997. Antara sinden, bajidor, dan uang. *Pikiran Rakyat*, February 15, 14.

———. 1999. Erotis sinden yang bikin heboh. *Pikiran Rakyat*, June 10, 14.

Murgiyanto, Sal. 1991. *Aspects of Indonesian Culture: Dance*. New York: Festival of Indonesia Foundation.

———. 1998. Indonesia: Sundanese Dance Traditions. In *International Encyclopedia of Dance*, edited by Selma Jeanne Cohen. New York: Oxford University Press.

Myers, Douglas. 1992. Jaipongan: A Seed Takes Root. *Archipelago* (5):44–46.

Narawati, Tati. 2003a. Citra kesatria ideal dalam seni pertunjukan Sunda. In *Seni dan pendidikan seni: Sebuah bunga rampai*, edited by R. M. Soedarsono. Bandung: UPI.

———. 2003b. Sumbangan Cirebon terhadap perkembangan seni pertunjukan di Priangan. In *Seni dan pendidikan seni: Sebuah bunga rampai*, edited by R. M. Soedarsono. Bandung: UPI.

Natapradja, Iwan. 1971. Karawitan Sunda. Unpublished manuscript.

———. 1975. Sundanese Dances. *Selected Reports in Ethnomusicology* 2 (2):103–8.

Notosusanto, Nugroho, and Sarah Weiss. 1995. Tayuban. *RIMA* 29 (1–2):119–24.

Oetomo, Dede. 2000. Masculinity in Indonesia: Genders, Sexualities, and Identities in a Changing Society. In *Framing the Sexual Subject: The Politics of Gender, Sexuality, and Power*, edited by Richard Parker, Regina Maria Barbosa, and Peter Aggleton. Berkeley: University of California Press.

Ortner, Sherry B., and Harriet Whitehead. 1981. Introduction: Accounting for Sexual Meanings. In *Sexual Meanings: The Cultural Construction of Gender and Sexuality*, edited by Sherry B. Ortner and Harriet Whitehead. Cambridge: Cambridge University Press.

Panitia Kamus, Lembaga Basa, dan Sastra Sunda [Dictionary Committee, Department of Sundanese Language and Literatures]. 1969. *Kamus Umum Basa Sunda*. Bandung: Tarate.

Parker, Andrew, and Eve Kosofsky Sedgwick. 1995. *Performativity and Performance, Essays from the English Institute*. New York: Routledge.

REFERENCE LIST

Pausacker, Helen. 2004. Presidents as Punakawan: Portrayal of National Leaders as Clown-Servants in Central Javanese Wayang. *Journal of Southeast Asian Studies* 35 (2):213–33.

Peacock, James L. 1968. *Rites of Modernization: Symbolic and Social Aspects of Indonesian Proletarian Drama*. Chicago: University of Chicago Press.

Peletz, Michael G. 1996. *Reason and Passion: Representations of Gender in a Malay Society*. Berkeley: University of California Press.

Pemberton, John. 1994. *On the Subject of "Java."* Ithaca, NY: Cornell University Press.

Peradotto, John. 1983. Oedipus and Erichthonius: Some Observations of Paradigmatic and Syntagmatic Order. In *Oedipus: A Folklore Casebook*, edited by Lowell Edmunds and Alan Dundes. New York: Garland.

Perlman, Marc 1998. The Social Meanings of Modal Practices: Status, Gender, History, and Pathet in Central Javanese Music. *Ethnomusicology* 42 (1):45–80.

Planasari, Sita. 2005. Ronggeng dan jangeran dalam Orkestra. *Koran Tempo on the Web*. http://www.korantempo.com/korantempo/2005/10/04/Budaya/ krn,20051004,64.id.html (accessed October 4, 2005).

Pleyte, C. M. 1916. De Eerste ronggeng. *Tijdschrift voor Indische taal-, land- en volkenkunde* 57:270–72.

Poerbatjaraka. 1954. Keterangan kata-kata: Najub, najuban; Tor-tor; Galuh; Bagèlan, Kalimantan dan namanja; Batu-tulis Plumpungan; Dimana tempatnja rumah Mpu Bharadah? dan Belas. *Bahasa dan budaja* 3 (2): 3–40.

Probonegoro, Ninuk I. K. 1987. Teater topeng Betawi sebagai simbol transisi masyarakat Betawi. *Jali-jali* 1:21–29.

Raden, Franki. 2008. Djamin, Yazeed. *Grove Music Online*. http://www.grovemusic .com.

Raffles, Thomas Stamford. 1965. *The History of Java*. Vol. 1, *Oxford in Asia Historical Reprints*. Kuala Lumpur: Oxford University Press.

Richardson, Vanessa. 1994. An Analysis of Culture, Gender, and Power in the Films *Nji Ronggeng* and *Roro Mendut*. *RIMA* 28 (2):37–52.

Rigg, Jonathan. 1862. *A Dictionary of the Sunda Language*. Batavia: Lange.

Rimmer, Valerie. 1993. The Anxiety of Dance Performance. In *Dance, Gender and Culture*, edited by Helen Thomas. New York: St. Martin's Press.

Roelcke, Gottfried, and Gary Crabb. n.d. *All around Bandung: Exploring the West Java Highlands*. Bandung: Bandung Society for Heritage Conservation.

Rogers-Aguiniga, Pamela. 1986. Topeng Cirebon: The Masked Dance Theatre of West Java as Performed in the Village of Slangit. Master's thesis, UCLA.

Rosdiani, Erni. 1997. Tari Srikandi-Mustakaweni dan Tari Cikeruhan. Diploma-3, Jurusan Tari, STSI, Bandung.

Rosidi, Ajip. 1961. *Sang Kurian kesiangan: Sebuah tjerita rakjat Sunda*. Bandung: Tiara.

———. 1984a. Ciri-ciri Manusia dan Kebudayaan Sunda. In *Masyarakat Sunda dan Kebudayaanya*, edited by Edi Ekadjati. Jakarta: Girimukti Pasaka.

REFERENCE LIST

———. 1984b. *Manusia Sunda: Sebuah esai tentang tokoh-tokoh sastra dan sejarah.* Cet. 1. ed. Jakarta: Inti Idayu Press.

Rouffaer, Gerret Pieter, and Jan Willem IJzerman. 1915. *De eerste schipvaart der Nederlanders naar Oost-Indie onder Cornelis de Houtman, 1595–1597; journalen, documenten en andere bescheiden.* 's Gravenhage: M. Nijhoff.

Rubin, Gayle. 1975. The Traffic in Women. In *Toward an Anthropology of Women,* edited by Rayna R. Reiter. New York: Monthly Review Press.

Rusliana, Iyus. 1989. *Mengenal sekelumit tari wayang Jawa Barat.* Bandung: ASTI.

Sagan, Carl. 1977. *The Dragons of Eden: Speculations on the Evolution of Human Intelligence.* New York: Ballantine.

Saleh, Sri. 1926. Dialek Bogor. *Poesaka Soenda* 4 (8):126.

Sarluy, J. 1920. Uit mijn vele en interessante ervaringen op Java van 1895 t/m 1920. KITLV: Leiden.

Sedgwick, Eve Kosofsky. 1985. *Between Men: English Literature and Male Homosocial Desire.* New York: Columbia University Press.

Sedgwick, Eve Kosofsky, and Adam Frank. 1995. Shame in the Cybernetic Fold: Reading Silvan Tomkins. In *Shame and Its Sisters: A Silvan Tomkins Reader,* edited by Eve Kosofsky Sedgwick and Adam Frank. Durham, NC: Duke University Press.

Sedyawati, Edi. 1983. Citra ballet Indonesia: Bunga rampai. In *Seni dalam masyarakat Indonesia,* edited by Edi Sedyawati and Sapardi Djoko Damono. Jakarta: Gramedia.

Sedyawati, Edi, Yulianti Parani, and Proyek Pengkajian dan Pembinaan Nilai-Nilai Budaya (Indonesia). 1995. *Ensiklopedi tari Indonesia.* [Ed. 1.]. ed. Jakarta: Departemen Pendidikan dan Kebudayaan Direktorat Jenderal Kebudayaan Direktorat Sejarah dan Nilai Tradisional Proyek Pengkajian dan Pembinaan Nilai-Nilai Budaya.

Seeger, Anthony. 1991. When Music Makes History. In *Ethnomusicology and Modern Music History,* edited by Stephen Blum, Philip V. Bohlman, and Daniel M. Neuman. Urbana: University of Illinois Press.

Seeger, Charles. 1977. *Studies in Musicology, 1935–1975.* Berkeley: University of California Press.

Seni Tari Sunda dalam Perajaan Pehtjun. 1955. *Star Weekly,* July 2, 4.

Sewell, William H. 1992. A Theory of Structure: Duality, Agency, and Transformation. *American Journal of Sociology* 98 (1):1–29.

Soebiantoro, Afwani, and Manel Ratnatunga. 1978. *Folk Tales of Indonesia.* 1st ed. New Delhi: Sterling.

Soedarsono. 1974. *Dances in Indonesia.* Jakarta: Gunung Agung.

Soeharto, M. 1992. *Kamus Musik.* Jakarta: PT Gramedia.

Soepandi, Atik. 1985. *Kamus istilah karawitan Sunda.* Bandung: Satu Nusa.

Soepandi, Atik, and Enoch Atmadibrata. 1976. *Khasanah Kesenian Daerah Jawa Barat.* Bandung: Pelita Masa.

Soepandi, Atik, and Maman Suaman. 1980. *Peranan dan pola dasar kendang dalam karawitan Sunda.* Jakarta: Institut Kesenian Indonesia.

REFERENCE LIST

Soepandi, Atik, Enip Sukanda, and Ubun Kubarsah. 1996. *Ragam cipta: Mengenal seni pertunjukan daerah Jawa Barat.* Bandung: CV Beringin Sakti.

Soeriadiradja, M., and I. Adiwidjaja. 1930. De Soendaneesche dans. *Djawa* 4–5:115–21.

———. 1949. Tari Sunda. In *Tari Djawa dan Sunda.* Djakarta: Noordhoff-Kolff N.V.

Solihin, Asep. 1986. *Perbendaharaan tabuh reog buhun pada perkumpulan seni Reog Mitra Siliwangi Bandung.* Bandung: ASTI.

Somantri, R. Tjetje. 1953a. Njarungum panemu Ki Hadjar Dewantara. *Budaja* 5:13–14.

———. 1953b. Sadjarah ibing di Pasundan: Ibing di Djawa Kulon. *Budaja* 1 (4):29–30.

Somawijaya, Abun. 1990. Perkembangan ketuk tilu buhun hingga jaipongan: Salah satu materi pelajaran pada ASTI Bandung. Bandung: ASTI Bandung.

Sontani, Utuy Tatang. 1962. *Sang kuriang; opera dua babak.* Djakarta: Bhratara.

Spiller, Henry. 1993. Sundanese Dance Accompaniment: The Career of Pa Kayat. *Balungan* 5 (2):15–18.

———. 1996. Continuity in Sundanese Dance Drumming: Clues from the 1893 Chicago Exposition. *World of Music* 39 (2):21–40.

———. 1999. Topeng Betawi: The Sounds of Bodies Moving. *Asian Theatre Journal* 16 (2):260–67.

———. 2001. Erotic Triangles: Sundanese Men's Improvisational Dance in West Java, Indonesia. Ph.D. diss., University of California, Berkeley.

———. 2004. *Gamelan: The Traditional Sounds of Indonesia.* Edited by Michael B. Bakan. World Music Series. Santa Barbara, CA: ABC-CLIO.

———. 2006. What Is "Traditional" Sundanese Dance? In Konferensi Internasional Budaya Sunda (KIBS) [International *Conference on Sundanese Culture*], edited by Ajip Rosidi, H. Édi S. Ékadjati and A. Chaédar Alwasilah. Bandung: Yayasan Kebudayaan Rancagé.

———. 2007. Negotiating Masculinity in an Indonesian Pop Song: Doel Sumbang's "Ronggeng." In *Oh Boy! Masculinities and Pop Music*, edited by Freya Jarman-Ivens. London: Routledge.

———. 2008. *Focus: Gamelan Music of Indonesia.* New York: Routledge.

STE. 1999. Indonesian Philharmonic Orchestra Embraces Ethnic Nuances. *Jakarta Post*, May 16, 9.

Stutterheim, Willem Frederik. 1956. A Thousand Years Old Profession in the Princely Courts on Java. In *Studies in Indonesian Archaeology*, edited by Willem Frederik Stutterheim. The Hague: Martinus Nijhoff.

Suanda, Endo. 1981. The Social Context of Cirebonese Performing Artists. *Asian Music* 13 (1):27–42.

———. 1983. Topeng Cirebon in Its Social Context. M.A. thesis, Wesleyan University.

———. 1985. Cirebonese Topeng and Wayang of the Present Day. *Asian Music* 16 (1):84–120.

———. 1988. Dancing in Cirebonese Topèng. *Balungan* 3 (3):7–15.

———. 1996. Tari dalam topeng Cirebon. In *Kapita selekta tari*, edited by Arthur S. Nalan. Bandung: STSI Press.

———. 1998. Java: Cirebon. In *The Garland Encyclopedia of World Music*, vol. 4, *Southeast Asia*, edited by Terry E. Miller and Sean Williams. New York: Garland.

Sudrajat, Undang. 2004. "Ronggeng Gunung" Mampukah Bertahan? *Pikiran Rakyat*, June 20.

Suganda, Her. 1996. Tjetjep Supriadi, kerisauan wayang golek. *Kompas*, June 14, 10.

———. 1998. *Bajidor dan sinden* (March 8, 1998). *Kompas Online* 1998. http://www.kompas.co.id/kompas%2Dcetak/9903/08/dikbud/baji20.htm (accessed December 6, 2000).

———. 2002. Nonton Ronggeng Gunung, jangan lupa bawa sarung. *Kompas*, October 5.

———. n.d. Deded . . . deded-deng: Ritme gendang Sunda yang seolah menyampaikan dialog. *Kompas*, 8–9.

Sugiharwati, Tutty. 1980. Ketuk tilu Ujungberung sebagai tari rakyat. Sarjana Muda Tari, ASTI Bandung, Bandung.

Suhaenah, Euis. 1996. *Ketuk tilu sebagai aset pariwisata: Tinjauan deskriptif terhadap tari ketuk tilu pada sanggar-sanggar ketuk tilu di kotamadya dan kabupaten Bandung.* Bandung: ASTI/STSI Bandung.

Suhaeti, Etty. 1986. Perkembangan gerak-gerak tari ketuk tilu di Bandung. Sarjana Seni Tari thesis, Jurusan Tari, Institut Seni Indonesia (ISI), Yogyakarta.

Suharto, Ben. 1980. *Tayub: Pengamatan dari segi tari pergaulan serta kaitannya dengan unsur upacara kesuburan.* Yogyakarta: ASTI.

Sujana, Anis. 1993. Tayuban di kalangan bupati dan priyayi di Priangan pada abad ke-19 dan ke-20. S-2 tesis, Humanoria, Universitas Gadjah Mada, Yogyakarta.

———. 1996. Tari kursus. In *Kapita selekta tari*, edited by Arthur S. Nalan. Bandung: STSI Press.

Sukarya, Chandra. 1997. Penyajian karya seni wanda kendang ketuk tilu. Diploma 3, Karawitan, STSI Bandung, Bandung.

Sumardjo, Jakob. 1988. Sangkuriang, Pantun. In *Ensiklopedi nasional Indonesia*. Jakarta: Cipta Adi Pustaka.

———. 2005a. Mitos Nyi Pohaci. *Pikiran Rakyat*, January 29.

———. 2005b. Silih Asah, Silih Asih, Silih Asuh. *Pikiran Rakyat*, January 14.

Sumarsam. 1995. *Gamelan: Cultural Interaction and Musical Development in Central Java.* Chicago: University of Chicago Press.

Sumiati, Lilis. 1996a. *Ketuk tilu sebagai sumber penataran tari kreasi baru.* Bandung: STSI Bandung.

———. 1996b. Tari Rakyat Jawa Barat. In *Kapita selekta tari*, edited by Arthur S. Nalan. Bandung: STSI Press.

REFERENCE LIST

Sunarto. 1990. *Motif-motif pukulan kendang jaipongan pada lagu Banda Urang.* Bandung: ASTI.

Sunarya, Asep Sunandar. 1998. *The Birth of Gatotkaca: A Sundanese Wayang Golek Purwa Performance from West Java.* Translated by Andrew N. Weintraub. Jakarta: Lontar Foundation.

Supandi, Atik. 1970. *Teori dasar karawitan.* Bandung: Pelita Masa.

Suryabrata, Bernard. 1974. Kesenian Cirebon. *Budaja Djaja* 7 (76):538–43.

Susilo, Hardja. 1984. Wayang Wong Panggung: Its Social Context, Technique and Music. In *Aesthetic Tradition and Cultural Transition in Java and Bali,* edited by Stephanie Morgan and Laurie Jo Sears. Madison: Center for Southeast Asian Studies, University of Wisconsin.

Sutherland, Heather. 1973. Notes on Java's Regent Families, Part II. *Indonesia* 17:1–42.

———. 1979. *The Making of a Bureaucratic Elite: The Colonial Transformation of the Javanese Priyayi.* Asian Studies Association of Australia, Southeast Asia Publications Series. Singapore: Heinemann Educational Books (Asia).

Sutton, R. Anderson. 1984. Who Is the Pesindhèn? Notes on the Female Singing Tradition in Java. *Indonesia* 37:119–33.

———. 2002. *Calling Back the Spirit: Music, Dance, and Cultural Politics in Lowland South Sulawesi.* New York: Oxford University Press.

Suwandono. 1978–79. Team kesenian Jawa Barat ke Hongkong. *Kawit* 19 (V–II): 7–9, 31.

Swartz, David. 1997. *Culture and Power: The Sociology of Pierre Bourdieu.* Chicago: University of Chicago Press.

Swindells, Rachel. 2004. Klasik, Kawih, Kreasi: Musical Transformation and the Gamelan Degung of Bandung, West Java, Indonesia. Ph.D. diss., City University, London.

Tamsyah, Budi Rahayu, Purmasih, Tati Purmawati, and A. R. Supratman. 1998. *Kamus Sunda-Indonesia.* Bandung: Pustaka Setia.

Thunberg, Charles Peter. 1795. *Travels in Europe, Africa, and Asia Made between the Years 1770 and 1779. Vol II Containing Two Expeditions to the Interior of the Part of the Country Adjacent to the Cape of Good Hope, and a Voyage to the Island of Java Performed in the Years 1773, 1774, and 1775.* 2nd ed. London: F. and C. Rivington.

Tirasondjaja, Gugum Gumbira. 1979–80. Ketuk tilu merupakan tari rakyat khas Jawa Barat. *Kawit* 23:19–27.

Tirasonjaya, Gugum Gumbira. 1988. Jaipongan, Tari. In *Ensiklopedi nasional Indonesia.* Jakarta: Cipta Adi Pustaka.

Tjarmedi, Entjar, Deded Suparman, Entis Sutisna, and Asep Resmana. 1997. *Pedoman lagu-lagu klasik dan kreasi gamelan degung Jawa Barat.* Bandung: CV Satu Nusa.

Tohari, Ahmad. 1982–86. *Ronggeng Dukuh Paruk; Lintang Kemukus Dina Hari; Jantera Bianglala (a trilogy).* Jakarta: Gramedia.

—. 2003. *The Dancer: A Trilogy of Novels* Translated by René T. A. Lysloff. Jakarta: Lontar Foundation.

Travers, Thomas Otho. 1960. *The Journal of Thomas Otho Travers, 1813–1820.* Edited by John Bastin. Memoirs of the Raffles Museum, no. 4, May 1957. Singapore: AG Banfield.

Truman, Benjamin Cummings. 1893. *History of the World's Fair.* Philadelphia: H. W. Kelley.

Turyati. 1996. Ketuk tilu gaya kaleran. Bandung: STSI Bandung.

Upandi, Pandi. 1977. Peranan kendang dalam tari Sunda khususnya Tarian Monggawa. Sarjana Muda Tari Skripsi, ASTI, Bandung.

—. 1997. *Biografi Encar Carmedi, seniman karawitan Sunda.* Bandung: STSI.

Veth, P. J. 1875. *Java, geographisch, ethnologisch, historisch.* 1st ed. Haarlem: Erven F. Bohn.

Walton, Susan Pratt. 1996. Heavenly Nymphs and Earthly Delights: Javanese Female Singers, Their Music and Their Lives. Ph.D. diss., University of Michigan.

Weintraub, Andrew N. 1997. Constructing the Popular: Superstars, Performance, and Cultural Authority in Sundanese Wayang Golek Purwa of West Java, Indonesia. Ph.D. diss., University of California, Berkeley.

—. 2001. Instruments of Power: Sundanese "Multi-Laras" Gamelan in New Order Indonesia. *Ethnomusicology* 45 (2):197–227.

—. 2004a. The "Crisis of the Sinden": Gender, Politics, and Memory in the Performing Arts of West Java, 1959–1964. *Indonesia* 77:57–78.

—. 2004b. *Power Plays: Wayang Golek Puppet Theater of West Java.* Athens: Ohio University Press.

—. 2006. Dangdut Soul: Who Are "the People" in Indonesian Popular Music? *Asian Journal of Communication* 16 (4):411–31.

—. 2008. "Dance Drills, Faith Spills": Islam, Body Politics, and Popular Music in Post-Suharto Indonesia. *Popular Music* 27:367–92.

Wessing, Robert. 1977. The Position of the Baduj in the Larger West Javanese Society. *Man (New Series)* 12 (2):293–303.

—. 1978. *Cosmology and Social Behavior in a West Javanese Settlement, Papers International Studies: Southeast Asia series no. 47.* Athens: Ohio University Center for International Studies.

Widodo, Amrih. 1995. The Stages of the State: Arts of the People and Rites of Hegemonization. *RIMA* 29 (1&2):1–36.

Williams, Sean. 1998a. Constructing Gender in Sundanese Music. *Yearbook for Traditional Music* 30:74–84.

—. 1998b. Java: Sunda. In *The Garland Encyclopedia of World Music*, vol. 4, *Southeast Asia*, edited by Terry E. Miller and Sean Williams. New York: Garland.

—. 2001. *Sound of the Ancestral Ship: Highland Music of West Java.* New York: Oxford University Press.

REFERENCE LIST

Wilson, Ian Douglas. 2002. The Politics of Inner Power: The Practice of Pencak Silat in West Java. Ph.D. diss., Murdoch University.

Wirakusumah, R. Sambas. 1953. *Hartos widji-widji ibing keurseus*. Rancaekek: Wirahma Sari.

Wright, Michael. 1978. The Music Culture of Cirebon. Ph.D. diss., UCLA.

Yampolsky, Philip. 1987. *Tonggeret* [album liner notes]. New York: Elektra Nonesuch/Icon Records 79173-2.

———. 1994. *Musik Populer Indonesia: Kroncong, Dandut, Langgam Jawa* [album liner notes]. Bandung: MSPI.

———. 1995. Forces for Change in the Regional Performing Arts of Indonesia. *Bijdragen tot de taal-, land- en volkenkunde* 151 (4):700–725.

Yohana, Yoyo. 1979. Tari rakyat ketuk tilu dari Ujung Berung Kabupaten Bandung pada F.T.R. Jawa Barat tahun 1979. *Kawit*:34–37.

Zanten, Wim van. 1989. *Sundanese Music in the Cianjuran Style: Anthropological and Musicological Aspects of Tembang Sunda*. Dordrecht: Foris.

———. 1995. Aspects of Baduy Music in Its Sociocultural Context, with Special Reference to Singing and Angklung. *Bijdragen tot de taal-, land- en volkenkunde* 151 (4):516–43.

Zimmer, Benjamin G. 1999. Unpacking the Word: The Ethnolexicological Art of Sundanese Kirata. *Texas Linguistic Forum: SALSA VI* 42:275–84.

Zoetmulder, P. J., S. O. Robson, Darusuprapta, and Sumarti Suprayitno. 1995. *Kamus Jawa kuna-Indonesia*. Jakarta: KITLV/PT Gramedia Pustaka Utama.

Index

Page references to figures and tables are in italics.

Abay Subardja. *See* Subardja, Abay
Ade Komaran. *See* Komaran, Ade
adeg-adeg, 130
Adiwidjaja, I., 14; "De Soendaneesche dans," 147
aduh bapa (dance movement), 46
"Adumanis" (piece), 70, 71, *72*
Aep Diana. *See* Diana, Aep
aesthetic teams, 171–76; as "angles," 182; male, 195
aesthetics: of dance, 184, 190, 200; challenging of, 209; of erotic triangles, 165–68; theories of, 166–67
Aim Salim. *See* Salim, Aim
akal, 84
ala genah. *See* ngala genah
alcohol. *See under* dance events
alihan, 149
alus (refined), 24, 32; Keeler's description of, 25
amateur, 102; male dancers as, 2, 10, 17, 110, 141, 161, 185–86; versus professional, 102–3, 172–73
ambiguity in drumming. *See under* drumming
ambiguity of leading and following, 158, 149–51, 196; in tari kursus, 156
Amelia, Lia, 112
amok, 30, 31–32
Ana Mulyana. *See* Mulyana, Ana
Anderson, Benedict, 26, 33,

173; "The Idea of Power in Javanese Culture," 27; on Islam and power, 100; on Muslim orthodoxy in Java, 146; on power, 61, 99
angklung, 7–9; buncis, 58
arak, 107. *See also under* dance events
arang-arangan, 203
Arcangel, Ben, 23, 221n5
Ardiwinata, D. K., *Tatakrama Oerang Sunda,* 145
aristocrats, 4; dances of, 10, 12, 13, 15, 19, 63, 91–92, 107, 111, 126, 179; dress, 157, 201; European customs and, 146; lifestyle, 117; patronage of dance, 14, 110; and power, 26, 118; relationship to drummers, 73, 75; upward mobility, 144–46
Arja, Sujana, 125, 141, 214n11
Arjuna, 25, 26
Arnold, Joseph, 105
artis dangdut, 94–95
Asep Sunandar Sunarya. *See* Sunarya, Asep Sunandar
ASKI (Akademi Seni Kawaritan Indonesia), 211n2
Atmadibrata, Enoch, xvi, 10, 44, 147; approach to Sundanese dance history, 17–18; on drumming's functions, 52; on etymology of tayuban, 218n11; on mincid, 214n10

INDEX

audio sense, 168–70
aural sense, 182
Austin, J. L., 219n14
authentic Sundaneseness, 158, 161, 162, 207

Badan Kesenian Indonesia (BKI), 19
badaya, 199
"Badaya" (dance), 15
Baduy, 8
bahasa Indonesia, x
Baier, Randal, 58–59
bajidor, 4, 34, 68, 138, 212n9; in Cikaum,
  Subang, 4–5, 187–89; kirata for, 34,
  212n10
bajidoran, 10, 34, 112, 127–34, 190, 212n9;
  as erotic triangle, 142, 187–89, *188*; as
  source for jaipongan, 13; drum grooves
  of, 128–34; interaction between men
  and sinden in, 128; reaction of audience
  to, 189; similarities and differences with
  dangdut, 135–37; similarities with ketuk
  tilu, 127
bajing, 34–35
"Bajing Luncat" (song), 35
baki, 159
baksa, 200–201
baksarai, 201
Bålådéwa, 26
Balkin, J. M., 41
ballroom dance, 10
bamboo, 8
"Banda Urang/Rendeng Bojong" (piece),
  71, *72*
Bandung, xvi, 3, 5, 12, 33, 67, 106, 113;
  geography of, 77. *See also* Bandung Zoo;
  CCF; IKIP Bandung; Sekolah Tinggi Seni
  Indonesia
Bandung Zoo, xvi, 47, 52, 101, 125, 127,
  184, 185; ronggeng from, 187
bangga, 28, 35, 104, 123, 138, 142, *167*,
  168. *See also* berani; pride
banggreng, 112
bangsing, 134
Banner, Hubert Stewart, 88, 110, 111
Barker, Joshua, 24, 31, 57
Barrow, Sir John, 109
Bartenieff, Irmgard, 129–30, 139
Barthes, Roland, 165–66; on myth, 120–21,
  122; *Mythologies*, 177
basa Sunda. *See* Sundanese language

Becker, Judith, 178; on configurative drum
  patterns, 54; *Deep Listeners: Music,
  Emotion and Trancing*, 48
Bejo Group, 137
Benamou, Marc, on professionalism, 102
berani, 30, 142. *See also* bangga; pride
bersih desa, 4
Between Men (Kosofsky), 40, 163–64
Bidin Suryagunawan, R. *See* Suryagunawan,
  R. Bidin
Bik, J. Th., 107
Bima, 26
binary oppositions, 78, 162–63, 166, 168; in
  wayang mythology, 174
BKI (Badan Kesenian Indonesia), 19
bloking, 160, 200–202, 203
bobodoran, 212n10
body types for dancers, 12
Boellstorff, Tom, 30
Bogor, 217n2. *See also* Buitenzorg
Bourdieu, Pierre, 48, 103, 178; on ideology,
  166
Brakel-Papenhuyzen, Clara, 83, 84
Brenner, Suzanne, 99, 101
bricolage, 41
Brinner, Benjamin, xvi, 214n7
bubukaan, 70
Buitenzorg, 105, 107, 217n2
bukaan (dance movement), 68–69, 130
bupati. *See* regents
Butler, Judith, 122, 165, 178; *Gender Trouble*,
  119

cadential patterns, 48, 51–56, *54–55*, 58, 63;
  in dangdut, 137; in jaipongan, 71, *72*,
  130–31; in ketuk tilu, 66, 115–16; in tari
  kursus, 153; in tepak melem, 56, *56*
Cali Pujang. *See* Kalipucang
"Cangkurileung," 204
capang (dance movement), 51, 68–69,
  130–31
cassette culture in West Java, 66–67
CCF (Centre Culturel Français) Bandung,
  205, 220n12
Cece Somantri. *See* Somantri, R. Tjetje
celempungan, 219n17
centeng, 113
Cepot, 74
character types: in Sundanese dance, 22; tari
  kursus, 150–51; topeng, 12, 22

240

INDEX

Chernoff, John, 124
choreographies: bloking and, 199–201; canonized, 67; conceptualization of, 68; for dance at 1893 World's Columbian Exposition in Chicago, 64, *65*; fixed, 67–68, 156, 164, 197; group dances, 200; increasing complexity of, 118; jaipongan, 68–73, *72*, 139; relationship of music to, 64; "Tari Cikeruhan," 203–5; tari klasik, 158; tari kursus, 150–53, *152, 154, 155,* 156; "Tari Tayuban," 160; two-part structure of in ketuk tilu, 66
Ciamis, 113
Cianjur, 105, 106
Cibodas, 107
Cicih Muda, 97
Cikaum, Subang, 4–5, 187
"Cikeruhan" (piece), 203
cindek (dance movement), 68–69
circumcision ceremonies, 9, 106
Citarum River, 77
congruence theorems, 181–82
Connell, R. W., 24
contradictions of masculinity. *See under* masculinities
Cook, Simon, 53
Cooper, Grosvenor, 54
Cooper, Nancy I., 40, 101; on *Ronggeng Dukuh Paruk* (Tohari), 96–97
Cosmology and Social Behavior in a West Javanese Village (Wessing), 27
cosmology, Sundanese, 39
costume: of male dancers, 159, 185; and masculinity, 205; of ronggeng, 159, 185; for "Tari Cikeruhan," 205–6; for tari kursus, 157
Couperus, Louis, *The Hidden Force,* 109
cursus, 148. *See also* tari kursus

Dahlan, Mas Nana Munajat, 4, 68–69, 212n10
dalang, 26, 193–94, 196; and ronggeng/pasinden, 92–93, 127
dalang topeng, 12, 22–23, 125, 214n11
Damarwulan, 12
dance. *See* dancing
dance events: agricultural roots of, 10, 21, 84; and alcohol, 107, 111, 118; association with illicit sex, 114; common features among, 112;

comparison of upper- and lower-class versions, 111; contexts for, 106–7; dangdut and, 37; European participation in, 109; and Islam, 100; as myth, 121–22; and Oedipal triangle, 81–82; order of dancers in, 105–6, 111; participants in, 105, 107; protocols of, 104–11; as sites for performing masculinity, 36; status and, 108–9; trigonometry of, 181; women's reactions to, 108, 111. *See also* erotic triangle
dance movements: basic stance for jaipongan, 190; European impressions of, 88; funny, 203; mincid, 116; for "Tari Cikeruhan," 204–6; for tari kursus, 149–55, *152, 154, 155,* 160, 201
dance, Sundanese. *See* Sundanese dance
dance triangle. *See* erotic triangle
dancers, male. *See* male dancers
Dances in Indonesia (Soedarsono), 18
dances, wayang, 11–12
dancing: aesthetics of, 116, 140, 199; exploration of masculinity through, 139–40; floor plans of (*see* bloking); and freedom (*see* freedom in dancing); learning, 110, 124–25; and malu, 138–42; as men's activity, 197; motivations for, 139; participatory versus presentational, 11–13, 17, 37, 192; plausible deniability in, 33; reception by audiences of, 17, 207–8; relationship of drumming to, 116, 126, 149–51, 185; and sexual desire, 35; social, 10–11; style, 105, 109–10, 114, 124; style in bajidoran, 130; style complexity, 118; style individuality of, 133; style in ketuk tilu, 115–16; vicarious enjoyment of, 138, 177, 140–41, 188; as visual experience, 20, 157
dancing girls, 63–64, 86, 106, 108
dangdut, 1, 94–95, 134–38, 198, 209; accompaniment for, 95; as accompaniment for men's social dance, 11; artis (*see* artis dangdut); and bajidoran, 135–37; differences with traditional music, 134; drumming for, 11, 135; ensemble for, 134–35, 137; and erotic triangle, 142; ketuk tilu elements in, 137; and malu, 137; as onomatopoeic name, 46–47; reasons for popularity, 37; videos, 37–38

241

INDEX

Danoeredja, R., *Serat-Sinerat Djaman Djoemenengna Raden Hadji Moehamad Moesa*, 93

Daratista, Inul, 11, 217n17

Darul Islam, 114

Dasimah, Nyi, 93

"Daun Pulus/Keser Bojong" (Gumbira), 71, *72*

Daun Pulus/Keser Bojong (Jugala), 189, 190

Davis, Martha Ann, 129–30, 139

Dawkins, Richard, 178

Dayang Sumbi, 76–77

"De Eerste Ronggeng" (Pleyte), 216n6

de Montesquieu, Baron Charles-Louis de Secondat, 213n12

"De Soendaneesche dans" (Soeriadiradja and Adiwidjaja), 147

Deceit, Desire, and the Novel (Girard), 221n14

Deep Listeners: Music, Emotion and Trancing (Becker), 48

deep listening, 48

"Deep Play: Notes on the Balinese Cockfight" (Geertz), 216n9

degung. *See* gamelan degung

desire, 164, 206; Lacan on, 80–81; male homosocial, 163, 164; as response to arbitrary prohibitions, 121; sexual, 99; signification of, 99

devadasi, 84

Dewi Sri (rice goddess), 7, 8, 39, 83, 84, 168, 173; insemination by rain of, 10

Dian (recording company), x

Diana, Aep, xii, 51, *51*, 68

divine nature of drumming and ronggeng, 173

Djajadiningrat, Pangeran Aria Achmad (P. A. A.), on ronggeng and tayuban, 91

Djamin, Yazeed, *Nyi Ronggeng* (symphonic composition), 97

Djawa (periodical), 147, 211n5

Doel Sumbang. *See* Sumbang, Doel

dogdog, 7, 49–50, 75, 214n9; as icon of egalitarianism, 58, 75; patterns, 55–59

doger, 112

Don Quixote (Cervantes), 163

Dostoïevski: Su double à l'unité (Girard), 221n14

double standard, 23

doxa (Bourdieu), 178

Droste's Cocoa and Chocolate Company, 108

drummer, as consumer/producer of visual messages, 170–71; gender of, 174–76; as professionals, 102–3, 141

drumming, 38, 39, 163, 207; ambiguity in, 2, 44, 48, 62; as audio message, 170–71; basic grooves for Sundanese dance, 136; cadential patterns, 53–55; combining mincid and cadential patterns, 63; for dangdut, 11, 135–36; for degung, 53; as disembodied impulse, 173; at 1893 World's Columbian Exposition in Chicago, 64; as element of erotic triangle, 122; as exclusively male activity, 174–76; and freedom, 149; as icon of egalitarianism, 58; imitation of by dancers, 164; imitation of in kacapi music, 55; for jaipongan, 192–93, 194–95; jokes about, 74, 175–76; for ketuk tilu, 66, 75; leading and following, 67, 71–73, 75; as liberating and regulative, 39, 43; loosely coupled (with dance) versus tightly coupled, 117, 150; as metaphor for power, 44, 61–63, 75, 163–64, 174; mnemonics, xiv, 45–48, 50–51, 189; and movement, 43–48, 57–58, 59, 62, 74, 90, 185, 116, 126; and musical rhythm, 51–52; notation for, 50–51, 68; physical requirements for, 175; and power, 48, 163–64, 206; relationship to dance movements, 43, 74, 185, 116, 126; relationship to presentational dance of, 149–51; rhythmic groupings of three in, 54, 136; signals, 64, 149–50; for tayuban, 75

drums. *See* dogdog; kendang; kulanter; terbang

dua wilet, 159

Durban Ardjo, Irawati, 14–15, 200; approach to Sundanese dance history of, 19–20; *Perkembangan tari Sunda*, 19; *Tari Sunda tahun 1880–1990*, 19

Earl, George Windsor, 106, 108, 109, 110, 111

ecstasy (drug), 137

effort-shape, 129–30, 219n20

egot, 4, 128, 187

Ekadjati, Edi S., 39

Elements (Euclid), 213n13

elmu, 9, 124

engkeg gigir (dance movement), 46, *152, 154, 155*

INDEX

Entis Sutisna. *See* Sutisna, Entis
"Erang" (piece), 115, 116
erotic triangle of Sundanese dance, x, xiv,
40–42; and aesthetics, 165–68; "angles"
and "sides" of, 41–42, 177, 182, *183*;
congruence of, 181–84; dance events
as, 41, 176–80; deformation of, 172–73,
179–80; elements of, 38, 122, 167–68;
as flexible framework, 143; incomplete,
193; jaipongan as, 191–94, *191*, *192*,
195–96, *195*, *197*; ketuk tilu as, 184–87;
meaning of, 179; noncongruent dances
and, 197–207; in a nutshell, 207; "Tari
Cikeruhan" (Salim) as, 206; tari kursus
as, 148–51; tayuban as, 144
erotic triangles, 40, 76, 103, 142; as model
of desire and gender division, 165;
Sedgwick on, 163–64; traffic of women
and, 165
Errington, Shelly, 174
etiquette, 145–46, 175, 220n3
Euclid, *Elements*, 213n13
Euclidian geometry, 41, 168, 181, 183, 184,
198; triangle congruence theorems of,
41
Euis Komariah, 47–48
European customs, Sundanese aristocrats
and, 146

female entertainers. *See* ronggeng
females, physical capabilities of, 175
Fessler, Daniel, 28–30, 31
field (Bourdieu), 178, 208
Foley, Kathy, 114; on goong strokes, 52; on
ronggeng, 85–86; on singers in wayang
golek, 92
Foley artist, drummer as, 155
following. *See* leading and following
Frank, Adam, on Silvan Tomkins and
shame, 29–30, 31
freedom, 161, 203, 206; in dancing, 2, 4,
35–36, 38, 68, 75, 104, 114, 115, 116,
119, 123–26, 129, 148, 156, 164, 196,
207; in dangdut, 136; illusion/myth
of, 16, 36; in "Tari Baksa," 202–3; in
tari kursus, 148, 156; in tayuban,
144
Freud, Sigmund, 119, 166; on Oedipus
myth, 78–79
Fryer, Ruth, 92
Fryke, Christopher, 86

gamelan degung, 6; klasik pieces for, 53;
kawih, 6
gamelan salendro, 128; instrumental parts
for, 152; instrumentation of, 151–52;
retuning of, 93; singers in, 91, 207; as
wayang golek accompaniment, 194
Gandakusumah, R., 92, 146–47
Gardner, Stephen L., 123, 126; *Myths of
Freedom*, 36
Garut, 107, 113
Gatotkaca, 194; as ideal hero, 26. *See also*
Jabang Tutuka
"Gawil" (dance), 15, 201
"Geboy" (piece), 215n15
gedig, *152*, 153, *154*, *155*
Geertz, Clifford, 27, 138; on cockfights,
123; "Deep Play: Notes on the Balinese
Cockfight," 216n9
gendang, 49, 135. *See also* kendang
gender, 143; in dancing, 174–76;
performativity of, 119–20; and triangles,
40–42
gender identities, 22, 23, 162;
contradictions in, 1; feminine, 23–24;
masculine, 1; performance of, 199;
structuralist approach to, 162–63;
gender ideologies, Sundanese, 86, 162
gender symbolism in agricultural rituals, 21
Gender Trouble (Butler), 119
"Gendu" (piece), 159
geometry of dance events, 168–80
geometry theorem, 192
Gerak Maya (dance group), 147
Geusan Ulun Museum. *See* Prabu Geusan
Ulun Museum
Giddens, Anthony, 40
Gilman, Benjamin Ives, 63
Girard, René, 163–64; *Deceit, Desire, and the
Novel*, 221n14; *Dostoïevski: Su double à
l'unité*, 221n14
Goldsworthy, David, 83, 114; on cadences,
54; on dance event protocols in
Southeast Asia, 104; on gongs, 52
golok, 204
gong. *See* goong
"Gonjing Miring" (piece), 204
goong, 3; significance of strokes, 52, 146
"Gotong Singa" (dance), 15
goyang, 74, 95, 204
"Goyang Karawang" (Bobby S. and Muchtar
B.), 38

243

INDEX

"Graeni" (dance), 15
Gugum Gumbira Tirasondjaja. *See* Gumbira
  Tirasonjaya, Gugum
Guinness stout, 4
Gumbira Tirasonjaya, Gugum, 112, 128,
  189–90; on threeness, 39
Gummock, 109, 111

habitus, 166, 178, 208; of listening, 48
Hadidjah, Hajah Idjah, 94, 190
hajat, 67–68; types of entertainment at, 95
halus. *See* alus
Hanan, David, 141; on *Nyi Ronggeng*, 95–96
Harjantho, Jen, 96
Harrell, Max, 54
Hartos Widji-widji Ibing Keurseus
  (Wirakusumah), 148
Hefner, Robert, 83
Heins, Ernst, on gender in Sundanese music,
  175–76
Hesselink, Leisbeth, 146
heterosexual matrix, 121, 176–77, 178
heterosexuality, compulsory, 79, 119
hiburan, 21
Hidden Force, The (Couperus), 109
History of Java (Raffles), 8, 6
Hobsbawm, Eric, 17–18, 220n10
hormat, 145. *See also* etiquette
houses, Sundanese, 39

ibing. *See* ngibing
ibing keurseus. *See* tari kursus
ibing najoeb, 147. *See also* tayuban
ibing pintonan, 17
ibing silaturahmi, 17
ibing tayub, 144; as invented genre, 159. *See
  also* tayuban
Ibu Haji Siti Rokayah, 174
"Idea of Power in Javanese Culture, The"
  (Anderson), 27
identities: gender (*see* gender identities);
  regional West Javanese, 199; Sundanese,
  197–98
Idjah Hadidjah. *See* Hadidjah, Hajah Idjah
IKIP Bandung, 47, 205, 206, 220n12
Imik Suwarsih. *See* Suwarsih, Imik
incest, 77, 79
Indonesian Independence Day (August
  17), 9
Indonesian language, x
Indrawati Lukman, 200

Inul Daratista, 11, 217n17
invented tradition, 220n10; in Java, 19; tari
  tayub as, 157. *See also* Hobsbawm
Irawati Durban Ardjo. *See* Durban Ardjo,
  Irawati
isin, 27. *See also* malu
Islam, 28, 146; association of terbang with,
  49; and dance events, 100; and power,
  100; and ronggeng, 84, 100, 113–14
Iti Narem, 93
Iwan Natapradja, 7, 20
Iyar Wiarsih, 89, 92, 190

Jabang Tutuka as metaphor for Indonesia,
  26. *See also* Gatotkaca
jago, 34, 87
jaipongan, ix, 4, 6, 13, 66, 114, 125, 126,
  185, 198, 200, 207, 208; accompaniment
  for, 190; basic stance for, 190; as erotic
  triangle, 142, 191–94, *191, 192,* 193,
  195–96, *195, 197*; form of, 70–71;
  history of, 189–91; inspirations for, 190;
  introductory sections of, 70; mincid
  in, 69; origin of term, 46–47, 189;
  reasons for success of, 162; ronggeng
  and dancing in, 94; standard phrase of,
  51, 69–70, *70, 73,* 136; as "traditional"
  Sundanese performing art, 190; in
  wayang golek, 193–97
jajangkungan (dance movement), 199
jalak pengkor (dance movement), 51,
  68–69, 130–31, 132
jangkung ilo (dance movement), *152,* 153,
  154, 155
Java Village (1893 World's Columbian
  Exposition), 63
jawara, 33–34, 204
"Jeruk Manis" (Rokayah), 174
"Jipang Kraton" (piece), 159
joged, versus ngibing, 14, 135
jogedan, 149
juara. *See* jawara
Jugala (recording company), 189, 215n16
Juju Masunah, 47–48
Jukes, J. Beete, 87
juru kawih, 91. *See also* pasinden
juru sekar, 91. *See also* pasinden

kabupaten, music patronage at, 14
kacapi, 55, 77 174
Kadewan (dance troupe), 206, 220n12

Kalipucang, 106, 217n3
karaoke, 6
Karawang, 10
"Kareangan" (piece), 215n13
Karlina, Lilis, 38
Kartodirdjo, Sartono, 144–45
kaul, 32, 68, 138; relationship to malu of, 138
Keeler, Ward, 25, 27–29, 31, 32
kembang (flower) of penca silat, 9
"Kembang Kalang" (dance), 15
"Kencana Wungu" (Sudiredja), 12
kendang, 3, 135, 213n2; in bajidoran, 128; description, 49–50; function in ensembles of, 49–50; imitation of dogdog patterns by, 59; indung, xii, 49; in popular song videos, 40
kendang mulut, 45–46
kendang penca, on radio, 9
kendang rampak, 213n3
kendangan, 53, 55
kentongan, 57
keris, 117
keroncong, 55
kesurupan, 118
ketuk, 3, 84
ketuk tilu, ix, 1, 47, 111, 190, 199, 206, 207; accompaniment for, 39, 64–66, 115, 184, 185, 204, 216n7; application of term to dance events, 10, 112; association with illicit sex of, 114; dance style of, 114, 115–16; drumming for, 66, 73, 116; as erotic triangle, 142, 184–87, 186; form of, 66, 112–17; history of, 112–14; kaleran style, 127; mincid in, 66; other terms for, 217n7; in Paneungteung (Lembang), 2–4, 184–87; popularity of, 66, 113, 126; on radio, 90; similarities with bajidoran, 127; similarities to tayuban, 92, 111
ketuk tilu perkembangan, 189. See also jaipongan
ketukan, 69
keupat, 60, 152, 153, 154, 155, 155; etymology of, 214n10
khas Sunda, 90. See also authentic Sundaneseness
"Kidung" (piece), 3, 115
Kincheloe, Joe L., 41
kirata, 33–34, 219n13; for bajidoran, 212n10

"Klana" (dance), 15
Kleden-Probonegoro, Ninuk, 87, 216n5
kliningan, 127; other meanings of, 219n17. See also bajidoran
Komaran, Ade, 69, 70, 136, 140
Komariah, Euis, 189
konkurs (dance competitions), 147
Kost, K. S. See Kostaman, K. S.
Kostaman, K. S., 91, 92, 93
kostim, 118
Krakatau, 113
kraton, 14
kreasi baru, 12, 17
krisis sinden, 93
kroncong, 55
kuda lumping, 58
kuda-kuda, 130
kulanter, xii, 49. See also kendang
Kunst, Jaap: on drumming, 50; on kuda lumping, 58
kunstkring, 211n1. See also lingkung seni
kursus, 148. See also tari kursus
Kusumadilaga, R. Tumenggung, 146
Kweekschool voor Inlandsche Onderwijzers (teachers' school), 146

Laban, Rudolph, 129
Lacan, Jacques, 119, 121, 122, 177; on Oedipus myth and desire, 80–81
lagu, 66, 115–16
lalamba, 151
Lamster, J. C., 108–9, 111
lawakan, 62
leading and following, 155, 164, 177; ambiguity in, 62, 149, 156, 173–74
lek, 27. See also malu
Lembang (city in West Java), 2, 21
Lenyepan (tari kursus character type), 151–54, 154
Lesmana, Ono, 12
Leunyay, Yayah, 4
Lévi-Strauss, Claude, 120, 122, 216n3; on Oedipus myth, 78–79; Structural Anthropology, 78
Leyepan. See Lenyepan
Lia Amelia, 112
life-cycle ceremonies, 9, 95, 126. See also hajat
Lilis Karlina, 38
lingkung seni, xvi, 211n1. See also LS
live music, preference for over recorded, 67

lontang (dance gesture), 160
LS Kandaga Kancana, 113
LS Manggu Sari, 3, 184, 194
LS Rawit Group. *See* Rawit Group
Lubis, Nina Herlina, 93, 117, 146, 220n3
Lukman, Indrawati, 200

macapat. *See* pupuh
maen goong (dance movement), 153, *154, 155*
Mahabharata, 11, 25, 193
male dancers: as consumers of visual messages, 170–71; costumes of, 185; as producers of tactile messages, 171; response to malu of, 32; subjectivity of, 185–86
male gaze, 141. *See also* dancing, vicarious enjoyment of
malu, xiv, 27–31, 39, 44, 104; and dangdut, 137; equivalent terms for, 212n7, 212n8; and masculinity, 31; physical expressions of, 30; and sexuality, 35
mamandapan (dance movement), 151
Mamat, Yetti, 200
"Manangis" (song), 85
Manggu Sari. *See* LS Manggu Sari
Martakusuma, Tubagas Oemay, 19
martial arts. *See* penca silat
Marx, Karl, 122
Mas Nana Munajat Dahlan. *See* Dahlan, Mas Nana Munajat
masculinities: alternative, 26; behaviors of, 99; contradictions of, 1–2, 23, 33–34, 120, 139–40; double standard of, 26–27; illicit sexuality and, 108; and sexual prowess, 35; standards of, 24–27; Sundanese, 208; tari kursus and, 162; theories of, 24; wayang characters as models of, 26
masculinity, 23–24, 141, 207; hegemonic, 24; as unmarked category, 24
Masunah, Juju, 47–48
Mataram kingdom, 8, 144
meme, 178, 208
"Menak Jingga" (Sudiredja), 12
Menak stories, 11
Mendonça, Maria, 215n15
Meyer, Leonard B., 54
mincid, 60, 70, 115, 129, *152, 154, 155*; in bajidoran, 131–32; description of, 131;

etymology of, 214n10; in ketuk tilu, 66, 116; in penca silat, 9; rangkep, 71
minta goong, 56
mirror stage, 80
misrecognition (Bourdieu), 167
mnemonics. *See* drumming, mnemonics
Mochtar, Tosin, 6–7, 46, *47*, 55–56, 70, 71, 128, 157–58, 203
modes, Sundanese, 115
monggang, 212n9
Monggawa (tari kursus character type), 151
movement clusters. *See* dance movements
Muda, Cicih, 97
Muda, Mas Nanu, 134, 212n10, 212n11
Mulvey, Laura, 141
Mulyadi, Salam, 2, 90, 91, 124, 140, 216n13
Mulyana, Ana, 69
Murgiyanto, Sal, approach to Sundanese dance history of, 20
music, relationship of choreography to, 64
myth, 120–22, 165–66; of Oedipus (*see* Oedipus); of Sangkuriang (*see* Sangkuriang)
Mythologies (Barthes), 177
Myths of Freedom (Gardner), 36

nafsu. *See* passion
Nagara Kertagama (fourteenth-century Javanese poem), 83
Nano S., 97
Narawati, Tati, 25
Narem, Iti, 93
Natapradja, Iwan, 7, 20
nayuban, 144. *See also* tayuban
New Order, 20, 24, 26; cultural policy of, 19, 90
ngabaksaan, 201
ngala genah, 69, 132, 133–34
Ngalana (tari kursus character type), 151
ngibing, versus joged, 14, 135
nibakeun (dance movement), 69
Notosusanto, Nugroho, "Tayuban" (short story), 100
Nugraha Sudiredja. *See* Sudiredja, Nugraha R.
Nyatria (tari kursus character type), 151
nyembah (gesture), 4
nyered, 66, 115, 204
Nyi Dasimah, 93
Nyi Mas Warnasari, 93

INDEX

Nyi Pohaci. *See* Dewi Sri
Nyi Ronggeng (film by Surawidjaya), 95–96, 141
Nyi Ronggeng (symphonic composition by Djamin), 97
nyorong. *See* nyered

Oedipus, 78–82, 119, 177, 216n3; dance events and, 81; kinship and exogamy rules and, 80; similarities to Sangkuriang, 78–79
Oemay Martakusuma. *See* Martakusuma, Tubagas Oemay
Oetomo, Dede, 24
ogel, 57. *See also* reog
oncor, 39, 114, 115
Ono Lesmana, 12
Opleiding School voor Inlandsche Ambtenaren (OSVIA), 146
oray-orayan, 116. *See also* ketuk tilu
Oray Welang (Jugala), 189, 190
Otong Rasta. *See* Rasta, Otong

Pajajaran kingdom, 144; Baduy as descendents of, 8
pakbang (dance movement), 46
palacuran, 82. *See also* prostitution
pamogoran, 82. *See also* prostitution
panambih, 55
Pandi Upandi, 156
Paneungteung (village near Lembang), 2–4, 184–88
Panji stories, 11
pantun, 77
"Panyembrana," 199
Parahyangan, x. *See also* Preanger; Priangan
pasinden, 204; dancing in wayang golek performances by, 127; as immobilized ronggeng, 90, 94; popularity of, 93; as singers in gamelan salendro, 91
pasinden crisis. *See* krisis sinden
Peacock, James, 25
peaks of culture (cultural policy), 19, 20, 149
pelog, 37, 38, 93, 115, 151; Western tunings and, 37
Pemberton, John, 19
penca silat, 9, 17, 45, 125, 185; buah (fruit) of, 9; five tepak of, 211n3; form of, 66; in Paneungteung, 4

pencugan (dance movement), 69
Peradotto, John, 216n3
performativity, 119–20, 168; versus performance, 165
Perkembangan tari Sunda (Durban Ardjo), 19
phallus, 81
Pigeaud, Theodore, 83
Pleyte, C. M., "De Eerste Ronggeng," 216n6
pola, 51, 68, 73, 164
pola ibing, 69, 128
porno, 11, 52
poststructuralism, 2, 178
power, 143, 149, 162, 179, 196; in dance, 173–74; displays of, 100; and drumming (*see* drumming); Javanese concepts of, 27, 61, 99–100; masculine, 162; of ronggeng, 101; Sundanese concepts of, 28, 61; and Sundanese gender ideology, 162; and tattoos, 31; and women, 99
Prabu Geusan Ulun Museum, tayuban at, 126, 158
Preanger, x, 107. *See also* Priangan, Parahyangan
Preangerstelsel, 144
presentational dance, jaipongan as, 190
Priangan, x, 107, 109, 112, 144
Priangan system (Preangerstelsel), 144
pride, 28–30, 168. *See also* bangga
professionalism, 102–3, 171–73, 187
prostitution, 87, 108, 146, 216n9
proverbs, Sundanese, 43, 74, 99
pupuh, 212n6
Pusbitari (dance troupe), 15, *16*

qasidah, 49

Radio Republik Indonesia (RRI) Bandung, 9, 90
Raffles, Sir Thomas Stamford Bingley, 23, 88, 105, 106, 107–8, 110, 111; *History of Java*, 86
Rama, 25
Ramayana, 11, 25, 93
Rancaekek, 147
Rasta, Otong, xi , 92–93; on gamelan retuning, 93; on goong strokes, 52
Rawit Group, xii, xiv, 62
reason, 84
rebab, 3, 84, 203
rebana. *See* terbang

247

INDEX

Red Bull energy drink, 4
regents, 144–46
renggana, 82
renggong, derivation from ronggeng of, 88
rengkong, 55–56
reog, 49, 57, 59
Reog Mitra Siliwangi, 57
rerenggongan, 55, 152
"Reumbeuy Bandung" (Rokayah), 174
reversal of causes and effects, 164
rhythm: of drumming, 51–52, 54, 136;
   embodiment of by Sundanese, 45;
   noncongruent treatment, 54
rice farming, 8
rice goddess. See Dewi Sri
Richardson, Vanessa, 96
ritual, as context for performing arts, 7–9
Rokayah, Ibu Haji Siti, "Reumbeuy
   Bandung" and "Jeruk Manis," 174
ronggeng, 38, 82–103, 174, 196, 207;
   absence of in tari kursus, 148;
   appearance of, 87; at Bandung Zoo,
   125; characteristics of, 101; compared
   to other female performers of, 94, 98;
   as consumers of audio messages, 171;
   contradictions of, 76, 82, 89, 98, 164–65;
   costume of, 90, 185, 159; dancing style
   of, 91; as Dewi Sri, 86, 168; as element of
   erotic triangle, 86, 122–23; elimination
   of in tari kursus, 161; etymology of, 82;
   European impressions of, 88; fictional,
   95–97; folk tale about, 84; image of,
   97–99; immobilization of, 90, 94, 187;
   men's reaction to, 98; microphones and,
   90; mobility of, 147; motivations of,
   100–102; negative connotations of, 10,
   87, 149, 160–61; as objects of desire, 82;
   origins of, 83–86; other terms for, 82,
   216n5; payment of, 101, 105, 111, 117;
   physical beauty and, 97–98; in popular
   song videos, 40; and power, 85, 99–101;
   as producers of tactile/visual messages,
   170–71; as professionals, 102–3, 141;
   as prostitutes, 87; relationship to
   male partners' movements of, 116; as
   representations of feminity, 85; role
   of, 100; as serial monogamists, 87–88;
   singing style of, 87–88, 165; subjectivity
   of, 100–103, 142, 165, 171–72; in
   tayuban, 158
"Ronggeng" (Sumbang), 95

Ronggeng Dukuh Paruk (Tohari), 96–97
ronggeng gunung, 82, 85, 112, 127, 219n16
ronggeng wayang, 92. See also pasinden
Rubin, Gayle, on Oedipus myth, 79–80, 119
runtuyan. See pola

Sagan, Carl, 219n15
Salam Mulyadi. See Mulyadi, Salam
Saleh, Tati, 189; as film star, 96; as
   jaipongan artist, 94
salendro, 115
Salim, Aim, 157–58; "Tari Baksa," 200
Sallustius, on myth, 219n15
Sambas Wirakusumah, R. See Wirakusumah,
   R. Sambas
Sancho Panza, 163
sandiwara, 61–62
Sangkala (recording), x
Sangkuriang, 76–78, 82, 177; ambiguities in,
   77; bibliography of, 215n1; similarities
   to Oedipus of, 78–79
santana, 146
Sarluy, J., 87, 105, 106, 114
Saussure, Ferdinand de, 120
schema, 40–41
Sedgwick, Eve Kosofsky, 178–79; Between
   Men, 40, 163–64; on ideology, 122; on
   Silvan Tomkins and shame, 29–30, 31
Seeger, Anthony, on history, 37
Seeger, Charles, 173; "Speech, Music, and
   Speech about Music," 168–69
sekar ageung, 55
Sekar Pusaka (dance group), 147
Sekolah Tinggi Seni Indonesia (STSI), xv,
   7, 15, 17, 23, 51, 211n2; jaipongan
   and, 190; tayuban at, 126, 156; "Tari
   Cikeruhan" and, 203–6; tari kursus and,
   201
Semar, 173
sembah, 145–46
senses, 168–70, 182
sepak soder, 201
Serat Centhini, 218n12
Serat-Sinerat Djaman Djoemenengna Raden
   Hadji Moehamad Moesa (Danoeredja), 93
sesajen (offerings), 3
Sewell, William H., 177–78; "A Theory of
   Structure," 40–41
shakti, 84
shame, 29. See also malu
silat. See penca silat

silih asah, silih asih, silih asuh, 39

sinden. *See* pasinden

sisindiran, 194

Siti Rokayah, Ibu Haji, 174

Siti Samboja, 85

Soedarsono, 44, 114; approach to Sundanese dance history of, 18–19

Soeharto period. *See* New Order

Soepandi, Atik, xii, 44, 51, 212n9; on drumming's function, 52; on drum notation, 51

Soeriadiradja, M., 14; "De Soendaneesche dans," 147

Solihin, Asep, 57

Somantri, R. Tjetje, 13, 19, 148; as notable choreographer, 18; "Tari Kupu-kupu," 199–200; "Tari Merak," 199–200; "Tari Puja," 199; as teacher at OSVIA, 146

Somawijaya, Abun, 67, 74

songs: for ketuk tilu, 115; musical accompaniment and, 89; ronggeng style for, 89; sense of freedom in, 116

sorog, 115; and Western tunings, 37

"Speech, Music, and Speech about Music" (Seeger), 168–69

standard pattern, 132. *See also* pola ibing

Structural Anthropology (Lévi-Strauss), 78

structuralism, 2, 162, 208; critiques of, 177–78

STSI Bandung. *See* Sekolah Tinggi Seni Indonesia, Bandung

Suaman, Maman, on drum notation, xii, 51

Subang (city), 4–5, 10, 13, 15, 94, 97, 112, 127, 128, 137, 185, 187–88, 212n9, 212n11, 219n18

Subardja, Abay, 92, 153, 157–58

subjectivity, 171–73; male, 196–97

Sudiredja, Nugraha R., 12

Suganda, Her, 45, 46, 67, 219n18

Suhaeti, Etty, 90

Suharto, Ben, 83–84

Sujana Arja. *See* Arja, Sujana

Sukarno, 26, 190

suling. *See* bangsing

Sumarna, Undang, ix

Sumarsam, 218n12

Sumbang, Doel, "Ronggeng" (song), 95

Sumedang, 12, 92, 106, 112, 146, 147, 221n6; Prabu Geusan Ulun Museum of, 126, 158

Sumiati, Lilis, 200

Sunarya, Asep Sunandar, 173–74, 193, 215n20

Sundanese dance: canons of, 13–14; character types of, 22; classifications of, 17–20; developments in twentieth century, 207–8; at 1893 World's Columbian Exposition in Chicago, 64; as invented tradition, 20; levels of, 14; men's improvisational dancing as "missing link" in, 15; Natapradja's categories of, 7; overview of, 7–20; as visual symbol of identity, 21

Sundanese language, x; in dangdut songs, 11; levels in, 145

Sundanese names, xi–xii

Supandi, Atik. *See* Soepandi, Atik

Supriadi, Tjetje, 94, 127

Suratno, Nano. *See* Nano S.

Surawidjaya, Alam, *Nyi Ronggeng* (film), 95–96

Suryagunawan, R. Bidin, 73, 147

susuk, 98

Sutherland, Heather, 144

Sutisna, Entis, xi, 90, 91, 92; on joged and ngibing, 135–36

Sutton, R. Anderson, 20, 100

Suwanda, 128, 190

Suwarsih, Imik, 90

Sweeney, Amin, on professionalism, 102

Swindells, Rachel, on gender in Sundanese music, 175

tactile sense, 168–70, 182

Taman Budaya, Bandung, 200

tandak, 63, 109, 110; etymology of, 214n11

Tangkuban Prahu, 77

tantrism, 84, 173

"Tari Baksa" (Salim), 199–203, 209; as incomplete erotic triangle, *202*

"Tari Cikeruhan," 203–7, 209; costume for, 205–6; dance movements for, 204–6; as erotic triangle, 206; musical accompaniment for, 206

Tari Djawa dan Sunda (Soeriadiradja and Adiwidjaja), 211n5

tari klasik, 11, 13, 198, 207; etymology of, 144; in twenty-first century, 208

"Tari Kupu-kupu" (Somantri), 199–200

tari kursus, xiv, 12, 18, 143–62, 118, 179, 193, 207; as basis for tari klasik, 143; character types of, 150–51; compared

tari kursus (*cont.*)
with tayuban, 157; costume for, 157; elimination of ronggeng in, 161; as erotic triangle, 148–51, 158, 193; etymology of, 148; form of, 150–54, 160; gestures of, 150, 201; leading and following in, 15; as a "peak of culture," 149; reasons for popularity of, 148–49, 162, 208; unusual musical changes in, 215n13; variability in choreography of, 153; as visual spectacle, 157

"Tari Merak" (Somantri), 199–200, 201

"Tari Puja" (Somantri), 199

Tari Sunda tahun 1880–1990 (Durban Ardjo), 19

tari tayub, 147; as invented tradition, 157. *See also* tayuban

tarompet, 9

Tasikmalaya, 113

taste, 166

tatakrama, 145. *See also* etiquette

Tatakrama Oerang Sunda (Ardiwinata), 145

tattoos, 31, 33

tayub. *See* tayuban

tayuban, ix, 10, 91, 100, 112, 144; alcohol at, 158; cleaning up of, 146–48; compared with tari kursus, 157; compared with ketuk tilu, 92, 111; in east Java, 83–84; efforts to modernize, 89; as erotic triangle, 142, 144, 179; etymology of, 117, 119, 218n11, 218n12, 219n13; kirata for, 219n13; leading and following in, 73; popularity of, 126; protocols of, 117–19; staged performance of, 159–60; tari kursus dances at, 159

"Tayuban" (Notosusanto), 100

teams, aesthetic. *See* aesthetic teams

tepak, 44, 45; for penca silat, 9, 211n3

tepak kocak, 46–48, 52–53

tepak melem, 55–56, 56; etymology of, 214n8

terbang, 49–50

"A Theory of Structure" (Sewell), 40–41

Thunberg, Charles Peter, 105

"Tiga Kedok" (Sudiredja), 12

tindak tilu, *152*, 153, *154, 155*

Tirasondjaja, Gugum Gumbira. *See* Gumbira Tirasonjaya, Gugum

Tirasonjaya, Gugum Gumbira. *See* Gumbira Tirasonjaya, Gugum

Tjarmedi, Entjar, 55, 90, 213n5

Tjetje Somantri. *See* Somantri, R. Tjetje

Tjetje Supriadi. *See* Supriadi, Tjetje

Tjibodas. *See* Cibodas

Tohari, Ahmad, *Ronggeng Dukuh Paruk*, 96–97

Tomkins, Silvan, on shame, 29–30

topeng, 12, 147, 148, 208; assimilation of in Sundanese dance, 18; character types of, 22; gender roles in, 22; tayuban and, 127

topeng banjet, 203

topeng Betawi, 84

Tosin Mochtar. *See* Mochtar, Tosin

tradition, invented. *See* invented tradition

transcribing drumming, system for, xii–xiv

Travers, Thomas Otto, 106

triangles, and binary oppositions, 162–63; association with gender and power of, 40–42, 208; congruence of, 181–82; as models for dance, 212n11; noncongruence of, 198; as resolution of contradictions, 121. *See also* erotic triangle

trias politika, 213n12

trigonometry of Sundanese dance events, xiv, 180, 181

triping, 10, 137

tri tangtu, 39–40. *See also* trias politika

Tubagas Oemay Martakusuma. *See* Martakusuma, Tubagas Oemay

Tumang, 76–77

Undang-undang Dasar (Indonesian constitution), 19, 149

University of California, Santa Cruz (UCSC), ix

upacara adat, 6

Upandi, Pandi, 156

upward mobility, 145–46

van Zanten, Wim. *See* Zanten, Wim van

Veth, P. J., 87

visual sense, 168–70, 182

"Waled" (piece), 159

Walton, Susan Pratt, 90

wanda anyar, 135–36

wanda klasik, 135–36

waranggana, 91

Warnasari, Nyi Mas, 93

wawayangan, 199

wayang dances, 11–12, 15, 17, 18, 19, 22

INDEX

wayang golek, 25, 92–94, 173; accompaniment for, 194; competition with ketuk tilu of, 127; dancing ogres in, 193–97; erotic triangle and, 142; jaipongan in, 193–97; reasons for popularity of, 193

wayang priya. *See* wayang wong

wayang priyayi. *See* wayang wong

wayang wong, 11–12, 63. *See also* wayang dances

weddings, 5–7, 9, 95, 105, 106, 189, 138, 193

Weintraub, Andrew, 74, 173–74, 193; on krisis sinden, 93

Weiss, Sarah, 100

Wessing, Robert, *Cosmology and Social Behavior in a West Javanese Village*, 27–28

Wiarsih, Iyar, 89, 92, 190

Widodo, Amrih, 88

Williams, Sean: on gender in Sundanese music, 175–76; on kaul, 138

Wirahmasara (dance group), 17, 147

Wirakusumah, R. Sambas, 147; *Hartos Widji-widji Ibing Keurseus*, 148

wiraswara, 204, 206

Wisma Cahaya Garuda, 5

World's Columbian Exposition, Chicago (1893), 63

Yampolsky, Philip, 94, 136; on creation of jaipongan, 192

Yayah Leunyay. *See* Leunyay, Yayah

Yazeed Djamin. *See* Djamin, Yazeed

Yetti Mamat, 200

Yohana, Yoyo, 112–13

Yoyo Yohana. *See* Yohana, Yoyo

zaman kaset, 67

Zanten, Wim van, 8, 55, 74, 99, 174

Zoo, Bandung. *See* Bandung Zoo